SPAIN 1914–1918:
BETWEEN WAR AND REVOLUTION

This work analyses the Spanish experience of the First World War in terms of the general crisis in Europe at this time. In Spain, as elsewhere, the impact of four years of devastating conflict resulted in ideological militancy, economic dislocation and social struggle.

The author examines the slow decay of the ruling liberal monarchy during the war years, and the failure of the neutrality policy to save the existing regime. He looks at challenges to the administration from the labour movement, the bourgeoisie, the army, and international powers.

Romero Salvadó shows a politically apathetic population galvanized by the war into fierce debate about belligerence or neutrality. The debate divided the nation and the new political awareness led to a questioning of the administration's authority. There was also vast economic and social change, as Spain exploited its privileged position as supplier to both sides in the war. These factors led to galloping inflation, civil unrest and political turmoil, finally resulting in the revolutionary strike of 1917.

Spain 1914–1918: Between War and Revolution explores a crucial episode in the history of Spain and Europe. Romero Salvadó offers an insightful analysis of a society in transition from tradition to modernity, and from oligarchy to mass politics.

Francisco J. Romero Salvadó is a Senior Lecturer in Modern European History at London Guildhall University. He has written extensively on Spain's liberal monarchy and the revolutionary crisis of 1917.

ROUTLEDGE/CAÑADA BLANCH STUDIES ON
CONTEMPORARY SPAIN
Edited by Paul Preston and Sebastian Balfour
Cañada Blanch Centre for Contemporary Spanish Studies, London

1 SPAIN 1914–1918: BETWEEN WAR AND REVOLUTION
Francisco J. Romero Salvadó

Also published in association with the Cañada Blanch Centre:
SPAIN AND THE GREAT POWERS
Edited by Sebastian Balfour and Paul Preston

SPAIN 1914–1918:
BETWEEN WAR AND
REVOLUTION

Francisco J. Romero Salvadó

London and New York

First published 1999
by Routledge
11 New Fetter Lane, London EC4P 4EE

Simultaneously published in the USA and Canada
29 West 35th Street, New York, NY 10001

Routledge is an imprint of the Taylor & Francis Group

Typeset in Garamond by
The Running Head Limited, www.therunninghead.com
Printed and bound in Great Britain by
St Edmundsbury Press, Bury St Edmunds

British Library Cataloguing in Publication Data
A catalogue record for this book is available
from the British Library

Library of Congress Cataloging in Publication Data
Romero Salvadó, Franciso J., 1960–
Spain, 1914–1918: between war and revolution / Francisco J.
Romero Salvadó
Includes bibliographical references and index.
1. World War, 1914–1918 – Spain. 2. World War, 1939–1945 –
Influence. 3. Spain – Politics and government – 1886–1931.
4. Spain – Social conditions – 1886–1939. I. Title.
D520.S8R66 1999
946′.074–dc21 99–10069 CIP

ISBN 0–415–21293–6

A mi madre Montserrat Salvadó
y en memoria de mi padre Rigoberto Romero

CONTENTS

CONTENTS

PREFACE

The First World War constituted a turning point in modern European history. It was a devastating conflict which produced massive economic dislocation, social distress and discontent throughout the continent. Hitherto the existing governing elites had managed to cling to power through a variety of liberal political systems which in fact disguised the monopoly of power enjoyed by the privileged propertied classes. After the First World War that would no longer be possible. It heralded the arrival of a new era, that of mass politics. Europeans would irretrievably move away from the world of 1914 as the dominant forms of hierarchical, clientelist and elitist politics broke down. The ruling orders were confronted with the unwelcome prospect of more genuine democracy, and from 1917 with the fast-advancing threat of socialism. The war initiated a period of ideological militancy and political mobilization without precedent in Europe since 1848.

Spain was not an exception. In fact, the Spanish case has to be regarded as a regional version of the general crisis which engulfed Europe during those years. The impact of the Great War inflicted a deadly blow on the Restoration monarchy which had ruled the country since 1875. The Spanish governing classes struggled in vain to keep the country free from the conflict. The official neutrality of the state did not save its political system. Spain did not enter the war, but the war entered Spain and its economic and political impact eroded the fragile foundations of a political system which had so far been based on the passivity and subservience of the population.

A chronological order has been adopted for the narrative so as to facilitate a sense of evolution. The analysis traces developments from the outbreak of hostilities in Europe to the subsequent disintegration of the ruling political system in Spain throughout the years of the conflict. The first chapter is an introduction in which particular emphasis is placed on the fact that foreign problems played an important part in the growing loss of hegemony of the Restoration monarchy. The second examines the socio-economic impact and the ideological split in the country produced by the war. The third and fourth chapters have particular importance. The period covered, December 1915–April 1917, has traditionally been ignored by most historians, yet it constituted the crucial moment when the crisis of the ruling system could no longer be concealed. In the third chapter, the rebellion of key institutions (the labour movement, bourgeoisie and army) is analysed. In the fourth, the secret war fought in Spain between the Allies and the Central Powers, and the process by which the country came close to abandoning neutrality, are both thoroughly investigated. In the fifth, the insurrection of the military, the subsequent mobilization of all the progressive forces of the state and the crisis of legitimacy of the governing elites are scrutinized. In the following two chapters, the attempts by the Catalan bourgeoisie to reform the system peacefully and the showdown in August 1917 between government and working class are investigated. In the eighth, the destruction of the ruling political system is studied. The ninth chapter is an account of the failure of the governing elites to find a new stable political settlement. The bankruptcy of the new political solutions in both the domestic and international fields is fully examined. The tenth and last chapter is a brief examination of the aftermath of the First World War. Like the rest of Europe, Spain was caught in the social warfare, economic dislocation and political turmoil which followed the Bolshevik triumph in Russia and the collapse of the Central Powers. The ailing liberal regime managed to cling on for five more years until it was finally overthrown by the military in September 1923.

ACKNOWLEDGEMENTS

Like any academic enterprise, this project has benefited from the assistance and support of many people and institutions. First of all, I am grateful to the British Academy, the University of London, the Central Research Fund, the Centre for Contemporary Spanish Studies and the British–Spanish Joint Research Programme (Acciones Integradas) for their financial aid. Also of great help was the assistance received in different archives and libraries. In particular, I must mention the staff at the Fundación Pablo Iglesias and Fundación Maura in Madrid, the Centre d'Estudis d'Historia Contemporánia (Biblioteca Figueras) and the Arxiu Nacional de Catalunya in Barcelona.

I am indebted to my Ph.D. supervisor at the University of London, Paul Preston, for his patience, encouragement and stimulation in prodding this work along. The comments of and discussions with my friends and colleagues at the Centre for Contemporary Spanish Studies were extremely helpful. In particular, I would like to thank Helen Graham, Sebastian Balfour, Paul Heywood, Enrique Moradiellos, Chris Ealham, Lola Elizalde, Pablo La Porte and Inés Roldán. I would also like to mention Lawrence Butler, Maria Sophia Quine and Jonathan Smele from Queen Mary and Westfield College and Frank Snowden, formerly at Royal Holloway and Bedford New College. Their support and advice were of inestimable value.

Alison Pinington and Elizabeth Speakman helped me enormously with their proof-reading and accurate remarks. Their patience and hard work were admirable. Finally, I would like to thank all those friends who had to put up with my difficult moods when I was absorbed and distracted by this project: Anthony, Melanie, Joanna, Frederick and all the kids in 47 Landor Road, and Javi, Carlos, Lucy, Helena and all the friends in Madrid who with their warmth and friendship made easier my stay in Spain.

Without the support, help and encouragement of all these friends and colleagues, my book would probably have never been completed. Of course, any errors in the text are entirely mine.

1

INTRODUCTION

At the time of the outbreak of the First World War constitutional and liberal political systems were dominant in most countries in Europe. None of them could be described as a real democracy. Elections, parliaments and other liberal trappings were widely used to conceal the fact that the privileged governing elites preserved their political hegemony through patronage, social subservience, prestige and tradition.

Spain followed that pattern. Since 1875 the country had been ruled by a constitutional monarchy. The architect of the new ruling order was the shrewd politician Antonio Cánovas del Castillo. His main objective was to reach a political settlement which would put an end to the years of civil strife, military coups and general instability which had characterized the earlier part of the century. He was to be largely successful. The restoration of the Bourbon monarchy in the person of Alfonso XII and the constitution of 1876 were his achievements. The new political system seemed to be modern and democratic. It conceded freedom of expression and association, political parties and trade unions were allowed to exist, and, in 1890, universal male suffrage was introduced.

In fact, the Restoration settlement was far from democratic. All the constitutional paraphernalia actually served to conceal the monopoly of power enjoyed by a governing elite. For the following four decades two monarchist or 'dynastic' parties rotated in office: the Conservatives, headed by Cánovas himself, and the Liberals, led by Práxedes Mateo Sagasta. The succession in government of these two groups was so systematic that the Canovite order was known as *Turno Pacífico* (Peaceful Rotation).

The governing class was formed by the representatives of the dominant landowning oligarchies of Castilian wheat growers and Andalusian wine and olive oil producers. As the years went by, the group also included large financial interests such as banks, state companies and big concerns like railways.[1]

Thus liberal democracy in Spain, as in most European countries at the time, was a sham and a way to disguise the supremacy of these privileged groups in society. It perpetuated the co-existence of modern liberal institutions with a semi-feudal socio-economic order.

1

Yet Cánovas broke with a past marked by intolerance and *exclusivismo* (monopoly of office by one political faction). After 1876 both Liberals and Conservatives agreed upon a system of regulated rotation through which they shared the spoils of office, patronage and administrative graft. Neither dynastic formation was a modern political group seeking to win the vote with clear-cut and attractive programmes. They were artificial groups created from above. They did not even bother to campaign before polling day, as the system was based on electoral falsification. During the Restoration period elections did not produce governments in Spain. The Ministro de la Gobernación (Minister of the Interior) manipulated the results so that the government always obtained an overall majority. The ruling system avoided confrontation and instead sought compromise and stability. The party in power at election time respected the strongholds of the dynastic opposition and even the most important seats of such enemies as the Republicans on the Left and the Carlists on the Right.

At the top of the Canovite edifice was the Crown. The monarch was not only the Commander in Chief of the army but also had the power to appoint and dismiss governments. He was the one who ensured the smooth functioning of the *Turno*. Any Prime Minister to whom the king gave the decree of dissolution of parliament knew that the new elections would inevitably give him an overall majority to rule comfortably. At the bottom, the *caciques* were the kingpins of the entire political structure. They were the local notables, the bigwigs and influential bosses of each locality, landowners or their agents, officials, moneylenders, lawyers or even priests. It was they who delivered the expected majorities to the governments in Madrid. The *caciques* made universal suffrage, granted in 1890, inoperative, ran their areas as personal fiefs, and had unlimited powers to settle local affairs, choose judges, appoint officials, undertake public works and even levy taxes in accordance with their will. No government would dare to move against them as its position in office depended on them. They filled the gap left by the lack of real political mobilization and took advantage of their key role as links between the central administration and the country. Hence the *caciques* could systematically violate the law with impunity and build a clientelist network based on patronage and self-interest. Their friends were rewarded and promoted and their enemies coerced, arrested and in some cases even murdered.[2]

The Canovite system worked relatively smoothly during the first two decades after 1876. Its continuity depended on mass apathy and political demobilization, which was facilitated by the nature of Spanish society in the last quarter of the nineteenth century. High levels of illiteracy, poor transport and communication systems, the lack of national integration and the slow process of urbanization favoured the development of the patron–client network in which *caciquismo* was rooted. It was obvious that as the country advanced economically, socially and culturally the Canovite status quo would begin to run into increasing difficulties. Nevertheless, foreign policy problems contributed significantly to the erosion of the foundations of the *Turno Pacífico*. Three dates were to be crucial: 1898, 1909 and 1914.

Defeat in the war against the United States in 1898 and the subsequent loss of the remnants of the overseas Empire – Cuba, Puerto Rico, Guam and the Philippines – further discredited the regime. The feeling of impotence and decline was such that a movement of criticism against the ruling system was born.[3] This so-called *regeneracionismo* found in the *caciquista* system the epitome of all that was wrong in the country, the proof that Spain was backward, undeveloped and divorced from progress. An elite of intellectuals known as the *Generación del 98* became the leading force denouncing the corruption of the dynastic elites.

Simultaneously, the *Turno* parties began to lose ground in the most important cities. They could not ignore the fact that an increasing number of Republicans were elected in the larger towns. It was apparent that the urban population was politically aware and elections could not be easily rigged there. The vote was still conducted in the old way but more repression and bribery were needed to get the desired results. Catalonia, the economically most advanced area, was the first to destroy the grip of the *caciques*. It had been worst hit by the loss of the lucrative Cuban markets for its textile goods. The Catalans called into question the nature of the Restoration system and created their own parties. In 1901 the newly established Lliga Regionalista, representative of the Catalan industrial bourgeoisie, obtained a sweeping victory.[4] After 1905, Regionalists and Republicans were in control of Catalan politics. Furthermore, the two ruling parties were affected by internal problems. By the turn of the century the two historical leaders, Cánovas and Sagasta, were dead. Based not on ideological lines but on patronage, their parties were bound to be divided by factional squabbles. Additionally, the new king, Alfonso XIII, took advantage of the new situation to attempt a restoration of royal prerogatives. He would further the disintegration of the *Turno* by repeatedly trying to implement the maxim 'divide and conquer'.

After 1898, the dynastic leaders also abandoned their traditional caution in foreign policy. Hitherto the Restoration politicians had applied in international matters the so-called *recogimiento* or isolation from the two hostile blocs which were being formed in Europe. After her defeat at the hands of the United States, Spain, without throwing in her lot with either of the two camps, initiated a timid approach towards France and Britain to guarantee the status quo in the Western Mediterranean. A treaty signed with France in 1900 gave possession of Guinea and the Western Sahara to Spain. In a new treaty signed at Algeciras in 1906, confirmed one year later at Carthagena, France, Britain and Spain recognized one another's spheres of influence in the area and Spain was granted a strip of land in Northern Morocco.

Without possession of Tangier, the richest Moroccan port, which became an international city, the occupation of a desert zone in Morocco inhabited by fierce and rebellious tribes caused problems to Spain right from the start.

Imperialist adventures were very unpopular. Stories told by the thousands of soldiers returning from the lost colonies about the appalling state of the medical and logistical services of the army increased the lack of enthusiasm for any new colonial enterprise. Furthermore, with a chronically burdened state budget Spain could hardly afford to undertake new colonization projects. In 1909, the government was drawn into a minor war to defend Spanish mining concessions against continuous attacks by Moorish guerrillas. The call-up of reservists that summer, most of them married workers, was met by a General Strike against the Moroccan campaign. In Barcelona and other Catalan towns, the revolt got out of control. During the so-called 'Tragic Week' of July 1909, barricades were erected and churches burnt down. The riots were finally suppressed with great violence. Over 175 people were shot and five more were executed later.[5]

The sequel to those events was the fall of the Conservative cabinet in October. Its Prime Minister, Antonio Maura, was one of the exceptional dynastic leaders who had advocated a revolution from above. Realizing that in order to save the social order some political reforms were needed, Maura sought to replace the artificial *caciquista* mechanism with a modern programme which would attract the conservative and Catholic middle classes. His regenerationist experiment was halted by the events of 1909. Maura never forgave the role played by the Liberals. The latter, deeply upset by Maura's attempts to tamper with the ruling system, had fiercely opposed his administration and taken advantage of the situation created by the Tragic Week to oust him from power. Maura refused to alternate with them in office. In January 1913 Maura demanded power on his own terms and affirmed that the Conservatives under his leadership would never rotate with the Liberals. He stressed his refusal to return to the practices of the *Turno* and even coined the term *idóneo* to refer to any political formation prepared to rotate in power with the Liberals.[6]

In October 1913, Maura had to face the sad truth that the bulk of the Conservative party had abandoned him and, led by the ex-minister and rich lawyer Eduardo Dato, accepted the continuity of the *Turno* fiction. The *Idóneo* party had been created. A minority formed mainly of young Conservatives followed the dismissed leader and created the *Maurista* movement. Maura was the first and last dynastic politician who had a genuine mass following. This was the first serious split in one of the two dynastic parties.[7] It forecast the factionalism and loss of hegemony of the ruling notables which was to increase after 1914.

2

THE OUTBREAK OF WAR

Spain and her official neutrality

The outbreak of the First World War was to make it increasingly more difficult to continue the constitutional sham in every European state. Such a
devastating conflict brought about enormous social and economic strains which
altered the relation of forces in most countries. Food shortages, economic
dislocation, social distress, scarcity and inflation led to a political awakening
and ideological militancy of the masses. Under those pressures, the existing
forms of hierarchical, clientelist and elitist politics broke down. At the end of
the war, the traditional governing elites found it impossible to put the clock
back and return to the world of 1914.

Spain, if spared the human slaughter, experienced as much of the effects of
the conflict as the other European states. Her official neutrality could hardly
hide the intensity of the debate between the supporters of the Central Powers
and those of the Allies, nor could it check the increasing militancy and ideological awareness produced by the impact of the war on the daily lives of the
Spaniards. Having rested so far on the political apathy of most Spaniards, the
Restoration system entered a period of crisis; a crisis of hegemony produced
by the inability of the governing elites to face successfully the arrival of mass
politics and its subsequent challenge to clientelism and patronage as a source
of power.

The First World War destroyed the foundations of the Canovite status
quo. Ironically, a war in which Spain did not intervene was to have a decisive
influence on her contemporary history.[1] Most dynastic politicians were determined to keep Spain out of the conflict regardless of the price. They succeeded in doing so but it was beyond their power to prevent the conflict from
entering Spain.

The very day that hostilities broke out on the continent, the Conservative
cabinet declared Spain officially neutral. On 25 August Prime Minister Dato
wrote to his former chief Maura noting that the lack of commitments to
either side facilitated the country's neutral status. Yet he also pointed out
other very revealing facts:

5

Our position is not to abandon that policy. We would depart from neutrality only if we were directly threatened by foreign aggression or by an ultimatum . . . Germany and Austria are delighted with our attitude as they believed us committed to the Entente. France and Britain cannot criticize us as our pacts with them are limited to Morocco. Moreover, we do not owe them anything since in the dreadful year of 1898 they did nothing for Spain . . .

I do not fear that the Allies would push us to take sides with or against them . . . They must know that we lack material resources and adequate preparation for a modern war. Even if the country was ready to launch itself into a military adventure, our collaboration would have little consequence. Would we not render a better service to both sides by sticking to our neutrality so that one day we could raise a white flag and organize a peace conference in our nation which could put an end to the current conflict? We have moral authority for that and who knows if we shall be required to do so . . .[2]

Thus among the main motives behind Spain's neutrality were the recognition of her political and diplomatic isolation as well as the economic weakness and military disorganization of the country. Furthermore, the dispute in Europe was not regarded as affecting Spanish interests, while there was always the hope that by maintaining an impartial position Spain could play the leading role in organizing a peace summit and therefore gain in the diplomatic field what could never be achieved on the battlefield.

The view that Spain could not effectively wage a modern war and therefore should not get involved in the conflict was shared by nearly everyone in the country in the summer of 1914. On 1 and 7 August, the National Executive Committee of the Socialist party and its trade union, the Unión General de Trabajadores (UGT), published a statement which set out their opposition to intervention in such a terrible conflict where workers would be the main victims. In an article in *La Veu de Catalunya*, Francesc Cambó, the leader of the Catalan Lliga Regionalista, also commented that a poor and badly armed country like Spain should stay out of the European war. Equally, Antonio Maura wrote to Dato that he was prepared to go to the Cortes in order to applaud the decision taken by the government. Maura pointed out that the war would inevitably have a deep impact on Spain and regretted that the fate of the country might well be in the hands of foreign powers or depend on others' fortunes. Thus, when on 30 October 1914 the Cortes opened after the summer recess, the declaration of neutrality was warmly applauded by all the political parties. Dato firmly noted that Spain had not received the smallest provocation from any of the belligerent nations and desired to remain aloof from the horrors of the war. In the unlikely event of the country being provoked by an act of aggression, Dato promised that the government would hasten to appeal to parliament in order to defend the honour, liberty and independence of the nation.[3]

However, right from the start there were dissenting voices in the country. On the one hand, there were the ultra right-wing Carlists who, led by Juan Vázquez de Mella, wasted no time in disseminating their pro-German feelings. On the other hand, the Republican Radicals led by Alejandro Lerroux did not hide their support for the Allied cause and even began to campaign for open intervention in the conflict. There were rumours that there had been some discussion in military circles of whether Lerroux should be court-martialled and shot. Lerroux's reputation was that of a demagogue and a troublemaker. Hence the British ambassador, Sir Arthur Hardinge, felt deeply embarrassed when in early November he received a note from the Madrid committee of the Radical party requesting him to forward to the British Prime Minister their best wishes for the success of the Entente in the war. The British ambassador complied, but not before informing the Spanish Foreign Minister, the Marquis of Lema, of the Radicals' message.[4]

The attitudes adopted by Carlists and Radicals were hardly a surprise to anyone. The real shock came with the publication on 19 August 1914 of an article entitled *Neutralidades que matan* ('Fatal Neutralities') in *El Diario Universal*, mouthpiece of the leader of the Liberal party, Count Romanones. It was said that it had been written by the Count himself, although authorship was claimed by Juan Pérez Caballero, a former Foreign Minister under the Liberal cabinets of Segismundo Moret in 1906 and 1910. Even if Romanones did not write it, his was the inspiration. The article constituted a clear appeal to Spain to cast in its lot with the Entente:

> Geopolitical, economic and diplomatic imperatives impose collaboration with the Entente. Spain is surrounded by the Allies, the sea-lanes are controlled by them, the vast bulk of our trade is with France and Britain and theirs is the largest portion of foreign investment in our country. Moreover, Spain's economic life depends upon British coal and American wheat . . . our collaboration with them would only represent the logical continuity of the international policies undertaken by different Spanish governments between 1900 and 1913 . . .
>
> Neutrality unsupported by the neutral's own force is at the mercy of the first strong state which finds it necessary to violate it . . . The Balearic and the Canary Islands, the Galician coasts are undefended . . .
>
> If Germany wins, will she thank us for our neutrality? No, she will try to rule the Mediterranean. She will not take French continental territory. She will seize the African coast from Tripoli to Fernando Poo . . . We shall lose our hopes of expansion in Morocco. We shall lose our independence. We shall lose the Balearic Islands. Nor will German expansion in the economic and industrial domain

compensate us for the ruin of the countries with whom our interests in those respects have been up to now identified. On the other hand, if the Allies triumph they will owe us no debt of gratitude and will remodel the map of Europe as they think fit . . .

There are neutralities which are fatal![5]

The impact of the article was considerable. The leader of the Liberal party was publicly criticizing the policy adopted by the government at the outbreak of the war. Romanones's argument did not necessarily advocate entering the war but openly demanded that Spain should move closer towards the Allied camp. This was patently at odds with the strict neutrality declared by Dato. In the long term this was to hurt his own image as future Prime Minister. Romanones himself claimed in his memoirs that at this stage the king shared his views. The Count argued that although his intention was not to push Spain into the conflict, his duty was to let the Allies know that Spain was prepared to adopt a neutrality favourable to them. Realizing that he was not in tune with the country, Romanones tried a new approach. In *El Imparcial* of 4 September 1914 he insisted that neutrality did not imply isolation, as that would be inconsistent with the economic interests and conditions of modern Europe. He also denied any personal responsibility for the article 'Fatal Neutralities' and recognized the impracticality of abandoning neutrality. Dato's formal declaration of the Spanish position on the war, made in the Cortes on 30 October, was quickly endorsed by Romanones. The British Ambassador commented that neither Count Romanones nor any other responsible man would now venture to support a departure from neutrality.[6]

By the autumn of 1914, if the general consensus among Spaniards was to remain away from the battlefields, hopes for a short war or for a peaceful solution in which Spain could play a decisive role faded away. Both sides failed to destroy the enemy by achieving a quick and decisive victory. Germany, facing a war on two fronts, had planned for years to knock out France swiftly in the West and then turn her forces to the East before the Russians could mobilize their immense military manpower into full action. While the Austrians attacked Serbia, the German troops in a lightning campaign invaded neutral Belgium, causing the entry of Britain into the war, and swept through France. But by early September the German offensive had begun to peter out and was finally halted on the River Marne. A long and bloody war of attrition began on the Western Front. Hundreds of thousands of men lost their lives for the conquest of a few square miles of land. Unlike the atrocious stalemate in the West, the Eastern Front remained in constant movement. Millions of Russian soldiers advanced into Eastern Prussia and Austria but they were surrounded and annihilated in the battles of Tannenberg and the Matzurian Lakes. This pattern repeated itself during the following years: millions of Russian soldiers, badly trained and starved of supplies, managed to break the Austro-German lines and occupy thousand of square miles of territory, but sooner or later the offensive ran out of steam and ended in massive defeats.

As the war raged on, many nations which originally had remained neutral began to take sides and joined one of the two warring blocs. The Ottoman Empire and Bulgaria soon threw in their lot with the Central Powers, while Japan, Italy, Greece, Portugal and Romania joined the Allies. Spain, or rather the Spaniards, were inevitably affected by the continuation of the conflict.

By 1915 the effects of the war began to be evident. Ideologically, many Spaniards identified with one of the armed camps. Economically, the country was dramatically upset by the European dispute. The placid life of the *Turno* governments was nearing its end as Spain saw her normal existence altered by forces unleashed by the war. The Socialist journalist Luis Araquistáin caught perfectly the changing mood of public opinion towards the war issue. According to Araquistáin, this could be divided into three phases: during the initial stage the conflict was followed as if it were a game and people even placed bets on the outcome; a second and critical period began in 1915 when Spaniards started to take sides; with the outbreak of agitation and mobilization around the neutrality question, a final and active phase became evident by 1916.[7]

Most of the population, especially those in the countryside, regarded the ideological and political issues of the conflict with indifference. Their living standards were inevitably hurt by the hardships and shortages brought about by the war, but they did not understand the struggle of ideas and concepts behind the actual fighting. Yet for many social, cultural and political groups based in the cities, the European conflict became a question of obsessive concern. The war was almost immediately perceived as an ideological clash in which each of the warring factions came to symbolize certain transcendent ideas and values. The quarrel between the partisans of the Allies and of the Central Powers generated a violent debate around the issue of neutrality. Rather than merely reflecting contrasting opinions, it revealed a deep preexisting spiritual division within the Spanish people which the war did not create but only exacerbated. It was such a bitter polemic that it had the moral quality of a civil war, 'a civil war of words'. It represented a verbal clash between the two Spains which was a portent of the real civil war that still lay a generation in the future.[8] Passions reached such a pitch that families and friends were often divided and many cinemas refused to give news on the conflict in order to prevent fights.

The two dynastic parties generally kept to the formula of neutrality. Dato banned all public meetings on Spain's position towards the war in an effort to avoid the divisions that finally pushed Italy into the conflict in May 1915. Realizing the poor quality of the Spanish army, the Conservative government decided to pursue comprehensive military reform and sent a military and a naval commission, led respectively by Major Garrido and Captain Carranza, to Washington to purchase weapons and supplies. That operation would last until late 1917.[9]

As public opinion began to split, dynastic politicians clung desperately to formal neutrality. However, some of them could not avoid being identified with one side or the other. Romanones and his friends in the Liberal party had clearly cast their lot in with the Western Powers. For political rather than ideological reasons, those Liberals who disputed Romanones's leadership and backed that of his rival, the Marquis of Alhucemas, tended to be regarded as Germanophiles. Even within the Conservative party there were divisions. The Minister of the Interior and Eduardo Dato's right-hand man, José Sánchez Guerra, and the Minister of War, General Ramón Echague, were believed to support the Central Powers. In contrast, Dato and his Foreign Minister, the Marquis of Lema, were regarded as good friends of the Allied cause. As early as 7 August 1914 the Spanish ambassador in London, Alfonso Merry del Val, had called at the Foreign Office and stated under instructions from his government that Spain was desirous of doing anything she could for the protection of British interests and subjects. A few days later a Spanish request for a naval officer and one other Spanish officer to be allowed to follow the operations of the British army and navy was promptly granted. In 1915, British diplomats judged the existing Spanish administration to be the best possible given the existing conditions, and in June the French ambassador informed his British counterpart that insulting letters had been addressed to the Marquis of Lema by the German ambassador, Prince Ratibor.[10] Nevertheless, despite personal sentiments, both dynastic parties, with the outstanding exception of Romanones, managed to conceal their internal differences and give an image, until the end of the war, of cohesion regarding the declaration of neutrality.

There is abundant literature concerning the ideological division of Spain between Germanophiles and Francophiles.[11] Although an accurate definition of both sides in ideological, social or political terms is difficult, it can be affirmed that in general terms so-called 'official Spain' was Germanophile and 'real Spain' was Francophile. The more economically backward Castile supported the Central Powers and the more dynamic areas of the periphery the Allies. The Right wanted a victory for the imperial forces and the Left for the Western democracies. The main Germanophile voices in the country were those of the clergy, the army, the aristocracy, the landowning elites, the upper bourgeoisie, the court, the Carlists and the *Mauristas*. All regarded a victory of the Central Powers as a triumph for those who defended such Catholic and traditional values as monarchism, discipline, authority and a hierarchical social order. The main Allied supporters were the Regionalists, the Republicans, the Socialists, the professional middle classes and the intellectuals, those who wanted to transform the existing oligarchical liberalism into a genuine democracy.

As the conflict went on, neutrality began to lose its initial meaning. On the one hand, the friends of the Allied cause would increasingly regard it as a sham and thus would switch to positions ranging from benevolent neutrality to diplomatic rupture with Germany and even open intervention. On the other hand, it was evident even to the most rabid Germanophiles that with Spain surrounded by the Entente Powers and the British fleet controlling the seas, to join forces with Germany would amount to military suicide. Hence they became champions of a strict neutrality as the best way to support the Central Powers. They were not in fact neutral but pragmatism forced them to accept neutrality as the best solution. Their advantage was that their pro-German feelings could be easily disguised under a vague façade of patriotism, *españolismo* and opposition to foreign interference in Spanish affairs, while the case of the pro-Allied forces advocating entry into the war could be shown as a yielding to the work of foreign agents bordering on treason.

Many supporters of the Central Powers were Francophobes rather than Germanophiles. They put forward historical examples such as Morocco and Gibraltar to argue that Spain had nothing to gain from an Allied victory, while the triumph of the German armies could favour Spanish interests. Germany represented the best defence of the West against Russian barbarism. The most outstanding case of Francophobia was that of the Catholic church. Its hierarchy and its main journal, *El Debate*, portrayed the Kaiser as God's sword. Despite Wilhelm's Protestantism, he was regarded as a Catholic prince in disguise, raised up to chastise immoral and faithless France with divine vengeance and to restore the temporal power of the Pope. Throughout the four years of war, the church was the institution which offered the most unyielding position and the most coherent ideological support for the German cause. Not even the invasion of Catholic Belgium softened its stand. Many argued that it was God's punishment of a nation which had allowed the construction of a monument to Francisco Ferrer Guardia, the Spanish Anarchist executed in 1909 for allegedly being the mastermind of the week of riots and destruction of churches in Barcelona known as the Tragic Week. After the Bishop of Southwark's tour of Spain in October 1915, he declared that only the Bishops of Madrid and Ciudad Real were friendly towards the Allies; the Primate and the rest of the clergy had made clear their pro-German sympathies and hatred of French Republicanism.[12]

The army did not present the same cohesive front as the church. Most of the officers were not Germanophiles in the strictest sense of the word, but they admired the efficiency and discipline of the Prussian army. There were some outstanding examples of Francophile generals such as Miguel Primo de Rivera or Eduardo López Ochoa, but the majority were well aware of the inability of the Spanish army to participate in the European conflict and thus they loathed the idea of departing from the initial strict neutrality. Furthermore, Allied reports warned that there existed a military party, including among others the Minister of War, General Echague, which was not only very confident of a final German victory but was also hoping that if the Entente was badly beaten, Spain could, under some pretext or another, annex Portugal.[13]

Carlists and *Mauristas* were the two political parties which voiced Germanophile feelings more openly. Their strong Catholicism, monarchism and conservatism pushed them against Protestant Britain and Republican France.[14] The speech delivered by the Carlist spokesman Vázquez de Mella on 31 May 1915 marked the official U-turn from outspoken Germanophilia to an all-out defence of strict neutrality. The encirclement of Spain by the Allies, confirmed by Italy's entry into the war, made the supporters of the Central Powers in Spain realize that there was no way the country could side with Germany. Henceforth those journals close to Carlism and *Maurismo*, such as *El Correo Español*, *La Tribuna*, *El Universo* and *La Acción* adopted the line that patriotism and internal independence forbade a departure from neutrality. Ironically, the leaders of both movements disagreed with their followers. The Carlist Pretender, Don Jaime, was fighting in the Russian army, and Maura continually disappointed his Germanophile followers when he alluded to international affairs and stressed that Spain was inevitably linked by cultural and economic realities to the Western Powers. The Conservative statesman was inclined to defend a neutral stance which was clearly benevolent towards the Allies. The British ambassador, Hardinge, regarded Maura as a pro-Allied leader who had to act with caution so as not antagonize his pro-German followers. After Maura's speech at the Royal Theatre on 21 April 1915, the British ambassador wrote:

> Maura is too much of a statesman to believe in the possibility of Spain pursuing a policy of hostility to France and Britain which would have involved the repudiation of agreements such as that of Carthagena to which he had been a party himself . . . his followers were greatly taken aback when Maura proclaimed himself a convinced supporter of the Entente with the Allies . . . Least of all did they expect that his remarks would support the policy of Romanones.[15]

Similarly, Hardinge wrote after a speech by Maura in Berlanga on 10 September 1916:

> The important point in it was Señor Maura's account of his own part in the Carthagena agreement and of his defence of that agreement as dictated by the interests of Spain in Morocco and the Mediterranean, and by her natural affinities as a Western power . . . I am inclined to think that Señor Maura was playing to the gallery, for the clerical elements of his party were a little depressed by his evident attachment to the Carthagena agreement and only became responsive when he took to abusing Cardinal Richelieu and indulging in mournful references to Gibraltar. But these trimmings do not affect the general character of the dish which he served up to his political supporters . . . His present policy proved to be identical to that of Count Romanones.[16]

12

The court was the last important pro-German stronghold. It was led by the Queen Mother, the Austrian Archduchess María Cristina. A victory for the Central Powers was regarded as the best guarantee of survival for the old order. Naturally, the English Queen Victoria Eugenia, married to Alfonso in 1906, defended her country of birth. Alfonso XIII was regarded by all the Allied diplomats as a genuine and real friend of their cause. It was even alleged that the article 'Fatal Neutralities' expressed the feelings of the monarch and that it had been written by Romanones in order to please him. Most of Alfonso's apologists emphasized that he remained above political tendencies throughout the four years of war. The main objective of the Spanish monarch, however, was to consolidate his personal position at home and abroad so as to play a leading role in the new European concert. He aspired to the role of mediator in the conflict and if possible to benefit from it by enlarging the Spanish colonial empire. In order to achieve that purpose the king in 1915 set up a bureau to deal with prisoners' conditions, deportations, general information about missing citizens and soldiers of the belligerent countries, humanitarian aid and pardons. By the end of the war his role had been crucial in obtaining 50 pardons and 5,000 repatriations, tackling 25,000 cases of relatives in occupied territories and investigating the whereabouts of over 250,000 missing persons or prisoners of war.[17] However, after the March Revolution in Russia and the entry of the United States into the war, Alfonso adopted an increasingly Germanophile position which he attempted to conceal under the perfect cover of defending Spanish neutrality.[18]

The intellectuals constituted the main defenders of the Allied cause in Spain. They were the traditional adversaries of the church, competing for control of education and culture. The European conflict placed intelligentsia and clergy in different camps. The intellectuals were not only admirers of Republican France and democratic Britain but also Germanophobes who detested the authoritarian system that the Central Powers espoused. In a sense, by supporting Britain and France, the historic enemies of Spain, they were choosing Europe over Spain. They were opting for a future Europeanized Spain, modern, secular and democratic, in place of the tradition-ridden, priestly, oligarchical Spain that was. These intellectuals were known as the 'Generation of 1914'. Many of them, such as Benito Pérez Galdós, Miguel de Unamuno, Ramón Pérez de Ayala and Ramón del Valle Inclán, had been members of the Generation of 1898. They were now joined by younger poets, academics and writers, one perfect example being Manuel Azaña, President of the Madrid Atheneum. On 10 July 1915, the writer Pérez de Ayala published in the magazine *Iberia* the first expression of solidarity with the Allies.

In January 1917 a coalition of intellectuals presided over by Pérez Galdós formally established the anti-Germanophile League. They made no secret of their belief that the outcome of the conflict would determine the future political order of Europe. Thus a victory for the Allied forces would bring

13

about the democratization and modernization of the continent. Spain would then be able to free herself from the oligarchy, backwardness and *caciquismo* in which she had stagnated for so long. The magazine *España* was the main publication of the pro-Allied camp. It was edited until February 1916 by the philosopher José Ortega y Gasset and then by the Socialist Luis Araquistáin, who relied on British financial support to keep the magazine afloat. Spain's intelligentsia contributed articles to promote the Allied cause, and in its pages there appeared the first manifesto of the anti-Germanophile League. It called for the defence of liberalism and democracy and exhorted Spaniards to fight the false neutrality defended by the Germanophiles, whose real objective was to prevent the country from achieving the progress and liberties represented by the Western Powers. Pío Baroja and Jacinto Benavente were the two notable exceptions within Spain's cultural elite. Ironically, both seem to have been Germanophiles for the wrong reasons. The pseudo-Anarchist Basque author Baroja believed that Germany was the only power which could shatter clericalism in Europe. Benavente, for his part, published a manifesto in *La Tribuna* on 18 December 1915 which was signed by a long list of secondary figures in the artistic and academic world. He defended the pro-German neutralists in Spain from the accusations of reactionaries by alleging that, unlike those who based their international views on fatalistic and geographical imperatives, they were the defenders of an independent Spain, free to align with the countries she deemed appropriate. Furthermore, the playwright remarked that he believed in a future Socialist world order and this could be best created by Germany, the cradle of Socialism.[19]

Catalanists and Republicans were the principal political groups to side with the Allies. The main leader of the right-wing Catalan Lliga Regionalista, Francesc Cambó, never publicly departed from neutrality. On some occasions in the Cortes he even used the example of the German Empire to demand for Catalonia the same kind of autonomy that the German Länder enjoyed. However, the overwhelming majority of the Catalan political elite were outspoken Francophiles. Historical links with France and admiration for the principles and ideals defended by the 'sister' nation made most Catalanists believe that a French victory represented the best hope for the fulfilment of their nationalist aspirations. As early as August 1914, Catalans volunteered to fight for France. One year later a magazine, *Iberia*, was created to praise and defend their cause and a formal organization, the *Comité de Germanor*, was established in February 1916 in Barcelona to facilitate the recruitment of volunteers. In total, there were more than 2,000 Spanish soldiers, almost half of them Catalans, fighting as members of the French Foreign Legion. They took part in the main battles not only on French soil but also in the Dardanelles and Macedonia. The contacts between Catalan Nationalists and French Republicans created serious problems for many governments in Madrid.[20]

Republicans represented the opposite view to that of Carlists and *Mauristas*. Right from the start, they demonstrated where their sympathies lay. According to them, the country had to side with the Western democracies or it would remain a backward nonentity in Europe. Republicans from all the different groupings made clear that a French victory would be their own triumph as it would help accelerate the change of regime in Spain. Their papers, such as Alejandro Lerroux's *El Radical*, Marcelino Domingo's *La Lucha* and Roberto Castrovido's *El País*, were the mouthpieces of the Allied cause. During the conflict Lerroux became the leading pro-interventionist spokesman.[21] On more than one occasion he was attacked by hostile neutralist crowds and had to run for his life. His shady reputation, that of a political adventurer funded by Liberal administrations in Madrid just to create trouble for the Catalan Nationalists and woo the workers with false promises, did not help him, nor did it benefit the Allied cause. The British Embassy regarded him as an embarrassment. His speeches and actions were seen by the Allies, particularly in the first year of the war, as a gift to the Germanophiles and as a useless provocation to the government. On 26 May 1915, in a speech at Santa Cruz de Tenerife, Lerroux equated the kind of neutrality defended by the Dato cabinet with cowardice. In June 1915 there were all kind of rumours that the Radicals were plotting to bomb 27 German ships in Barcelona with a view to drawing Spain into the conflict. Earlier that year, Lerroux himself had become involved in the messy business of mediating in a transaction on behalf of Spanish groups who intended to sell rifles and ammunition to the British firm Vickers. Prime Minister Dato was enraged when he heard that Lerroux had asked for a commission of £120,000, partly for his own services and partly as an outright bribe to be offered to Dato himself.[22]

A different image was presented by the Reformist party led by the Asturian Melquiades Alvarez. Since its creation in 1912 that political group had adopted an accidentalist stand: without abandoning its Republican principles it had vowed to accept the existing regime if this was prepared to carry through a real process of democratization. Alvarez initially approved of the neutrality adopted by the government, but gradually moved to support a more benevolent attitude towards the Allies. On 1 May 1915 he declared in Granada that Spain should side with France and Britain even if they were defeated. This attitude was welcomed by the Allied diplomats as it appeared to be based on a principled assessment of the political reality, unlike that of Lerroux which seemed motivated mainly by profit or demagogy. In September 1915 Alvarez visited Paris, and on his return he became the chief spokesman for the Allied cause in Spain.[23]

The neutrality issue also had an impact on the labour movement. The organized working class in Spain was divided between Anarcho-Syndicalist and Marxist currents. The first was represented by the Confederación Nacional del Trabajo (CNT) and the second by the Socialist party (PSOE) and its trade union the Unión General de Trabajadores (UGT) These two organizations adopted different attitudes to the war. The CNT had been created in 1910 and had only just emerged from years of repression by the time of the outbreak of the hostilities in Europe. Its membership of only 15,000, mainly concentrated in Catalonia and Andalusia, meant that its influence was relatively small. The Anarcho-Syndicalists adopted an internationalist stand, condemning the war and refusing to take sides in what they regarded as a capitalist struggle. Despite the fact that some leading European Anarchists, such as the Italian Malatesta, the Russian Kropotkin and even the French Anarcho-Syndicalist trade union, the CGT, had sided with the Allies, the overwhelming majority of Spanish Anarchists and Syndicalists remained committed to neutrality. Their determination to adhere to that formula was confirmed in a Congress held in Ferrol in February 1915 which concluded with the slogan 'Revolution before War'. During the last years of the conflict, Anarchist intransigence and violent class warfare would become an asset to the Germans, who cleverly manipulated and used some of the extremist elements in the CNT for their own purposes.[24]

The Socialists presented a different picture. In 1914, with only one deputy in the Cortes and electorally allied to the Republicans since 1909, they still had a long way to go to catch up in size and influence with their European counterparts. Yet with almost 100,000 members in the UGT and with a solidly centralized and carefully built organization, the Socialists could claim to speak for the Spanish proletariat. The outbreak of the war caught them completely unprepared. Initially they proclaimed their internationalism and denounced the 'imperialist contest'. However, as it became clear that the Second International had failed to prevent the war and after Germany had invaded neutral Belgium in the summer of 1914, the Socialists began to change their initial stance. Soon the editorials in *El Socialista* were pointing to German militarism as the main cause of the war.

The Socialists' new position was clearly revealed in an article on 12 September, 1914 called 'Formas de Neutralidad' ('Ways of being neutral'). It portrayed the Great War as a struggle between the Central Powers defending the old order and the Entente which was fighting for progress and democracy. It argued that Socialists, unlike the reactionary elements in the country, believed that Spain should remain neutral because of economic and military deficiencies, but that neutrality should be benevolent towards the Allies. Thus Socialists and Republicans were in virtual agreement. This pro-Entente position was confirmed by the rhetoric of the old and authoritarian Socialist leader Pablo Iglesias. On 5 November 1914 Iglesias expressed in the Cortes his support for the Allied cause. A few months later Fabra Ribas, a member of the PSOE's National Executive, published a pamphlet entitled *El socialismo y el conflicto europeo. ¡Kaiserismo, He ahí el peligro!* ('Socialism and the European conflict. Kaiserism, the danger'). At the Tenth Congress of the party held at the Casa del Pueblo in Madrid between 24–31 October 1915, Iglesias and the PSOE's leadership defeated the internationalist opposition. Two questions were dealt with: the continuance of the *conjunción* or alliance with the Republicans and their attitude towards the war. Through its tight control of the party apparatus, the National Executive imposed its views on both matters. Iglesias himself and his right-hand man Julián Besteiro, a university professor, spoke in favour of continuing the *conjunción* and won by a narrow margin of 3,106 votes to 2,850. The internationalist motion was also defeated by 4,090 votes to 2,018. Henceforth, with the leadership firmly in control and the alliance with the Republicans confirmed, the Socialists became one of the outspoken defenders of the Allied cause in Spain.[25]

In the struggle to incline Spanish neutrality towards one or the other of the warring blocs, the Allies could count on important economic and geographic advantages. It seemed evident that unless the Western Powers were close to being badly beaten, no Spanish administration would contemplate the idea of moving closer to Germany. Yet these initial advantages were outweighed by an active and masterly strategy conducted in Spain by the Central Powers which gave them the initiative virtually throughout the four years of war. Their strategy can be divided into two phases: until early 1916, they followed a diplomatic campaign; for the remainder of the conflict, that campaign was reinforced by a very well organized intelligence network whose activities ranged from sponsoring press offensives against unfriendly politicians to financing both Anarchist groups in the peninsula and rebel guerrillas in Morocco. The objective was to ensure that Spain would never abandon her neutrality.

Until late 1915 there were hardly any references to German espionage in Spain. The dismantling of a wireless apparatus in a Carmelite convent at Portugalete (Bilbao) in October 1914 was probably an isolated case.[26] Yet by then the Director of the British Intelligence Service had already noted the close relations established between the German Embassy and the clergy, the military and the upper classes as well as Germany's influence on right-wing newspapers such as *ABC*, *El Correo Español*, *La Correspondencia Militar*, *El Debate* and *El Universo*.[27]

In fact, in the struggle to win the support of the Spanish ruling elites Germany had two important advantages over her rivals. First, the cause defended by the Central Powers could easily be portrayed as synonymous with that of the forces of order in Spain. Through its control of the right-wing media, the German offensive created an image of Germany as the best friend of the monarchy and the ruling political order, while the Allies were described as supporters of revolutionary and Republican groups in the peninsula. Secondly, Germany's efficient press campaign was far superior to that pursued by the Western Powers. The Allied press campaign did not take off until early 1916, and even then was mainly due to the activities of pro-Allied persons like Luis Araquistáin who managed to convince the British Secret War Propaganda Bureau to subsidize a propaganda offensive which could counter that of the Central Powers.[28]

One example of Germany's skilful propaganda was her ability to exploit the Portuguese case to create bad blood between the two peninsular states, and, indirectly, between Spain and Portugal's friends, the Entente. In October 1910, after a turbulent and violent decade, Portugal had proclaimed a Republic of a clear radical character. Subsequent relations with Spain, which certainly had a hand in some of the conspiracies to restore the Portuguese monarchy, were far from friendly. Unlike Spain's, Portugal's neutrality was openly benevolent towards the Allies. As early as October and November 1914, the British Embassy in Madrid was warning the Foreign Office that some Spanish circles and the king himself would be unhappy if Portugal threw in her lot with the Entente. The British ambassador, Hardinge, even wrote that Britain should never sacrifice her friendship with Spain to Portuguese ambitions or exigencies.[29]

Throughout 1915 the pro-German press in Spain continually referred to the support given by the Western Powers to the leftist Portuguese Republic. The British Foreign Office and the Ambassador at Lisbon, Lancelot D. Carnegie, believed that Portugal should not become a belligerent as she was more useful rendering services as a neutral. Furthermore, the active participation of the Portuguese Republic in the war would present Germany with a golden opportunity to promote ill-will between the two neighbours and would be unwelcome to almost all the dynastic politicians and the king. Carnegie was therefore instructed in July 1915 to let the Portuguese Foreign Minister Soares know that the British government was anxious that Portugal should not become a belligerent. During the following months both Hardinge and Carnegie pursued the same line with other Portuguese ministers and the President of the Republic, Bernardino Machado. The Portuguese politicians recognized that intervention in the war might make matters more difficult between the two peninsular states, and expressed their fear that if the Allies were badly beaten, reactionary and monarchist elements in Spain could either foment a revolutionary outbreak in Portugal to overthrow the Republic or find an excuse to proceed with a full-scale invasion. Hence they indicated that they were against declaring war on Germany, although the provocative and violent attitude of the latter finally forced the Portuguese to break off diplomatic relations and withdraw their ambassador in Berlin.[30] As a result Germany herself declared war on Portugal in March 1916. The Portuguese example and the extreme care displayed by the British diplomats revealed the Allies' deep insecurity with regard to Spain. They felt that Germany could always exploit her excellent relations with the Spanish court, army and church and embarrass the Entente on sensitive problems such as Portuguese intervention.

Additionally, Germany had ample room to manoeuvre on territorial concerns. It is highly unlikely that the Germans really believed that Spain could be tempted to the extent that she would decide to enter the war. Yet it proved to be an astute approach by which the Central Powers could both show their 'Spanish friends' the value of maintaining that friendship and also put sufficient pressure on the government to maintain strict neutrality in the conflict. Germany's asset was that her real aim was simply to prevent any Spanish administration departing from the position adopted in August 1914. Unlike Italy, where the territory coveted by the Italians belonged to the Habsburg Empire, the Germans could promise territories to Spain that did not belong either to themselves or their allies. Thus, knowing that geographic and economic factors barred Spain from aligning with her in the war, Germany could not only be generous with promises in exchange for an almost impossible alliance, but also hint that Spain's strict neutrality might be rewarded in the new European order following a German victory. By contrast, the Western Powers had to face the dilemma of either rejecting any territorial resettlement and thereby confirming the idea spread by the Germanophiles that they were historic enemies who had always sought to weaken and humiliate Spain, or else sacrificing valuable territory merely to secure Spanish gratitude.

German diplomacy was relatively successful in 1915. There is clear evidence of how its initiative permeated various Spanish political circles. Western diplomats were thrown off balance when friendly Spanish politicians, obviously reacting to Germany's territorial concessions, approached them with demands that they should match that offer. As early as January 1915, Prime Minister Dato confided to Hardinge that there were rumours that some extreme clerics and Carlists were looking to replace Alfonso XIII with an unnamed Prussian Prince to whom Tangier, Gibraltar and Portugal had already been promised by the German Embassy. Dato naturally dismissed them as pure fiction; nevertheless he noted that the strongest argument among Germanophiles was that Germany had never done Spain any harm in the past, and might conceivably do her some good.[31] One month later, the Spanish ambassador in London, Merry del Val, confirmed that his government and king were determined to maintain neutrality, but pointed out that the Germans were organizing regular propaganda by buying up newspapers and plotting with the clergy. They had also offered Spain Gibraltar and Tangier. The Foreign Office believed that what the German ambassador in Madrid, Prince Ratibor, had actually promised was that if Spain were to take Gibraltar and Tangier, Germany would not interfere.[32] The extent of the concessions the Germans were prepared to offer kept changing throughout the rest of the year. Sometimes only Gibraltar and Tangier were on offer; at other times they included control of Portugal and French Morocco as well. The sources of information cannot be doubted as they include such figures as the Count Romanones and the editor of the *Correspondencia de España*, Leopoldo Romeo, and also French and British citizens who had been in contact with the Spanish monarch.[33]

At the outbreak of hostilities the Allies had a certain interest in drawing Spain onto their side. On 17 August 1914 a secret report issued by the Admiralty War Staff on 24 December 1912 was circulated. The advantages of an alliance with Spain were underlined:

Under existing conditions, in the event of a war between the Triple Entente and the Triple Alliance, the strategic position in the Mediterranean limits in a marked degree the offensive operations of the Entente . . .

The accession of Spain to the Triple Entente as an active partner would introduce a change which may make its influence felt through all the plans of the Triple Alliance. Spain could possibly put an army of 50,000 men into the field, in addition to the reserves kept at home and the garrisons of distant positions . . . The mere knowledge that the Franco-British command of the Mediterranean was backed by 50,000 troops would introduce a fresh element into the situation which Italy could not afford to ignore, and which might in time help to weaken her adhesion to the Triple Alliance. Italy is peculiarly vulnerable to amphibious attack.

The other results of a Spanish adhesion to the Triple Entente would be, first, addition of the Spanish ships of war to the sea forces at the disposal of the Entente – which though providing a small increase of strength only, would be of considerable service in certain directions; and, secondly, the right of our own ships to use certain Spanish ports.

. . . To sum up.

Should Spain join the Triple Entente, the military situation would be improved to the extent by which the Spanish army could increase the effect produced by the Franco-British maritime supremacy in the Mediterranean in the later stages of a war. British overseas commerce in the Atlantic would be more safely conducted and more easily defended. No corresponding disadvantages worthy of consideration immediately present themselves.[34]

Simultaneously, in 1914 the British Foreign Office considered it vital to break up a possible German intelligence centre at Tangier and concluded that if France would agree, the best solution would be to let Spain have Tangier as the price of her alliance.[35] Yet, as emerged from the Admiralty's report, the Italian position was crucial when considering the advantages of a possible understanding with Spain. Italy's entry into the war on the side of the Western Powers in May 1915 certainly cooled the Allied initiatives towards Spain. Neither France nor Great Britain was unhappy with the neutrality adopted by Dato and there is no evidence that they tried to influence the Spanish government to reconsider its position. In any case, what the Entente probably expected was a formal approach from the Spanish administration offering intervention in exchange for territorial concessions; the Entente never intended to take the first step.

The Dato cabinet was not prepared to abandon neutrality. It rebuffed all German offers as well as avoiding any approach to the Allies. However, Spanish politicians, particularly those regarded as friendly, kept alluding to the necessity of obtaining some territorial gain. Their main objective was to acquire Tangier. Yet they did not and could not promise anything beyond their friendship and moral support. Obviously, the Entente could not consider this as an acceptable basis for discussion.

On 18 April 1915 Romanones spoke at Palma de Mallorca. He already hoped to succeed Dato in the government, and in order to do so he needed the support of all the factions of his Liberal party. Thus Romanones had to be careful not to lay himself open to charges of pro-interventionism. Therefore his former pro-Allied views were somewhat played down. Nevertheless, once more he insisted that Spain should remain loyal to the international line she had adopted before 1914. Isolation was not an option for any European state at that time. The Count believed that the war provided an opportunity to enlarge the Spanish empire in Morocco:

> The possession of the Moroccan coasts is one of the surest means of defending our interests in the Mediterranean . . . It is natural that the government should observe silence but we who have no such responsibility are obliged to declare that the possession of Tangier constitutes a national aspiration.[36]

Learning of Romanones's speech, the British Foreign Office instructed Hardinge not to push the question of Tangier. The French Foreign Minister wished to leave the question open.[37] A few days later, Maura repeated the same argument at Madrid's Royal Theatre: 'The future of Tangier must be Spanish and only Spanish . . . without Tangier, Spain cannot possibly fulfil her mission in the Protectorate . . .'[38] Two other leading Liberal politicians known for their pro-Entente sympathies, Manuel González Hontoria, a former Under-Secretary of State at the Foreign Office, and Juan Pérez Caballero, former Foreign Minister, reached a similar conclusion. In an article in *ABC*, the former pleaded for unity of purpose among the many Spanish factions in order to concentrate public opinion on a definite goal. That goal ought to be the ultimate acquisition of Tangier. Pérez Caballero declared in *El Mundo* that Spain had only one ambition in the Mediterranean and that was the occupation of Tangier. Moreover, he suggested that France had accepted that fact in 1902 and that Britain's interests would in no way suffer. However, such an object could only be obtained by loyalty and friendship towards France and Britain.[39] The king himself showed a keen interest in the subject. This was the impression that both Monsieur Cooreman and the Bishop of Southwark gained after their meetings with Alfonso in March and October 1915 respectively.[40] The Spanish monarch even obtained the goodwill of the Russian ambassador, Baron Budberg, in order to put pressure on the Allies to obtain Tangier.[41]

The Western Powers were open to any suggestions, but they were not prepared to give territory without gaining something in return. However, the king seemed to imply otherwise in his conversation with Monsieur Cooreman:

> His Majesty expressed friendly sentiments but said that he was in a difficult position between the Germans, who were supported by the Spanish Right and who offered him Gibraltar, Morocco and a free hand in Portugal, and the Allies who seemed not to feel gratitude for the services which he had rendered them. The king refrained from stating what he expected from the Allies, but Monsieur Cooreman derived the impression he had Tangier in mind. His Majesty did not apparently mention the nature of the services to which he made allusion.[42]

To the Allies, the strategy followed by the Spanish monarch and his politicians amounted to moral blackmail. Not lending their ears to the impossible German offers could not conceivably be regarded as services rendered to the Allied war effort. Between the months of May and November 1915 France and Britain had to consider how to deal with Spanish territorial claims. The British believed that active Spanish assistance could be of value and therefore an arrangement should be made in exchange for her intervention. In July, the British War Office supported the idea of giving Tangier to Spain, and together with the Admiralty was inclined to think in positive terms about exchanging Gibraltar for Ceuta. Simultaneously, however, objections were also being raised: the French had to agree and there was the problem of continuous anarchy in the Spanish zone in Morocco. It was seriously doubted that Spain could maintain order and assure security for European life and property. Thus there was always a strong case for not pushing matters and instead waiting for the Spanish government to make a formal approach both with its demands and with what it was prepared to offer in return. After talks between the British Foreign Minister Grey and his French counterpart, Cambon, this was finally the policy adopted by the Entente.[43]

Dato never contemplated the idea of departing from neutrality, and consequently he never approached the Allies with any proposal which could have jeopardized the non-involvement of his country in the conflict. Yet his problems were not over, for the impact in Europe was to make itself dramatically felt on the Spanish economy and society. Dato's inability to tackle the growing economic crisis brought about his downfall in December 1915.

During the conflict Spain underwent profound social, demographic and economic change. She took advantage of her neutral status to supply both camps; foreign competition was eliminated in the internal market and new outlets, which had to be abandoned by the belligerent nations, were taken over. The country experienced its first industrial take-off. The period of the Great War

Table 2.1 Spain's balance of trade between 1913 and 1920 (million pesetas)

Year	Imports	Exports	Balance
1913	1,308.8	1,078.5	−230.3
1914	1,025.5	880.7	−144.8
1915	976.7	1,257.9	281.1
1916	945.9	1,377.6	431.6
1917	735.5	1,324.5	589.0
1918	590.0	1,009.0	418.9
1919	900.2	1,310.6	410.4
1920	1,423.3	1,020.0	−403.3

Source: Instituto Nacional de Estadística, Comercio exterior de España: números índices, 1901–1956, Madrid, 1958, p. 27.

was a time of unexpected economic growth but it also seriously eroded the fragile foundations of the established ruling order. The war years were ones of extraordinary profits but equally of staggering price rises. They brought prosperity but also exacerbated the overall misery of the nation.[44]

During the first months after the outbreak of hostilities, the Spanish economy was in a state of disorder and confusion. There were difficulties in obtaining raw materials abroad and international credit was harder to procure. This adversely affected the stock market and financial and banking institutions. Yet by early 1915 a previously unknown phase of expansion of the economy began. The radical drop in imports together with the rising volume and prices of exports meant that a poor nation, almost overnight, saw a sudden flow of gold across her frontiers. Spain experienced a period of rapid accumulation of capital which was created by a highly favourable balance of trade (Table 2.1).

As exports grew and imports dwindled, the balance of trade registered an era of fabulous profits. Hundreds of new businesses and joint-stock companies were established and the Bank of Spain increased its gold reserves from 674 million pesetas in 1913 to 2,500 million in 1917. However, the amount of money in circulation also increased from 1,931 million pesetas in 1913 to 3,866.9 million in 1919. Consequently, the peseta lost half of its purchasing power. Prices shot up dramatically. By 1920 they were 223.19 per cent above those of 1914. This caused rampant inflation which led to shortages, widened the gap between rich and poor and initiated an internal migratory current that dislocated the weak foundations of the Spanish economy (Table 2.2).

Furthermore, this economic and financial growth was extremely uneven. Industrial production expanded more rapidly than that of agriculture and therefore the prices of manufactured products rose more rapidly than others. The boom benefited only certain regions and certain social classes. Profits were mainly monopolized by a rising industrial and commercial bourgeoisie.

Table 2.2 Evolution of prices 1914–1920

Period	Countryside	Cities
April 1909–March 1914	100	100
April 1914–September 1914	106	106.9
October 1914–March 1915	110.8	107.7
April 1915–September 1915	117.1	113.8
October 1915–March 1916	118.4	117.6
April 1916–September 1916	123.4	120.3
October 1916–March 1917	125.6	123.6
April 1917–September 1917	139.8	136.1
October 1917–March 1918	149.3	145.4
April 1918–September 1918	172.8	161.8
October 1918–March 1919	178.5	167.7
April 1919–September 1919	190	180
October 1919–March 1920	208.1	192.3
April 1920–September 1920	220.3	202.3

Source: Instituto de Reformas Sociales, *Movimientos de precios al por menor durante la guerra*, Madrid, 1923, p. 7.

Industrial regions entered a phase of feverish activity while other areas of the peninsula were devastated by shortages and inflation. The mining sector went through a golden age, particularly the production of coal in Asturias. The chemical and hydroelectric industries also expanded greatly. The Catalan textile concerns experienced a period of massive growth, as they could now not only supply most belligerent nations but also make inroads into traditional British markets in Latin America. The Basque steel, iron and shipping companies also increased their profits, especially the last, which benefited from the spectacular rise in transport costs. Finally, the banking sector was the other great winner of the period. In four years the number of financial companies and private banks doubled.

The war favoured the expansion of certain industrial and financial enterprises but also exacerbated the regional, social and economic differences in the country. The forced reduction of imports meant severe scarcities of foodstuffs and manufactured goods, rising prices and worsening living standards for rural and urban workers. Substantial profits were reaped, above all by speculators who exported virtually anything required by the war machine regardless of the consumption needs or welfare of Spaniards, and by profiteers who hoarded products in expectation of a boom in prices. Furthermore, the railway network proved unable to cope with the increased volume of traffic and virtually collapsed. The regions of central and southern Spain suffered most tragically from the effects of the war. A current of migration from the countryside to the cities and from the south to the north began to assume significant proportions. Wages could not keep pace with the rising prices of such basic products as sugar, eggs, bread, potatoes, meat and dairy products.

There was widespread unemployment and scarcity. Consequently, for most people this period was one of crisis characterized by food shortages, a fall in real wages and severe material distress. It was a situation popularly described as a *crisis de subsistencias*.[45]

The uneven impact of the war on the Spanish economy and society continually sparked off food riots, mutinies and popular protests. The mobilization of social forces which had previously remained politically passive contributed to the breakdown of existing forms of clientelist politics, confronting the governing elites with the uncertainties of popular politics, the unwelcome appearance of more genuine democracy, and the rapidly advancing threat of socialism.

In 1915 the first signs of popular discontent, social unrest and economic hardship were becoming evident. The Dato administration proved unable to cope with these new realities. It initiated the nationalization of foreign-owned assets in Spain and of the external debt. However, the Conservative government failed miserably to solve the *crisis de subsistencias*. Rather Spain's socio-economic crisis rapidly deepened with the return of over 40,000 Spanish workers from other European countries and Latin America, the introduction by the belligerent countries of import quotas and restrictions on exports. Shortages, unemployment and inflation were the results. In September 1914 a *Junta de Iniciativas* was set up under the direction of the former Minister of the Interior and right-wing Conservative Juan de la Cierva. Its objective was to channel, co-ordinate and implement a series of initiatives to deal with the crisis. In February 1915 Cierva resigned and the *Junta* was dissolved.[46] Thereafter *Juntas Provinciales de Subsistencias*, formed by the Civil Governor, the Mayor and a delegate from the Treasury, were created in each provincial capital. None of their attempts to control and regulate prices and exports of basic products led to any positive outcome as prices kept rising and profiteers and speculators prospered. The Conservative cabinet, like the following *Turno* administrations, proved unable or unwilling to fight those who benefited from the exceptional circumstances provided by the war. This was scarcely surprising, as those profiting were most often the very same local notables and *caciques* to whom the political class owed its votes. Simultaneously, the attempt in June 1915 by the Minister of Finance, Gabino Bugallal, to raise a loan to cover the Treasury Debt fell very short of expectations as capitalists preferred to invest in the shares of shipping or textile companies.

By late 1915 the government seemed to have abandoned its efforts to find solutions for the economy. Dato insisted that the military reforms should take precedence in the list of parliamentary business over every other item, including the budget. On 6 December, the Liberal leader, Count Romanones, backed by the Republican, Radical and Carlist minorities, presented a proposal which amounted to a motion of censure. He requested the Chamber to declare that the duty of the government had been to submit an integrated package of economic and financial measures appropriate to the crisis facing the country. Romanones demanded that the Chamber should proceed without delay to the introduction and discussion of such a bill and to a budget suited to the internal needs of the country and to the most pressing requirements of its Treasury. Realizing that he had lost the 'goodwill' of the other dynastic party, Dato resigned.

3

THE ROMANONES
ADMINISTRATION

The domestic challenge

After the fall of Dato in December 1915 the Liberal leader, Count Romanones, rapidly formed a new government. The Count, a Spanish grandee, was known for his cynical approach to politics, a shrewd ability in party manoeuvring, a skilful gambler's style with regard to important issues and for his good contacts at court. He was regarded by many as the perfect example of the *Turno* professional politician: a man without ideological principles or political ideas, but able to remain in power by his clever manipulation and control of the electoral machinery and its *clientelista* foundations. The novelist and leading figure of the cultural *Generación del 98*, Miguel Unamuno, wrote that the ultimate semantic paradox was that Romanones should be the leader of Spanish liberalism.[1]

In fact, Romanones's deviousness and opportunism was above that of his peers. In 1909 he was one of the Liberal notables who encouraged the then party leader, Segismundo Moret, to take advantage of the turbulent situation created by the crushing of the anticlerical and antimilitarist riots of that summer to join forces with the Republicans and oust Antonio Maura, the Conservative Prime Minister, from office. Once this was achieved, Romanones exploited the fact that Moret was too close to the Republicans to end both his premiership and his leadership of the party and replace him with the more malleable José Canalejas. After Canalejas's murder in November 1912 Romanones took over the leadership of the Liberal party, defeating all other faction leaders. With the king's complicity he outmanoeuvred them by claiming the right to take 'temporary' charge of the premiership as the Speaker of the Lower Chamber.[2]

There were increasing rumours that the other Liberal notables, annoyed by the Count's rise to power, were plotting his downfall. Romanones was not prepared to let his main rival, the Marquis of Alhucemas, form a new cabinet which might have represented the end of his supremacy in the Liberal party. Instead he preferred to relinquish office to the Conservatives. Maura's refusal to rotate with those whom he had regarded since 1909 as unprincipled and treacherous Liberals was an obstacle to Romanones's scheme. However, anxious to regain power the Conservatives ditched Maura and, led now by the rich lawyer and former minister Eduardo Dato, resumed office on 29 October 1913. The *Turno Pacífico* survived but the Conservative party was irretrievably divided between *Mauristas* and *Idóneos*.[3]

Romanones's second administration was to last from December 1915 to April 1917. This period is crucial to an understanding of the crisis of hegemony of the ruling system. A process which had begun in 1898 now accelerated dramatically as the dynastic politicians lost their leading role in political society and found their exercise of power increasingly questioned by all sections of the political spectrum.

The programme Romanones outlined at the opening of the Cortes in May 1916 was widely welcomed. The government promised to solve the *crisis de subsistencias* by stimulating the economy through a vast plan of economic and financial measures to fight shortages, inflation and unemployment, foster agriculture, public credit and transport, prevent the export of capital and emigration, strengthen national defence, modernize the judicial and educational systems, reduce expenses in Morocco and maintain strict neutrality.[4] Yet the impossibility of delivering any of these promises confirmed the mounting evidence that both *Turno* parties lacked the ability to adapt themselves to the changing circumstances brought about by the war and increased the general disillusionment with the established order. Now the *Zeitgeist* was the spirit of corporatism.[5] The rapid economic, social and ideological changes produced by the Great War meant that the regime's lack of grass roots support or popular appeal in a period of mass mobilization could no longer be concealed. Different social groups (the labour movement, industrial bourgeoisie and the army), upset by the inability of the government to satisfy their demands, resorted to corporatist solutions through which their particular interests would be better protected. Additionally Romanones, unlike the other dynastic leaders before or after him, took an active interest in the international question. Spain under his government came very close to joining the Entente. This was to cost him the premiership. On his departure from office Romanones left a country more polarized than ever before by the neutrality debate; his own party was split and broken, and the proletariat, bourgeoisie and army were eagerly awaiting the moment to strike against the *Turno*. The seeds of destruction of the existing order had been planted.

1 The labour movement

The organized labour movement had always been divided ideologically and geographically between two antagonistic camps: a Marxist tendency concentrated in Castille, Asturias and the Basque Country and an Anarcho-Syndicalist current dominant among the workers of Catalonia, Levante and Andalusia. Their evolution and strategies were very different.[6]

Marxism was represented by the Spanish Socialist Party (PSOE) and its trade union, the Unión General de Trabajadores (UGT). Spanish Socialism suffered from several deficiencies which to a large extent explain its failure to establish a hegemony within the organized labour movement. The Socialist leader, Pablo Iglesias, and the National Committee based in Madrid exercised their authority through their tight control of the party, trade union and daily newspaper, *El Socialista*. Lacking an intellectual tradition, they interpreted Marxism through the writings of French Socialists such as Jules Guesde and Paul Lafargue, which actually bore little relation to the Spanish situation. They defended reductionist, rigid and deterministic positions. The preservation of the purity of the movement was considered paramount and thus the PSOE isolated itself from contacts with other progressive forces which might 'contaminate' it with bourgeois ideas. They had an almost blind faith in the future victory of Socialism in the world. Official party rhetoric was therefore full of revolutionary fervour and promises of a classless society after the establishment of the dictatorship of the proletariat. In practice, however, Spanish Socialists employed an extremely moderate and reformist strategy. They concentrated on the daily struggle to obtain immediate gains, and under the strict control of Iglesias emphasis was laid on discipline and organization. Moreover, in spite of the corrupt character of the *Turno Pacífico*, the PSOE had subordinated the economic struggle to political and electoral initiatives. In fact, the first Socialist councillors were not elected until 1905. The hollowness of this strategy, torn apart by internal tensions between revolutionary theory and legalist action, limited the appeal and hindered the growth of the movement. Absorbed by political matters, they established their headquarters in Madrid when industrial Barcelona should have been the main focus of their activities. The evolution of Spanish Socialism was thus slow and even painful but built on a solid organizational basis. Its strength mainly lay among the labour 'aristocracy' of Madrid, the Asturian miners and the workers of the steel and shipping concerns of the Basque Country.

On the other hand, Spanish Anarcho-Syndicalism had always followed an irregular evolution: moments of euphoria and mass membership were often followed by state repression and the virtual disappearance of the movement. Yet socialist centralism, authoritarianism and politicism hardly appealed to Catalan workers or Andalusian landless peasants. Direct action and violent methods were not alien to them, since they could not obtain redress for their grievances from a corrupt political system that either failed to understand the Catalan class struggle or was completely dependent on the votes delivered by the Andalusian *caciques*. Nevertheless, far from constituting a real threat to the regime, Anarchist terrorism and insurrectionalism were regarded by the authorities merely as a nuisance to be dealt with by police repression. Moreover, the loose character of its organization facilitated its destruction. By the turn of the century, the movement had been crushed and only in 1907 did a revival seem to take place when Solidaridad Obrera was created in Barcelona to organize the local trade unions regardless of their ideological leanings.

After the Tragic Week of July 1909 and the subsequent repressive response of the state the two movements came to different conclusions. The Socialists abandoned their traditional isolationist stand and in November 1909 established a *conjunción* or electoral alliance with the Republicans. During this period, the UGT made a more systematic use of the strike weapon, initiating a series of nation-wide strikes in 1911 and 1912. Yet the leadership's main concern remained the electoral and organizational aspect of the *conjunción*. This seemed to pay off when Pablo Iglesias became the first Socialist deputy in May 1910. Furthermore, a number of important intellectuals like Julián Besteiro, Luis Araquistáin and Andrés Ovejero decided to join the party.

Shortly after the creation of the Republican–Socialist alliance, Solidaridad Obrera and other non-Catalan and non-Socialist trade unions met at Barcelona in October 1910 with the objective of setting up a national organization: the Confederación Nacional del Trabajo or CNT was created. From the beginning the newly created CNT was divided between a moderate Syndicalist tendency and an Anarchist hard line. The former seemed to gain the upper hand when terrorist methods of 'propaganda by deed' were discarded and instead emphasis was placed on the creation of a powerful organization. Nevertheless, the CNT continued to be more militant than the UGT. Revolutionary Syndicalism borrowed from the French Confédération Générale du Travail constituted its main ideological philosophy. It rejected parliamentarian politics and concentrated on the economic struggle by means of direct action spearheaded by a powerful trade union movement. Thus the Syndicalists were soon behind a series of ill-timed and badly co-ordinated strikes. At the end of 1911 the CNT was declared illegal by a Barcelona judge. Then, following the assassination of the Liberal Prime Minister Canalejas in November 1912, a crackdown on the organization forced the CNT to resort to a clandestine existence.

After the outbreak of the First World War the Socialist movement, with experienced cadres, a patiently built organization and 84,762 members in the UGT, was clearly the most important force in the Spanish labour movement. The CNT did not really begin its reconstruction until 1915 and then had only 15,000 militants. Apart from the traditional tactical and ideological differences, the pro-Entente position of the Socialist leaders, as opposed to the neutral stand of the Anarcho-Syndicalists, seemed to widen the gap between both organizations. The impact of the war was such, however, that for the first time the dream of the unity of the Spanish proletariat was almost realized.

The hardship and distress brought about by the European conflict bore mainly on the working classes. While some areas in the north and the east of the country experienced a dramatic economic boom and industrial expansion, the centre and the south were hit badly by unemployment and recession. The workers' conditions therefore varied according to region. In Valencia, Barcelona, Vizcaya, Asturias, Santander and León, salaries during these years increased by more than 100 per cent, but in Extremadura and Andalusia by only 50 per cent. At no time did salaries catch up with prices.[7] The enforced return of thousands of Spaniards working abroad, internal migration from the agrarian south to the industrial cities of the north or Madrid, the sudden end of crucial imports and the rising trend towards exporting basic products all combined to destroy the semblance of social harmony in the country. Furthermore, while fortunes were being amassed by industrialists, galloping inflation was eroding the living standards of the workers. In many cases, recently arrived migrant workers to cities such as Barcelona had to endure appalling living conditions, derisory wages and insecurity of employment. To make matters worse, the entrepreneurial inefficiency of the parvenue bourgeoisie was matched only by the prodigality with which it squandered its profits. Much new-found wealth was frittered away on ostentatious display rather than rationally invested in industry or agricultural modernization. Such cavalier disregard for the living conditions of those on whose backs the wealth was created could hardly fail to antagonize Spanish workers.[8]

In early 1916 the *crisis de subsistencias* had become a reality. In only two years the prices of basic staples had risen alarmingly: 1 kg of bread by 24.3 per cent, 1 kg of beef by 33.5 per cent, 1 kg of cod by 57.8 per cent, 1 kg of potatoes by 35.2 per cent, 1 kg of chick-peas by 20.2 per cent, 1 kg of rice by 10.5 per cent, 1 kg of sugar by 18 per cent, a litre of milk by 13.8 per cent and a dozen eggs by 30.9 per cent.[9] As workers' wages could not keep pace with prices, resentment, discontent and hatred against the authorities mounted. Food riots, social unrest and violent clashes with the Civil Guard became a common feature all over Spain.

After a steady loss in membership during the first year of the war, from late 1915 onwards the labour movement experienced a remarkable advance in numbers of militants and simultaneously achieved a previously unknown strength in national politics. Membership shot up within this period mainly for two reasons: the employers' willingness to satisfy workers' demands for fear of losing markets at this extraordinary moment when huge profits could be made, and the inflationary cycle which pushed workers to fight in order to maintain their basic living standards. Between 1910 and 1918 the industrial proletariat grew by 60 per cent. In particular the numbers of miners, dockers, textile workers and those engaged in transport and metallurgy increased.[10]

As in other European countries, this was a crucial moment in which the organized labour movement in Spain began to become aware of its strength and potential to challenge the status quo. In 1916 social unrest and strike activity increased dramatically. A total of 2,415,304 working days were lost in comparison to 382,885 in 1915. The violent and militant mood of the workers could be seen all over the country. During the first months of 1916 Barcelona was rocked by a wave of strikes. Initially only bricklayers, metal workers and bakers were involved but by March it had become almost a general strike. There were numerous bloody events: 'scabs' were often attacked and even shot by Syndicalists. Several workers were also wounded by the police or arrested. In late January there were popular protests in Valencia, Castellón, Palencia and Bilbao. In February there were demonstrations demanding jobs and bread in Málaga, Santander and Saragossa and a general strike began in Valencia. In March social unrest spread to Murcia, Valladolid and La Rioja. There were riots in Logroño leaving one dead and five wounded. There were violent clashes in the docks of El Ferrol and the mines of La Carolina (Jaén), Río Tinto (Huelva) and La Unión (Cartagena). In La Unión alone nine people were killed and fifty wounded.[11]

Despite the revolutionary mood of the workers and the general spirit of militancy, the Socialist leadership did not change its traditional attitude: fierce rhetoric in speeches and articles in *El Socialista*, extreme moderation and caution in practice. Pablo Iglesias and his colleagues showed more interest in international issues and the electoral campaign. There was an evident gap between the ruling elements of the party and the workers.[12]

During the first months of 1916 *El Socialista* and *España* published a series of defiant and aggressive editorials which attacked the Romanones administration for not dealing with the *crisis de subsistencias* satisfactorily and accused the government both of condoning violent repression of the strike movement and of siding with the employers in the social conflicts.[13] In practice, however, the Socialist leadership continued to be as cautious and legalist as usual. As early as 20 January 1916 the provincial federation at Orense called upon the UGT's National Committee to organize a general stoppage across the country to force the government to deal with the social crisis. The National Committee brushed aside the idea, deeming it harmful for the organization. Instead delegations from party and union visited Romanones at least three times between January and March to apprise him of the dissatisfaction of the workers, to protest against the repressive methods used by the authorities and to demand relief measures to solve the crisis.[14] Romanones's personal record hardly suggested that he would heed the calls for redress.

Romanones's chicanery was rapidly confirmed when on 25 February the Count sacked his Minister of Finance, Angel Urzaiz, one of the very few *Turno* politicians who was regarded by both right and left as an honest man trying to seek genuine remedies for the social distress. Romanones insisted that he was forced to dismiss his Minister because Urzaiz had frequently acted on his own without consulting the other members of the Cabinet. Yet Urzaiz argued that the real reason he had to go was that his economic measures were damaging certain privileged interests.[15] He was replaced by Miguel Villanueva, Logroño's main *cacique* and one of the leading Liberal notables, who immediately reversed Urzaiz's measures.

The PSOE continued to devote most of its energies to campaigning for the general elections scheduled for 9 April. Romanones once more proved himself a master in the art of trickery and deception. He promised to organize clean elections and even spoke against article 29, which permitted the automatic return of deputies when they were unopposed in their constituencies and thus constituted the most important weapon in the armoury of the local *caciques*. In fact, a record 145 deputies, more than a third of those in the Congress, were returned by means of article 29. Among them were all the five candidates for the province of Guadalajara, Romanones's stronghold. In the elections of March 1914, 93 deputies had been elected in this way. Under the Minister of the Interior, Santiago Alba, the elections were fixed as usual in Madrid.[16]

The new chamber of April 1916 had a majority of 235 Liberals and 86 Conservative *Idóneos*. The Republican–Socialist *conjunción* returned only 13 deputies, among them just one Socialist, Pablo Iglesias. It was such a shameful spectacle – all the main dynastic leaders had several family members in the Congress with them – that it became known as the 'Cortes of the Relatives'.[17]

The tone of the Socialist editorials suggested that their authors were genuinely surprised and outraged by the way in which the elections had been conducted – as if this were the first time that polls had been rigged in Spain. Both *El Socialista* and *España* concluded that Spain was not yet ready for Socialism. They distinguished between reactionary plutocracy and progressive bourgeoisie. The former was represented by the monarchy and the oligarchies, the latter by the Republican and Regionalist parties. The Socialist press revealed that the best-known dynastic politicians were members of the boards of the main national companies. They affirmed that this was proof that within the existing system the country was dominated by a few privileged interests. The Socialists believed that it was in the interest of both proletariat and bourgeoisie to remove the Bourbon monarchy and replace it with a modern bourgeois republic.[18]

The Twelfth Congress of the UGT held at the Casa del Pueblo in Madrid on 17–24 May was a turning point in the history of the Spanish labour movement. The seeds for the mobilization of its militants in an open challenge to the state were sown there. Moreover, the first initiatives were made towards a pact with the CNT. They were adopted reluctantly by a leadership under constant pressure from the rank and file.

Two days before the opening of the Congress, the UGT's National Committee had been discussing different solutions to deal with the socioeconomic crisis. Iglesias, backed by his right-hand man, the Madrid-born councillor and moderate leader of the plasterers' trade union, Francisco Largo Caballero, argued that the working class consciousness had not yet been formed. Thus the workers should avoid a direct confrontation with the state. Iglesias stressed that it was not prudent to call for a general strike. The people were hungry and under such conditions they could only carry out 'epileptic movements'. The UGT should therefore work towards disciplining and organizing

33

the proletariat and not push it into dangerous initiatives. In the end a motion presented by the railway workers' leader Daniel Anguiano and backed by Largo Caballero was endorsed by the rest of the National Committee. This argued that in order to give an impression of strength a campaign of agitation should be initiated through meetings and demonstrations to force the government to tackle inflation and unemployment.[19] Julián Besteiro, a moderate Socialist and Professor of Logic at Madrid University, was commissioned to draw up the final resolution. It was put on the agenda of Congress on 22 May and received overwhelming approval. The main points were the following:

> The current crisis is not only hurting the proletariat. A good part of the bourgeoisie is also suffering from this obsolete regime which is sacrificing the welfare of the majority of the citizens for the sake of a minority of plutocrats.
>
> Therefore this message is directed to all those being hurt by the policies of the present government and whose agreement is deemed fundamental for a common campaign of national protest.
>
> It is proposed:
>
> 1   To demand once more from parliament and government: the reduction of transport fares; the implementation of public works; the regulation of exchange and trade; the suppression of industrial privileges; an end to unproductive expenditure, particularly the criminal war in Morocco.
> 2   To prepare the public and to secure a response from parliament and government, the UGT is to organize an intense campaign to attract as many militants as possible.
> 3   After that campaign a day of demonstrations and meetings is to be held throughout Spain in order to attract as many people as possible.
> 4   The National Committee with reports from the provinces and the collaboration of the regional delegates is to be empowered to determine in a period of three months whether it is feasible to organize a one-day nation-wide stoppage.
> 5   If after the one-day nation-wide stoppage government and parliament do not give a satisfactory response, the National Committee is to summon the regional delegates and together decide what line of action should be adopted.[20]

The motion was carefully phrased in very moderate and legalistic terms. The Socialists regarded government and parliament as the preferred solution to the crisis. Only if they failed to provide one would more active initiatives be adopted. Yet this motion constituted the party's first response to the demands from below. Moreover, the Socialists' scheme not only sought to appeal to the proletariat through a long campaign of propaganda and mobilization but also insisted that the objective was to win over all those damaged by the crisis. Consequently, the UGT–PSOE leaders took an important step forward in becoming the champions and main partners of the Republican–Socialist *conjunción*.

At the same Congress, a crucial boost was given to hopes of working class unity. A resolution from the Asturian delegates, Isidoro Acevedo and Manuel Llaneza, calling for the collaboration of both trade unions was overwhelmingly approved. It may appear contradictory that while the Socialist leadership were stressing their Republican commitments, they were also making overtures to the more radical CNT. However, this rapprochement can be explained by several factors.

First, there had always been a hope that workers' unity could be achieved. There was a general consensus among the rank and file of both CNT and UGT in 1916 that the gravity of the situation made it essential. On 4 May 1916, the Madrid bricklayers' trade union had demanded that the UGT's National Committee initiate contacts with the CNT. On 23 May, during the Twelfth UGT Congress the marble workers' trade union had also argued the need for both organizations to work together for common goals. Later there was the motion introduced by the Asturian miners. The pressure of the militants could no longer be ignored by the Socialist leadership.[21] Nevertheless the UGT's old-guard reformist leaders had historically been reluctant to collaborate with their Anarcho-Syndicalist counterparts. The Socialists were concerned with the discipline and centralization of the movement and despised the lack of co-ordination and violent methods of the Anarcho-Syndicalists. Even Acevedo and Llaneza themselves did not believe in alliances with the CNT. They had been obliged to move such a resolution against their own views since this was a compromise voted in Asturias by the miners whose interests they represented.[22] Iglesias and his colleagues must have felt that they could not turn down the proposal as this would have infuriated the Socialist rank and file. They probably realized that with the CNT struggling to re-emerge and still with a very low membership this was the best moment to clinch a pact on their own terms. The UGT would, they hoped, become the leading force within a unified labour movement.

Secondly, it was a particularly opportune moment because the CNT, whose Congress was taking place in Valencia at the same time as the one held by the UGT in Madrid, had clearly expressed its desire to collaborate with the Socialists. On 11 May, the Anarcho-Syndicalists stated that aim and were invited to send a delegation to Madrid. The fact that the CNT was largely controlled by moderate Syndicalist leaders such as Salvador Seguí and Angel Pestaña, who were concerned mainly with the organization of the movement, and the temporary decline of those Anarchists bent upon doctrinal purity and violence, made the idea of joining forces more attractive to the Socialists.[23]

There was hardly any revolutionary aspiration in the Socialist strategy. When at the UGT Congress the CNT delegate, Mauro Bajatierra, spoke in defence of the use of sabotage in the economic struggle, Iglesias quickly opposed the idea, arguing that in such a case the labour force would become the main victim of its own tactics and that it would place the workers in an inferior moral position.[24] Furthermore, on 6 June a delegation of the UGT headed by Julián Besteiro visited the Prime Minister. It handed him the conclusions of the Congress, exhorting him to solve the problems of shortages, unemployment and inflation. Once more, the Socialist leaders were behaving as moderate bureaucrats, informing the government well in advance of their plans in an attempt to avoid having to take more active measures.[25]

Nevertheless, such revolutionary stirrings could not be extinguished. The final push came from Angel Lacort, a leading Anarchist from Saragossa, who organized in his city a meeting of delegates from both the UGT and the CNT. The UGT was represented by Largo Caballero, Julián Besteiro and the moderate Vicente Barrio, who had presided over the Socialist Congress the month before, and the CNT by Salvador Seguí and Angel Pestaña. On 17 July 1916 the historic Pact of Saragossa was signed by both parties. For the first time in the history of the Spanish labour movement the two rival movements had decided to form a common front in order to force the government to take action over the socio-economic crisis. Romanones panicked and ordered the arrest of all those who had been present in Saragossa.

To add to Romanones's worries, the UGT–CNT alliance had arrived in the middle of the most important strike in Spain since 1912: that of railway workers against the Compañía del Norte which had begun on 12 July. The importance of this strike lay in the fact that the workers' demands were not only for the customary pay rises but also for official recognition by the company of the existence and right of the local trade union to represent its militants. The company categorically refused as it preferred to deal with workers on an individual basis, encouraging personal contracts and opposing their organization into a trade union. Both government and company were to suffer a dramatic defeat while the labour force gained one of its most important victories. Yet it was to be a pyrrhic triumph.

Right from the start, the cabinet revealed its true colours. Rafael Gasset, Minister of Public Works and owner of the newspaper *El Imparcial*, one of the most important Liberal mouthpieces, refused to act as mediator and openly sided with the company. At that stage, the railway workers' leaders Trifón Gómez, Daniel Anguiano and others would have backed down with the blessing of the UGT's National Committee if it had not been for the resolution of the militants. Alleging that a transport strike was a national disaster, the government made good use of all its resources to defeat the workers: the Cortes was quickly closed, constitutional guarantees suspended, martial law declared, leading trade unionists arrested and the militarization of the rail services ordered.

Andrés Saborit, a member of the UGT's National Committee, had been surprised in Asturias by the outbreak of the strike. In an exceptional and unexpected display of audacity and against the orders of the National Committee, on 16 July Saborit succeeded in persuading the Asturian miners to launch a strike in solidarity with the cause of the railway workers. Romanones lost his nerve. Despite all his tricks, he did not have the ruthlessness to order a bloodbath. Romanones was a politician who preferred to do a U-turn and seek a solution which would permit everyone to save face. This was achieved when on 18 July all the conflicting parties accepted the mediation of the Institute of Social Reforms headed by the moderate, veteran Republican Gumersindo Azcárate. On 29 July the Institute ruled in favour of the workers' demand for official recognition of their trade union. On 9 August a Royal Decree passed by the government recognized the legal character of the trade unions as the representative of the workers in their disputes and forced the companies running public services to accept that fact.[26]

The crucial victory in the railway strike gave an important boost to the morale of the labour movement, now strengthened and united by the alliance sealed in Saragossa. The campaign of mobilization proposed in May and temporarily disrupted by the events of July was therefore resumed with greater zeal. It began with a rallying call on 30 September in *El Socialista*. At the Casa del Pueblo, Madrid's Socialist headquarters, an appeal was made to public opinion to join with the united working class in demanding from the government solutions to unemployment, inflation and shortages. Five days later *El Socialista* accused the plutocratic regime of being unable to fight speculators and *caciques*. The Socialist newspaper proposed a number of remedies for the crisis including a tax on farmland, nationalization of uncultivated land and prohibition of exports of those basic commodities which were scarce at home.

The tension between fierce rhetoric and moderate demands still remained. A regime which was deemed incompetent and corrupt was given plenty of advance warning about every single initiative adopted by the labour leaders. Romanones, denounced during the summer by the Socialists as one of the main shareholders of the largest mining company in Morocco and therefore a prime example of the plutocracy in power, was still approached and briefed on all matters by these very same Socialists.[27]

On 15 October, a day of demonstrations and meetings was organized in Madrid at which Francisco Roldán, the General Secretary of the CNT, joined forces with the leading elements of Spanish Socialism. For more than a month after that, UGT and CNT members shared the same platforms in rallies all over the country. Despite the apparent collaboration and goodwill between Anarcho-Syndicalists and Socialists, there were always tensions which were never fully resolved. Yet until late 1917 the UGT–PSOE was to be the dominant force and the CNT would follow their lead – with a certain reluctance.

There were always petty local clashes in the mutual competition for control of certain sectors of the labour force. One of the most important incidents took place in Barcelona when Anarcho-Syndicalists tried to take over La Naval, a dockers' trade union which constituted one of the few remaining Socialist strongholds in the city. Largo Caballero had to travel to the Catalan capital twice in August and September 1916 to obtain a promise from the Syndicalist leaders that they would persuade their militants to back down.[28]

Another source of conflict, more damaging in the long term to the relations between the two organizations, was their different attitudes towards the European war. The growing pro-Allied stand displayed by most Socialists clashed with the neutralism of the Anarcho-Syndicalists. The victory of the pro-Republican and pro-Allied position proposed by the Socialist leadership in the PSOE Congress of October 1915 represented the start of an all-out campaign in favour of the Western Powers' cause. On 26 November 1916, a final attempt by neutralists in the Madrid section of the party to pass a motion which called on the workers to concentrate on the labour struggle and remain aloof from the imperialist conflict was swiftly defeated by the official party line espoused by Saborit and Besteiro.[29]

The tone of editorials in *El Socialista* and *España* became more and more unrestrained in supporting the Allied cause. From the second half of 1916 onwards, a clear commitment to the Entente and standard attacks on German militarism gave way to a more belligerent mood. In December 1916 *El Socialista* used patriotic slogans, questioning why the country had incurred the disaster of 1898 and the senseless adventure of Morocco yet was doing nothing to defend the national honour when Spain's fleet was being sunk by German submarines. The Socialists stopped just short of advocating intervention when in the first months of 1917 they accused Germany of breaching Spain's neutrality and began to press the government to break off diplomatic relations with her. News of the Russian Revolution in March 1917 was received with enthusiasm and regarded as an Allied victory. In a series of articles under the headline 'Against the German Spirit', *El Socialista* argued that the overthrow of Tsarism was a proof that the Russian people wanted to carry on fighting. It was therefore a defeat for those traitors seeking peace with the Central Powers. Now the end of absolutism in Russia had helped clarify the real nature of the war: a struggle between democracy and autocracy.[30]

On the other hand, the CNT never abandoned its early internationalism. The message was that the workers should not waste their time on a bourgeois war. The Anarcho-Syndicalist newspaper *Solidaridad Obrera* attacked interventionism and argued that faced with the idea of fighting an alien war the proletariat should stage a revolution.[31] On 16 September 1916, the CNT confirmed its intention to participate in the campaign of mobilization organized by the UGT and queried the attitude the Socialist trade union might adopt if the Romanones cabinet was to declare war on one of the two sides.[32] The question was ignored by the UGT. The international conflict was thus not deemed an issue worth spoiling the UGT–CNT honeymoon period. Nevertheless, there was always the danger that if Spain did enter the war they could find themselves in hostile camps.

Finally, another factor which threatened the survival of the labour alliance was that the impatience shown by the CNT towards the blatant passivity of the government totally contradicted the caution and prudence advocated by the UGT. The impotence or unwillingness of the Romanones administration to deal with the economic crisis was revealed in full. Its only positive response came with the passing of the *Ley de Subsistencias* on 6 November 1916. This law basically amounted to the same emergency measures adopted by the Conservatives a year earlier, but was now complemented with tough talk: the government was empowered to reduce tariffs in order to allow the import of basic commodities, to acquire foodstuffs and raw materials and sell them at regulated prices, to expropriate production which was deemed essential for the life of the nation, and finally to create a 'Junta Central de Subsistencias' to supervise the whole affair.[33] This Junta was quickly set up on 14 November and two Socialists, Mariano García Cortés and Matías Gómez, accepted the invitation to join it. The bankruptcy of the new body was unmistakable. Lacking any executive powers, it could only offer advice and ideas which mostly went unheeded by an administration too weak or too frightened to take measures which might harm the interests of those *caciques* and speculators making profits out of the *crisis de subsistencias*.

The Socialists were not prepared to endorse hasty actions. On 19 October Francisco Roldán, General Secretary of the CNT, declared that an all-out strike should be launched within a period of 30 days. The UGT's National Committee was shocked and decided to appeal over Roldán's head to Seguí and the other Syndicalist leaders in Barcelona. The impasse remained for exactly one month. On 19 November, Francisco Roldán and two Anarchists, Gabriel Calleja and José Villanova representing Saragossa's labour movement and Barcelona's textile workers respectively, met at the Casa del Pueblo in Madrid with the UGT's National Executive Committee and all the Socialist regional delegates who had led the campaign in the provinces. A final strategy was to be decided. Yet what Roldán and the other two did not know was that a few hours earlier the UGT leadership had met with its appointees to the Junta Central de Subsistencias and had supported the proposal presented by Andrés Saborit that a nation-wide stoppage of only 24 hours should take place on 18 December and that time should be given to the government to assess whether the *Ley de Subsistencias* and the Junta were working successfully. Hence Roldán and the two Anarchists found themselves isolated at the gathering. The CNT Secretary was even reminded by Julián Besteiro that when his colleagues had signed the Saragossa Pact they had accepted the conclusions approved in the UGT's Congress in May.[34] It was a diplomatic way of letting the CNT know that its initiatives had to be subordinated to the decisions adopted by the Socialists. The next day *El Socialista* published the resolution to call a 24-hour nation-wide stoppage on 18 December, and just in case Romanones had failed to read the paper a Socialist delegation visited him that night.

The actual 24-hour stoppage on 18 December was a complete success for the labour movement and a model of organization and efficiency. Romanones himself recognized and praised this in the pages of *El Liberal*. The Conservative press had a different opinion and regarded it as the tyranny of the trade unions endeavouring to impose their will on the rest of the nation. They believed it was the weakness of the Liberal government that encouraged the labour movement to continue with its damaging campaign.[35] The same night another Socialist delegation, headed by Besteiro, once again informed the Prime Minister of the distress of the working class and warned him of more resolute actions yet to come unless the government adopted radical measures.

During the first months of 1917 the economic situation worsened, social unrest increased and the government was found wanting. In Barcelona carpenters declared a strike which was particularly violent, with numerous clashes involving firearms. The Catalan textile industry was hit by strikes in Sabadell. In Bilbao in January, the metal workers went on strike paralysing its most important industrial concern, Altos Hornos de Vizcaya. In Cadiz, a transport strike disrupted the life of the city for several weeks. There was a general strike in Saragossa in February. The dispatches of civil governors revealed their impotence faced with the distress of their provinces. In February the governor of La Palma de Gran Canaria suggested the creation of soup kitchens to feed the starving population. The collapse of the orange export industry and the closure of many mines brought unemployment and misery to eastern and southern Spain. Food riots and popular demands for bread and work became a common feature in the provinces of Valencia, Castellón, Murcia, Seville, Córdoba, Jaén, Almería and Huelva. The government was bombarded with letters from the local authorities asking for extraordinary measures to avoid the economic collapse of these areas. The impotence of the Romanones administration showed not so much its wickedness as the bankruptcy of the existing system. Madrid was a perfect example of this incapacity. There the Socialist councillors and members of the Junta de Subsistencias demanded the introduction of fixed prices for bread and the seizure of livestock. This was attempted in February, but a concerted offensive by wheat-growers and cattle-owners forced the government to back down.[36]

However, even the moderation of the Socialists had limits. Under pressure from the rank and file and the CNT and getting only hollow promises from the government, they realized that the time for action was approaching. They decided to put themselves at the forefront of a modernizing movement in Spain, stressing that far from adventurism, their objective was a political revolution which would bring about the democratization of the country.[37]

The Socialists' strategy was thus to throw in their lot with the middle classes in order to appear not as dangerous radicals but as partners in the achievement of the long-delayed bourgeois revolution.

In January Pablo Iglesias observed that one would think the king had gone to a mental hospital and chosen the nine most dangerous patients to form a government. Yet the Socialists' central dilemma still remained: the tension between their traditional prudence and the urgency to take active steps to topple the regime. The PSOE–UGT waited for two months before embarking on an active course. The lack of positive measures to fight inflation and unemployment, the sudden closing of the Cortes in February and then the report of García Cortés and Matías Gómez describing the Junta de Subsistencias as a powerless and useless institution finally prompted the Socialists to adopt a more forceful stance.[38]

On 1 March the Republican alliance was consolidated when Besteiro, Ovejero and García Cortés, members of the PSOE's National Executive Committee, shared a platform at the Casa del Pueblo in Madrid with Roberto Castrovido, the leading Republican deputy and editor of *El País*, and Marcelino Domingo, the fiery Catalan Republican. The message was that by closing the Cortes, Romanones had confirmed that the ruling system could not respond to the needs of the country. Only a Republic could bring about democracy and answer the demands of public opinion.[39] On 6 March the regional delegates arrived at the capital to report the general mood of their areas. The following day, *El Socialista* gave a full account of what had been discussed and agreed. The conclusion was that the stoppage of 18 December had not been enough. Living standards kept on falling and prices rising. The dramatic situation demanded drastic action.[40]

Hostility towards the regime reached its peak a week later when the Minister of Finance, Santiago Alba, launched a plan to tackle the debt of the Treasury not by resorting to direct taxation but by appealing to the patriotism of the country and issuing bonds for a loan of a nominal value of almost 1000 million pesetas, redeemable over 50 years by means of quarterly repayments to bear interest at the rate of 5 per cent per annum. *El Socialista* described it as a total victory of plutocracy and *caciquismo* over those in the system who still had hopes that it could be reformed from within. While hunger kept spreading across the country, the Socialist journal observed, this administration was still studying the problem and promising solutions in the near future. Their time was up. The only valid solution was to get rid of a regime which only cared about the privileges and interests of a minority.[41]

On 25 March the CNT published a manifesto calling for a workers' assembly to discuss the gravity of the crisis which they described as 'now or never'. Thus, on 27 March, delegates from both trade unions met at the Casa del Pueblo in Madrid. Julián Besteiro, who had become the virtual stand-in for a chronically ill Pablo Iglesias, again drew up the manifesto, which was unanimously approved and signed by Seguí and Pestaña for the CNT, by representatives from the UGT's National Committee and by the regional delegates. The main points of this remarkable document were:

> To the Spanish proletariat and to the country:
>
> After our campaign of protest . . . against the abuses of the administration and the political class of this country . . . the general strike of 18 December 1916 . . . should have produced some relief from the evils suffered and recognized by everyone. Nevertheless, despite our pacific warnings and our constant complaints . . . unemployment and the *crisis de subsistencias* every day bring more discomfort and misery to the proletariat.
>
> Is there any Spanish ruler who could affirm that our unbearable living conditions are not the consequence of a regime of privileges, of a constant orgy of private ambitions, of an unchecked immorality, which find shelter in our public institutions which should instead be providing for the fundamental interests of the people? . . . Railway companies, shipowners, mining concessions, industrialists, cattle-dealers, wheat-growers, profiteers, middlemen, trusts . . . find protection in our governments while people perish or emigrate . . .
>
> It is no longer possible to deceive the country with promises or brilliant speeches . . . Why should we keep complaining or what is the use of the general recognition of the justice of our demands by the very same rulers if a solution is not provided?
>
> All these evils, perceived every day by the workers, have convinced them that the partial struggle of each local trade union against the employers is not enough to solve their grave problems.
>
> The organized labour movement has therefore concluded that it must be united in the common fight against a system of government which protects exploitation. Responding to this belief, representatives of the Unión General de Trabajadores and of the Confederación General del Trabajo have unanimously agreed:
>
> 1 After considering that neither government nor parliament have done anything to meet the demands presented by the representatives of the working class and in order to force the ruling class to introduce fundamental changes which guarantee minimum decent living standards, the general strike, the most powerful weapon in the hands of the proletariat, is to be used for an indefinite period of time.
>
> 2 Henceforth, without interrupting its campaign of social demands, the labour movement is to adopt all those measures deemed necessary to proceed with success in the preparation of the general strike.

3   The signatories to this document feel it their duty to organize
    and lead the movement and to determine the date on which the
    general strike is to take place . . .[42]

Romanones responded with the usual methods adopted by the *Turno* leaders
when they felt that their world was being challenged: workers' centres were
closed, constitutional guarantees suspended and those who had signed the
manifesto arrested. This decision was encouraged by the monarch, who told
the British ambassador that the government had to show resolve because
workers were threatening the state.[43] The only disturbances and clashes took
place in Valladolid and were organized by the local Socialist leader, the controversial maverick Oscar Pérez Solís, against express orders from Madrid.[44]
Nevertheless, the workers' leaders had to be released on 3 April. There was a
consensus in Spain that with the passing of the *Ley de Subsistencias* the government enjoyed a monopoly of power. It could regulate prices, impose quotas
and take all sorts of measures; yet those faculties were not being exercised.
The cabinet was accused of choosing to repress social turmoil instead of preventing it by offering positive alternatives.[45]

In the spring of 1917, the labour movement was more united than ever
before. The Socialists, never truly committed to revolution, had managed so
far to mobilize the proletariat and lead the CNT in an open challenge to the
state. Yet their strategy rested on the belief that they should behave not as
agents of agitation but as constructors of democracy. Thus the manifesto
signed in March was not a declaration of war on capitalism. On the contrary,
it was an invitation to the bourgeoisie to assume its hegemonic position in
society and collaborate with the working class in the removal of the oligarchical regime.

2 The bourgeoisie

In 1914 Spain constituted one of the most clear examples of the 'persistence
of the old regime'.[46] The bourgeoisie had failed throughout the nineteenth
century to complete its historical task and seize control of the political apparatus of the state. The Restoration system devised by Cánovas represented the
consolidation of a reactionary coalition formed by the crown, the army and
the financial and landowning oligarchies of southern and central Spain. The
more dynamic commercial and industrial bourgeoisie were minor partners of
this ruling coalition. They were granted social peace and economic protection, but if they were not completely denied access to the major political
decision-making centres, they did not have an important part to play.

The Spanish defeat of 1898 at the hands of the United States paved the
way for the consolidation of different political forces which had been left out
of the *Turno Pacífico*. In 1901 the Catalan industrial bourgeoisie backed the
formation of an autonomous political party, the Lliga Regionalista: a socially

conservative group pragmatic in its politics, which envisaged a decentralized modern capitalist economy with its representatives holding the reins of power in Madrid. Its strategy consisted in using the autonomist lever to exert pressure on the central government and obtain economic concessions for Catalonia.[47]

In Barcelona in 1905 army officers, offended by what they regarded as intolerable anti-Spanish editorials and cartoons, ransacked the offices of both the Catalan satirical magazine, *Cu-Cut* and the Lliga Regionalista's newspaper, *La Veu de Catalunya*. The inability of the government in Madrid to reassert the authority of the civil power provided the first opportunity for all the Catalan Republican and Regionalist groups to join forces in the so-called 'Solidaritat Catalana' under the leadership of the Lliga and its spokesman, the lawyer Francesc Cambó. Only the fiery anticlerical demagogue Alejandro Lerroux remained hostile. The elections of 1907 smashed *caciquismo* once and for all in Catalonia when Solidaritat won 41 out of the 44 parliamentary seats. Yet the alliance was short-lived as the Lliga was soon to reveal the ambiguity of its programme. The anarchy, violence and disorder of the Tragic Week in 1909 stretched to the limit the conservatism of the Lliga whose leaders, frightened by the revolutionary events, rapidly moved away from Solidaritat and preferred to pursue on their own Home Rule for Catalonia. The remaining Republican factions formed a *conjunción* or electoral alliance with the Socialists in November of that year. The *conjunción* was soon to lose the two strongest Republican factions: the Republican Radical party created by Alejandro Lerroux in 1908 and the Reformists set up in 1912 by the Asturian pragmatist Melquiades Alvarez as a moderate and 'accidentalist' Republican formation which was prepared to accept the monarchy in return for a real democratization of the regime.

Since 1914 ideological and economic factors had been prompting the new zeal with which the industrial bourgeoisie attempted to storm the *Turno* stronghold. The European conflict produced unexpected economic prosperity and rapid industrialization which stimulated democracy and self-determination movements. The nation no longer possessed the overwhelmingly backward economy and peasant social structure on which its deep-rooted oligarchical system had rested. Urbanization, economic growth, political awareness and social mobilization strengthened the positions of both bourgeoisie and proletariat and diminished that of the landowning classes. As a result the new rising forces tried to wrest political power from the traditional governing elites. Spain did not constitute an isolated example on the continent: it was the regional version of the crisis of hegemony which engulfed the other European states during these years. Generally, this crisis featured a mutinous officer corps, dissident national minorities, a radicalized proletariat, alienated intellectuals, shortages of food and raw materials, general strikes and peasant uprisings.[48]

During the Romanones administration the Lliga Regionalista led by Cambó initiated its frontal offensive against the dynastic politicians. The industrial

44

and commercial bourgeoisie was the main beneficiary of the economic profits reaped from its control of war production. As the bourgeoisie grew richer, its confidence increased and so did its desire for political power.

In 1915 Catalan industries discovered seemingly endless opportunities to export their products. The textile mills in particular were inundated with orders from north of the Pyrenees and had to work around the clock to meet demand. In other sectors of Catalan industry, the disappearance of European competition from the Spanish market acted as a firm stimulus to import substitution. Among the industries to benefit from this development were electrical goods, engineering, metallurgy and vehicle construction. A similar process of capitalist development took place in the Basque Country, Asturias and Santander. The main beneficiaries were the Basque metallurgical and shipping companies and the coal-mine owners of Asturias.[49] Soon business and industrial organizations throughout Spain, and particularly the employers' organizations in Catalonia, were sending a constant stream of demands and petitions to Madrid, where the Lliga politicians forcefully advocated the virtues of advanced capitalism. The two major demands were for Barcelona to be declared a free port, and for export subsidies. The Lliga was met by delaying tactics from the Dato administration and finally felt insulted when Cadiz, a non-industrial town, was granted the status of a free port. Moreover, the conflict between Catalan industrial interests and Castilian wheat lobbies was exposed when the latter campaigned in Valladolid against the Catalan demands.

The situation worsened when the Liberals, the dynastic party most clearly identified with Castilian agrarian interests and with Spanish centralism, returned to power in December 1915. Santiago Alba, the rising star in the Liberal party and an ambitious politician with regenerationist ideas for Spanish agriculture but also the leading *cacique* of Valladolid, the wheat lobby's stronghold, was appointed Minister of the Interior and therefore the man to supervise the elections scheduled for April 1916. The Lliga felt provoked when Alba organized the so-called Castellana Pact, an extensive coalition of diverse forces in Catalonia ranging from the remnants of dynastic groups to Lerroux's Radical Party and left-wing Catalanists in order to beat the Regionalist party.[50] The result was the opposite of what was intended: the Lliga Regionalista not only managed to increase its vote in the city of Barcelona, where it obtained an overwhelming victory, and to maintain the size of its vote in the rest of the region, but also was prepared to mount an all-out offensive against the ruling oligarchies in Madrid.[51]

The objective of the Lliga was to consolidate the hegemony of Catalan capitalism in Spain. This was to be accomplished by selling the idea of an *Espanya Catalana* whereby a politically autonomous Catalonia offered a backward agrarian Spain a blueprint for the creation of a modern capitalist economy.[52] To achieve that, the Catalan party knew it had to gain access to positions of power in Madrid and this was barred as long as the *Turno* politicians were in full control of the situation. For this task, Francesc Cambó proved to be one of the shrewdest statesmen of the Restoration period. A man with the ability of creating, leading, organizing and changing all sorts of coalitions of often disparate groups in which the Lliga was to be the dominant force.[53] He had already masterminded Solidaritat Catalana in 1907 and would repeat the manoeuvre ten years later. The difference was that whereas in 1907 it was a struggle for political hegemony in Catalonia, now it was a battle for control of the entire country.

Cambó's offensive began on 21 May 1916 in a speech given on the day of the *Fiesta de la Unidad*. In a threatening tone, the Catalan leader declared that Catalonia was a nation with its own characteristics and identity and promised to discuss in the Cortes the recognition of Catalan as an official language and the question of Home Rule. Cambó's lieutenants, Peret Rahola and Joan Ventosa, gave similar speeches the same day in Barcelona.[54] The promise was fulfilled when the subject was first raised on 4 June by the Regionalist Senator Raimon d'Abadal in the Senate and then on 7 and 8 June by Cambó himself in Congress. Cambó demanded a profound modification of the structure of the state, stressing that Catalonia was a nation which demanded recognition of its own language, and an Assembly with its own executive to administer the internal business of the region. He caused a major upset when he warned that if his demands were not satisfactorily dealt with, his party would seek redress at the peace conference at the end of the hostilities in Europe.

The Catalan issue took up a great deal of the parliamentary agenda during June 1916. Most newspapers in Madrid accused the Lliga of separatism. There was a succession of deputies, including many of those returned from Catalan provinces, who to a greater or lesser extent criticized the Regionalist initiative and emphasized that the Lliga with just 13 out of 40 Catalan parliamentarians could only claim to speak for a minority in Catalonia. Lerroux, prone to opportunist demagogy, embraced Romanones in the corridors of the Cortes and promised the government his total support to fight Catalan separatism. Eventually, the Prime Minister himself declared on 8 June that he was not going to take part in a dialogue with the Lliga which actually amounted to political blackmail. Romanones showed more moderation a week later when he recognized the existence of a Catalan question. Yet he observed that there were other pressing problems which needed to be urgently examined by the Cortes. His government, he declared, was prepared to listen to anyone, providing no threats were uttered. Taking a very mild and appeasing stance, the Count denied that he had refused a dialogue but confirmed that there was an immense gap between what his cabinet could grant and what the Regionalists demanded.[55]

The Lliga only found a degree of sympathy from the *Maurista* movement, yet even they were divided in their attitude. Maura and Cambó had established cordial relations in 1907 when the former had been Prime Minister and the latter had been a leading member of Solidaritat Catalana. Unlike Liberal administrations characterized by centralism and veiled support for people like Lerroux, Maura had sought to meet some of the Regionalist demands with his ill-fated *Ley de Administración Local*. He always regarded the Lliga as the Catalan example of what he sought for the rest of the country.

In 1913, when in an internal coup the Conservative elite ousted Maura from the leadership of his party, a unique phenomenon in Restoration politics took place. A *Maurista* movement from below, mainly formed by conservative middle-class youth, emerged to rally around the dismissed leader. However, their total devotion to Maura and their criticism of *Turno* politics could hardly conceal their internal differences. There were those with reformist and Christian Democratic leanings, whose most outstanding representative was the Aragonese lawyer Angel Ossorio. They sought to democratize and modernize the political system. On the other hand there were *Mauristas* like Antonio Goicoechea, leader of the *Maurista* Youth, and Manuel Delgado Barreto, editor of the party newspaper *La Acción*, who represented an authoritarian, nationalist and ultra-conservative current in Spanish politics.[56] Those differences became more evident from 1916. Angel Ossorio, who had been governor of Barcelona in 1909, showed a tolerant attitude towards the Lliga and the Regionalist question. On 31 May 1916 he published an article in *La Acción* called 'Catalan Warning' in which he praised the activities of the Lliga, describing it as a school of citizenship, and attacked the false *españolismo* of Lerroux. However, at the same time another leading *Maurista*, Gustavo Peyrá, the rabid centralist and hard-liner from Gerona, was writing to Maura with an opposite view. Peyrá claimed that the Lliga was a separatist party that exploited the weaknesses of the central governments in Madrid and whose activities should be investigated by the Spanish embassy in Paris. He also stated that he was in total agreement with the Captain General of Barcelona, General Alfau, that no concessions should be made to the Lliga.[57] Maura felt compelled to intervene in the debate. On 30 June and 1 July he adopted a middle course in the Cortes. He warned that separatism would be a national disaster, but he also applauded the noble spirit of the Lliga and invited its representatives to join other political forces to achieve common objectives.

Maura, Romanones and most politicians misunderstood Cambó's strategy. The Catalan leader was far from a separatist or isolationist. In fact, the Catalan question in parliament was not its sole aim, as many believed, but just part of a very carefully devised plan which had as its main goal the disruption of the activities of the governing elites. Cambó and his party were determined to show that Spain could no longer be ruled without the goodwill of the Catalanists. Amidst the heated debate on the Catalan question, the leader of the Regionalist minority revealed both his bitterness at the present position occupied by his party in Spanish politics and his determination to change it:

> We, the Regionalists, represent a unique case . . . We spend our time fighting governments, and yet we are a group of men prepared to govern, who have been born to govern, who are ready to govern, who have shown skills to govern . . . and nevertheless we seem doomed to remain in opposition.[58]

In his June speech Cambó had constantly attacked the artificiality and the hollowness of the *Turno*. He had in mind a realignment of political forces in the country in which the Lliga and Catalan industry would each play a leading role in the process of political and economic modernization of Spain. In the offensive against the dynastic parties, Alba was singled out as the man to bring down. Cambó wrote in his memoirs:

> The government formed by Romanones was weak . . . There was only one man with the aspirations and conditions of leader: Santiago Alba . . .
>
> Alba was not only clever, but also an intelligent man, with a political culture above the other Liberal notables . . .
>
> Alba regarded me as a future enemy, as the man who could deny him the post to which he aspired. Thus, from the first moment, his obsession was to fight me. By doing that, he was not only adopting a personal position, but also following his anti-Catalan feelings . . .
>
> Alba had chosen to do battle with me and I had accepted the challenge and was prepared to go on to the end . . .
>
> Alba constituted an obstacle not only to me personally but to any attempt at Catalan participation in the government of Spain. My duty was to stop him or at least to prevent him from seizing the leadership of his party.[59]

Leaving personal resentment aside, Cambó reveals how Alba was, because of his youth and personal charisma, the strong man in the *Turno*. If this was to be destroyed, Alba's rising career would have to be stopped. This task was facilitated by the fact that soon after the elections of April 1916 Alba abandoned his post of Minister of the Interior to become Minister of Finance. This was the position from which he could either reach the top or else expose by his fall the inadequacies and contradictions of the regime. In fact, the latter was to happen.

Alba endeavoured to increase his prestige with an ambitious scheme of economic and financial reforms. It gave the Regionalists the chance to mount an impressive coalition against the government. Alba's aim was to carry out a ten-year programme of public works, naval, military and cultural reforms representing a total expenditure of 2,134 million pesetas. However, prior to proceeding with his so-called Plan of National Reconstruction, the Castilian minister argued that it was necessary to solve the budget deficit which had kept growing particularly since the start of the Moroccan campaign in 1909 and which by 1916 amounted to 850 million pesetas. He therefore announced his intention of levying a tax on excess war profits earned by industry and trade, but not by agriculture.[60]

Industry and trade were not prepared to bear the brunt of the costs and sacrifice their recent gains while the landed oligarchy would be unaffected. Cambó was able to utilize Alba's tax proposal to build up a formidable co-alition of economic groups and hence become the undisputed leader of the industrial classes. The duel between Cambó and Alba in the Congress represented the clash between the rising industrial bourgeoisie and the ruling landowning oligarchy.[61] Yet Cambó's success was also determined to a great extent by two factors. First, the internal factionalism and personal rivalries which characterized the dynastic parties played strongly against Alba. Thus many dynastic notables, jealous of Alba's meteoric career, were happy to see him badly mauled in parliament. A glaring example was Romanones who saw his leadership endangered by the possible victory of his own minister. Cambó wrote: 'The Count had to make efforts not to applaud me . . . after that campaign Romanones kept giving me signs of his personal sympathy.'[62] Secondly, the very foundations of the existing system made it impossible to introduce a modern economic programme. The dynastic parties were prevented in practice from undertaking any lasting regenerationist measures by the glaring fact that to introduce a modern fiscal system would hurt the interests of those to whom they owed their positions.[63]

In Congress on 3 June and two days later in the Senate, Alba for the first time officially presented his economic and financial programme, including his tax on excess war profits made by industry and commerce but not by agriculture. A campaign was immediately launched to wreck it. The campaign was to be conducted both inside and outside of the Cortes.

Business and industrial concerns mounted an impressive and noisy protest against Alba's measures. It was a model of economic mobilization and organization previously unknown in Spanish history, reflecting the growing strength of the national bourgeoisie. At no time would it be matched by preparedness or willingness on the part of the government to defend its plans. Even before Alba had officially presented his programme in the Cortes, right-wing journals like *ABC* had published editorials showing their opposition. Catalan industrialists were the first to express their resolution to fight to the last the tax on excess war profits. In *La Veu de Catalunya*, the organ of the Lliga Regionalista, Cambó's lieutenant, Ventosa, described the tax as an economic monstrosity and a criminal attempt to hurt industry in Catalonia and Spain as a whole. Basque industrialists followed suit. Led by the shipowners, they demanded the withdrawal of the tax. Soon all the more important commercial and industrial organizations had joined forces. Most vociferous among them were the Fomento del Trabajo Nacional de Barcelona, the Asociación de Navieros de Bilbao, the Círculo de la Unión Mercantil e Industrial de

Madrid, the Cámara de Comercio de Zaragoza, the Unión Gremial de Valencia and the Industria y Navegación de Sevilla.

Several arguments were used to attack Alba's tax proposals. It was claimed that the tax would halt investment, frighten away capital and therefore hurt production. It was described as unfair since it affected industry and trade but not agriculture. Moreover, its retroactive character, the opponents suggested, would be anticonstitutional and would introduce an ominous fatal precedent. A more cynical argument, although probably true, was to point out that the lack of preparation by the administration made it impossible to implement successfully such an ambitious law. Obviously big business were not prepared to collaborate with the state and make matters easier. The peak of the protest was when representatives of the industrial elite attended a meeting on 28 June 1916 in Madrid at the Palace Hotel. The leading Basque industrialist Ramón de la Sota set out their conclusions: the tax was unfair and harmful. It had to be fought to the end. A commission then went to the Cortes to meet leaders of the different parties and inform them of their resolutions. Cambó was well aware of them. He had been present at the gathering and had declared his total support for the industrialist cause.[64] Like the labour movement, the industrialists were prepared to defend their interests in an open clash with the state.

In the Cortes, Alba fought with determination for his economic plans. He tried to appeal to the patriotism of the deputies and several times expressed his readiness to seek a compromise. It was all in vain. Cambó brilliantly marshalled the hostile campaign against Alba's Bill. On 17 June, Joan Ventosa fired the first warning shot. Four days later, Alba obtained a partial victory when a Royal Decree was passed establishing the personal liability of managers and directors of those companies which would be affected by the tax on excess war profits. This was bound to infuriate the opposition. On 24 June, Gabino Bugallal, Minister of Finance in the former Conservative cabinet, voiced on behalf of his party the distress of his group with regard to the retroactive character of the Bill. He also expressed his intense disappointment at the government's resort to Royal Decrees. On 26 June, Cambó initiated a destructive all-out offensive. The Lliga leader virtually echoed the arguments put forward by the industrialists and warned that the introduction of such Bills would signal a divorce between country and government. Cambó's speech was followed by others from the spokesmen of all the parliamentary groups. Antonio Maura, Gabino Bugallal, Juan de la Cierva, a right-wing Conservative and leader of his own parliamentary group, the Basque deputies (connected with shipping and iron interests) Fernando María Ibarra and Horacio Echevarrieta, Alejandro Lerroux, the left-wing Catalanist Felipe Rodés, Melquiades Alvarez and the parliamentary leader of the Republican–Socialist *conjunción*, Julián Nougués, all took part in the debate. All of them, to a greater or lesser extent, found fault with Alba's Bill. The only outright support came from Lerroux. This was unlikely to raise the spirits of the minister. That day nine Liberal deputies introduced a motion of confidence in Alba's programme. With all the other parliamentary groups absent, only 150 out of 235 Liberal deputies voted in favour. Subsequently Alba attempted a conciliatory approach, but all his calls for reaching an understanding went unheard. Cambó and his friends practised successful obstructionism throughout July. The position of the government, forced to take a defensive stand, was so desperate that many believed that the outbreak of the railway strike had provided the perfect excuse for closing the Cortes on 13 July. Alba vowed to continue the defence of his plans after the summer. Nevertheless, they had already been wrecked.[65]

Ironically, Alba could not count on the support of the left. He was neither trusted nor believed by the labour movement. His tax was deemed fair and necessary, but there was widespread scepticism as to whether such a corrupt system could introduce any progressive legislation. Luis Araquistáin expressed exactly the feelings of his fellow party members when in the magazine *España* he wrote: 'This tax is needed but I cannot see how someone like Alba can really be all for it.' He concluded that Alba's economic regenerationism was just a façade. The real issue was a struggle for power in the Liberal party. Araquistáin's suspicions were shared and continually voiced in editorials in both *El Socialista* and *España*. The Socialists argued that it was all a charade whose real object was to get more money from the people. In the end, the brunt of the expenditure would have to be borne by the working class. In contrast, Cambó, although regarded as the natural class enemy, was viewed in a comparatively favourable light as the man likely to develop modern capitalism in Spain. According to socialist theory, a bourgeois democracy had to be established in Spain before anyone could even think about the triumph of Socialism. Cambó seemed the appropriate politician to carry out a bourgeois revolution in the country. Cambó's attacks on the government were described as a catapult to destroy the obsolete regime. *España* even devoted its entire issue of 22 June to the Catalan question and the two leading figures of Catalan Regionalism, Francesc Cambó and Enric Prat de la Riba, contributed two articles. On 2 July, Cambó was invited by the PSOE to give a speech at the Casa del Pueblo in Madrid. There he won his audience over when he declared that the only two real forces in the nation were Catalan nationalism and Socialism.[66]

When the Cortes opened again in September the debate about the tax on excess war profits had to be abandoned since, as Alba himself recognized, the most urgent task was to present the budget for the following year. In fact, the tax was not going to be discussed ever again. It was effectively dead and buried. On 30 September the minister read to a packed chamber the final version of his economic programme. He divided his finance measures into two: an ordinary one and an extraordinary one, known as 'The Plan of National Reconstruction', which embraced a vast amount of naval, cultural and public works for the following ten years. Alba asked for the collaboration of the minorities to accomplish his programme and expressed his willingness to enter into a positive dialogue with them.

Alba's hopes were soon dashed. On 21 October his programme was rejected by the Assembly of Industry and Commerce. The industrial elites of the nation did not trust Alba and wanted his head. Cambó decided to go in for the kill. The Catalan politician wrote:

> Our purpose was not to let any of his Bills pass, not even the ordinary budget . . . we continued our campaign throughout 1916, analysing every detail of each Bill . . . He [Alba] had to watch one after another of his Bills being torpedoed before his eyes . . . He had to go through the shame of not just failing to get his grandiose project approved, but not even getting his budget passed like any ordinary minister.[67]

Thus the Lliga deputies in parliament launched themselves once more into a meticulous cross-examination and dissection of every single measure in Alba's programme. Cambó described the minister's projects as either tolerable, acceptable or unacceptable. He conceded that some measures of national reconstruction were imperative, but concluded that Alba's plan was not what the country needed. Many of Alba's proposals were certainly essential to the well-being and prosperity of Spain, but, however desirable in theory, they were unacceptable in the form in which they had been submitted; their details had not been thought out and they would be unjust in their operation. Cambó further contended that many of the items which figured in the extraordinary budget ought to have been in the ordinary one, and that their inclusion in the former was only a device on the part of the government to balance the accounts of the ordinary budget and to delude the public as to the actual annual deficit. The main cause of this, according to the Lliga's leader, was the 'senseless' Moroccan adventure.[68]

Political intrigues, personal rivalries and the growing unpopularity of the government played into Cambó's hands. Furthermore, a deadlock occurred when Reformists and Conservatives insisted on discussing the ordinary budget first while the government wanted to deal with the extraordinary one. The parliamentary debate on 20 and 21 November killed off any remaining hopes of passing the economic programme before the end of the year. Whereas Lerroux offered his total support, all the other parliamentary groups refused to give the government a blank cheque for a ten-year programme.[69] Two alternatives remained open to the government: either to decree a permanent session of the chamber – a most unpopular precedent – and try to force the budget through before the end of December, or else find a formula of consensus by means of which the old budget for 1916 could be adapted and revived for 1917. After hard bargaining, the second alternative was agreed on 16 December. It represented the final nail in the coffin of Alba's personal prestige and confirmed the loss of credibility of the *Turno* parties. The Conservative administration had been discredited for failing to provide solutions to the economic crisis and had not even managed to pass the budget. One year later, and after promises of marvellous improvements to come, only the *Ley de Subsistencias* had been passed and it soon proved to be an utter failure. The Liberal cabinet was in total disarray. Spain's economic life was dependent on a budget dating back to December 1914.

The former Liberal minister and close friend of Santiago Alba, Natalio Rivas, expressed clearly in his memoirs the state of bitterness and crisis which reigned over the Liberal camp in December 1916. On 11 December he wrote that Borbolla, *cacique* of Seville and one of the leading notables of the Liberal party in Andalusia, had told him that Alba, who still had the king's support, should be able to lead his own cabinet in January. Rivas wrote that Romanones was losing his grip on the party. There were many rumours of plots within the party to deprive him of the premiership. The leader of the rival Liberal Democratic faction, the Marquis of Alhucemas, or the Speaker of the Lower House, Miguel Villanueva, were those named as most likely to succeed. Two days later Dato's lieutenant, Sánchez Guerra, commented that Romanones regretted that the ordinary budget had not been passed, but he did not care at all about the extraordinary one. An unhappy Rivas noted: 'Romanones's continuous deals with Lerroux only confirm the general feeling of lack of authority . . . there is confusion, disorder . . . it would be better for us to fall than carry on like this.' The following week Alba confided his pessimism to Rivas. The Chancellor, urged by Rivas to make his move for the leadership of the party, remarked: 'I prefer to see all the fools of the party going for it first.'[70]

Alba's excessive confidence was ill-founded. His party in general, and he in particular, had been badly humiliated in 1916, defeated by Cambó in their personal duel. No legislation could be passed without the consent of the Catalan minority. In February 1917, and only after obtaining the agreement of the minority parties, two economic Bills were introduced. One was for the protection of industry and included the provision that in some cases the state should furnish 50 per cent of the initial capital. The other was the so-called *Ley de Autorizaciones* which sought to enable the government to adapt the budget to the needs of the various ministerial departments in the present exceptional circumstances resulting from the war. In early March, with a deficit of over 1,000 million pesetas and unable to resort to taxation, Alba had to appeal to the people and raise a loan. Subscribed 22 times over, the loan was a success, but it also demonstrated that no economic regeneration could be expected from the ruling system.

Cambó's political leverage had grown dramatically in one year. During the first months of 1917 he held frequent meetings with the Reformist leader Melquiades Alvarez, representatives of the Basque Nationalist Party and even with his traditional enemy, Alejandro Lerroux. The Catalan politician was courted by leading Conservatives like Dato and Cierva. In mid-April he was approached by Alba. The minister recognized that the existing administration had no future and proposed forming a new government which would have the support of the monarch and would include both Alba and Cambó, one in charge of the Treasury and the other of Public Works. Cambó suggested that he would be willing to enter into a national coalition if it was to be presided over by Antonio Maura.[71] Yet this was not Cambó's strategy. His plan was not to join in the petty squabbles of the dynastic politicians but to take advantage of them in order to form a new hegemonic power bloc with which to break the *Turno* once and for all.[72]

In April 1917 Cambó felt he was very close to attaining his objective. On 13 April he declared with confidence in *El Liberal*:

> The situation is becoming extremely serious and yet this government is not taking positive measures to deal with the general distress and the food shortages . . . This administration behaves as if hostilities had never broken out in Europe so that it can carry on with its normal attitude of total passivity . . . The political system as a whole has proved incapable of dealing with the present situation . . . Never before has a government been granted so much authority nor a country felt so great a need to be governed . . . and still nothing is being done . . . people feel politically orphaned.

Cambó was thus drawing attention to the political vacuum which he had done so much to create – in the hope of subsequently being able to fill it.

3 The army

In the long term, the worst peril for the constitutional system was military unrest. During this period of increasing breach between society and government, the attitude of the army officers began to acquire a dangerous dimension.

The armed forces had played a crucial role in the consolidation of Liberalism in Spain in the nineteenth century. They had defeated the Carlists or absolutists in the 1830s and the victorious generals controlled the political scene almost constantly for the next forty years. This can be explained by two facts: first, the landed oligarchy which emerged as the dominant force in the 1830s was heavily dependent on the army to keep at bay the threat of both the Carlists and the popular classes; and secondly, once a political clique held power, it could maintain its hold through fixing election results, a practice known as *exclusivismo*. As a consequence, political factions were normally headed by generals, and *pronunciamientos* or military coups provided the only mechanism for a change in power. Queen Isabel II, following her mother's fate, was sent into exile in 1868. General Pavía's *pronunciamiento* put an end to the First

Republic in January 1874 and General Martínez Campos restored the Bourbon monarchy, in the person of Alfonso XII, after another successful coup in December 1874.[73]

The governing elites which ruled Spain since 1875 did not seize power through a revolutionary process or as legitimately elected representatives, but gained control once more through the army. The agreement between the two dynastic parties, the *Turno Pacífico*, meant that the military was no longer needed as an instrument of political change. But the system could not operate without the active collaboration of the army.[74] The military remained very much an integral part of the power bloc. The officers were the ultimate guarantors of the existing order and the praetorian guard of the ruling oligarchy. As the gradual modernization of economy and society enlarged those groups previously excluded from political power, the industrial bourgeoisie and the urban proletariat, the financial and agrarian elites were obliged to rely increasingly on repression to retain their hegemony.

Officers were rewarded with promotions, appointments, seats in the Senate, aristocratic titles and representation in both dynastic parties. Politics was left in the hands of civilians but in exchange they were not to interfere in military matters. The post of Minister of War was occupied by generals from 1875 to 1917. Furthermore, the Law of the Constitution of the Army of 29 November 1878 underlined the important role that the army played in the power bloc. Its second clause stated that the armed forces, besides the normal tasks performed in a constitutional state, had as their primary function the defence of the nation from its internal enemies. The maintenance of public order was left entirely in their hands. The Civil Guard, the force in charge of policing the countryside, was placed under the control of the Ministry of War. During the Restoration era both parties quickly responded to any social or political unrest with the suspension of constitutional guarantees and the declaration of martial law, granting the army a totally free hand. This militarization of public life revealed the fragility of the constitutional system and facilitated the intervention of the army in politics.[75]

The army's control of its own internal affairs meant that any attempt to undertake even minimal reform was doomed. Its structural problem, the excessive number of officers in relation to the number of servicemen, went unchecked. This was a problem decades old, a product of military intervention in politics, incorporation of defeated Carlist officers into the regular army, and the colonial wars throughout the century. In 1900, the ratio was one officer to fewer than four enlisted men. By 1910 Spain still had 16,000 officers for slightly more than 80,000 troops. The officer ratio was two to three times greater than that in France or in Germany, with an army only one third the size. It represented a cancer for a state which devoted about 40 per cent of its expenditure to defence, while 70 per cent of the defence budget went on officers' salaries. Despite the financial burden, modernization and professionalization of the armed services were neglected.[76] Drastic reform was needed but could not come from the army itself, a staunch defender of the status quo, nor from the politicians who could not intervene in military matters. In 1887 General Cassola, Minister of War in the Sagasta cabinet, attempted to introduce a comprehensive programme to professionalize the services. Under heavy attack from his fellow officers and abandoned by Sagasta, Cassola was forced to resign one year later and his projects were dropped. This confirmed that the symbiotic relationship between army and the dynastic politicians grew out of their common antagonism to social and economic modernization.[77]

The loss of the overseas empire in 1898 and the subsequent return of thousands of troops to the peninsula coincided with the mobilization of political forces against the ruling system. There were terrorist outbursts and the birth of nationalist politics in Catalonia and continuous insurrections in the Andalusian countryside. The army was therefore pushed to the forefront to defend the established order and increasingly saw itself as the defender of a nation endangered by the divisive effects of regionalism and class conflict. As their activities in defence of the state multiplied the officers also became more intolerant of any criticism. As the 'guardians of the sacred values of the Patria' they regarded any attack on themselves as an attack on the nation. Additionally, they increasingly became an institution cut off from the rest of society. They resented the antimilitarist attitude adopted by most Spaniards after 1898. There were tales of corruption, incompetence and hardship from the Cuban campaigns of the 1890s. Almost 200,000 soldiers had died not in actual fighting but of disease and wounds due to the lack of a proper medical corps. In turn, the army blamed the politicians for the defeat and for their own unpopularity. Courted by the new monarch, Alfonso XIII, they began to act as the praetorian guard of the monarchy rather than the oligarchy.[78]

A common response to antimilitarist articles was an attack by angry officers on the newspapers' offices. In 1895 the victims were two Republican journals, El Globo and El Resumen. Not only did the officers escape unpunished but the newspapers were closed down.[79] This trend increased after 1898. On 5 May 1900 El Progreso of Játiva (Valencia) was attacked, followed one year later by El Correo de Guipúzcoa. More serious was the storming of and beating of employees in the offices of the satirical magazine Cu-Cut and La Veu de Catalunya, journal of the Lliga Regionalista, in 1905. A wave of popular anger spread throughout Catalonia. The Liberal cabinet presided over by Eugenio Montero Ríos resorted to the usual practice of suspending constitutional guarantees. It soon found itself caught between a political mobilization in Catalonia, which gave birth to the coalition of Catalan forces known as Solidaritat Catalana, and the rebel officers supported by the entire military corps. There were rumours that the officers were planning to attack the Cortes, and the Civil Guard made clear they would not fire against their brothers in arms. The king took an active role. The Montero Ríos administration was dismissed and replaced by another Liberal cabinet headed by Segismundo Moret and more willing to placate the army. On 20 March 1906 it passed the

'Law of Jurisdictions' to satisfy the officers' demands. Subsequently, any offence, however trivial, against army, king or *Patria* would be tried by military courts. This represented a significant limit on freedom of expression and confirmed the privileged role of the military within the power bloc. It was not a watershed in the Restoration period but a continuation of the rule established in 1878. The capitulation of the dynastic politicians revealed their weakness: unable to assert civilian supremacy and abandoned by the other source of constitutional sovereignty, the king, they provided the army with an opportunity to impose its demands on the state.[80]

A new crisis arose again in Barcelona when, in the last week of July 1909, the population revolted against the calling up of the reserves for service in Morocco. The so-called Tragic Week was brutally repressed by the army. Over 104 civilians were reported killed and 1,725 civilians were tried by military courts. Five of them were executed.[81] The armed forces proved once more to be the main bulwark of the regime against any social or political challenge. The Moroccan adventure, however, also marked a split within the services. The introduction of promotion on merit in 1910 contributed to the alienation of those officers based in the peninsula who envied the privileged positions and extra incomes enjoyed by the favourites in the Ministry of War and the king's military household, and the recognition and promotion extended to the *Africanistas*, men in elite units in Morocco.[82]

The First World War brought about the first major breach between the officer corps and the ruling system it was supposed to defend. The inflation and economic hardship caused by the conflict hurt army officers as much as other classes. The scale of hostilities on the continent served to emphasize the disparity between the Spanish and the modern European armies. It encouraged the government to break traditional policy and to intervene in military affairs. First, General Echague, Minister of War in the Dato administration, and then General Luque, holder of that office in the Romanones cabinet, tried to introduce reforms to tackle the system of merit promotion and the necessary cutbacks in officialdom. But those initiatives represented a departure from the agreement between army and dynastic politicians which had so far guaranteed the continuity and survival of the *Turno Pacífico*.

Any reform struck at the security of bureaucratic middle-ranking officers who were now also suffering from inflation, shortages and worsening living standards.[83] Tampering with the status quo was bound to anger the officers. In 1916 General Luque prepared a comprehensive military reform bill which attempted to increase the standing army to 180,000 soldiers, financed by a substantial though hardly radical reduction of officers. It also dealt with the sensitive question of merit promotion. This reform bill was a brilliant exercise in compromise: Luque minimized the necessary cutbacks and accepted that in the meantime the seniority principle would continue. However, provisions such as a promotion freeze and aptitude tests threatened officers below the rank of colonel.[84]

It was a secret to nobody that the Spanish army was in desperate need of military reform, but Luque's bill did not satisfy military opinion. All sorts of criticism began to be launched against it: priority was given to the reorganization of the higher commands by simply pensioning off most of the senior officers in order to make room for junior and doubtless often less capable successors; not enough attention was paid to the welfare of the troops and to the details of munitions, armaments and instruction. The final straw, however, came with the introduction of tests of intellectual and physical ability. A mistake was certainly made when these tests were first applied only to the infantry corps and in the particularly restive city of Barcelona. The anger of the men of that garrison was boundless.

The officers had been observing how the working classes were obtaining pay rises and concessions by joining trade unions and declaring strikes, measures barred to the armed forces by their code of discipline. Thus deeply disturbed by the erosion of their living standards and by mounting economic hardship, and incensed by the government reforms, the officers began to absorb some Syndicalist principles. From the second half of 1916 they set up the Juntas Militares de Defensa, a kind of officers' trade union. These Juntas were initially established in Barcelona but soon spread across the peninsula. By January 1917, the chairman of the Central Junta at Barcelona, Colonel Benito Márquez, was boasting that the Juntas had become a reality in all the garrisons of Spain with the sole exceptions of Madrid and Morocco.[85]

The language used and some of the objectives pursued by the Juntas could be linked to the general 'regenerationist' dynamic of the era. There were harsh words against the ruling *Turno*. The officers were also spurred by their hostility towards both the privileged members of the Palace clique, mainly based in the military household of the king, and the *Africanistas*. Unlike their colleagues in the peninsula where promotions were awarded in a bureaucratic order corresponding to seniority and regardless of merit and competitiveness, the *Africanistas* could advance relatively quickly by showing ability on the battlefield, bypassing the army's bureaucratic pyramid. Nevertheless, the set-up in Morocco had been characterized by nepotism and corruption with thousands of medals and awards being given for the simplest of reasons. Yet despite all the regenerationist rhetoric, the main objective of most officers was always the defence of the collective interests of the corps. According to their beliefs, this would be achieved by ending the favouritism and privileges enjoyed by the palace clique and the *Africanistas*, by imposing a rigid promotion system based on strict seniority and by organizing themselves in order to obtain pay increases.[86]

The Juntas de Defensa were initially not taken seriously and even seem to have been welcomed by the Captain General of Catalonia, General Felipe Alfau. After being presented with the regulations of the Juntas in early 1917, he supported and encouraged his officers. The Minister of War, General Luque, was well aware of what was going on and made no objection. In fact, both

Alfau and Luque wanted to use the Juntas for their own personal ambitions.[87] It was not until the Russian Revolution in March 1917, when the monarch feared that their existence constituted a potential threat to the regime, that Romanones ordered their dissolution. Alfonso drew a parallel between the soldiers' soviets in Russia and the Juntas de Defensa in Spain. The anti-oligarchical language of the Spanish officers and their attacks on the Palace generals made the king believe he could become the target of the Juntas' anger. He therefore forced his government to take action. In early April General Alfau was summoned to Madrid and told by Romanones and Luque that the Juntas had to be dissolved. The following week Alfau informed the authorities in the capital that he had done so with total success.[88] As events were to prove, this was far from true.

4

THE ROMANONES ADMINISTRATION

The international challenge

Until early 1916, although fierce fighting raged across the continent of Europe, Spain never considered departing from her initial strict neutrality. However, that position was seriously challenged during the Romanones administration. No other Prime Minister during the years of conflict became so much involved in the international dispute. Labour militancy, military reforms and economic plans were crucial issues during this period and yet they were almost overshadowed by the foreign question. In fact, the war seems to have dominated Romanones's agenda. This attitude led to a phase of active agitation and polarization of the country around the neutrality issue. Furthermore, the two warring blocs, in particular the Central Powers, turned their attention to Spain. For them, it became a new theatre of operations.

No dynastic politician had welcomed the outbreak of hostilities in Europe. They were aware that a conflict of such magnitude could damage their dominant position in political society. Most of them, regardless of their respective sympathies for one or other European camp, longed for a quick end to the war so that they could return as soon as possible to their normal political routine. As the conflict dragged on, they realized that it could spread to the peninsula. Thus they tried to bury their heads in the sand, ignore what was taking place beyond the borders and hope they had been forgotten.

Count Romanones was an exception. He was one of the very few dynastic leaders who believed that Spain should abandon its formal neutrality. As early as August 1914 he had stated his views openly in the famous editorial 'Fatal Neutralities'. According to him, the only way in which Spain could rebuild her empire in Northern Africa and strengthen her economy was through closer collaboration with France and Britain, the main naval and colonial powers, and not through diplomatic isolation. Because of economic realities Spain should ally with the West (See Table 4.1). Moreover, personal reasons also influenced his determination to cement links with the Entente. He was one of the largest shareholders in the mining industries of Morocco, and in coal and iron mines in Asturias and Southern Spain whose production went to France to prop up the Allied war effort.

60

Table 4.1 Spain's balance of trade with the two warring camps in 1913 (million pesetas)

	Imports	*Exports*	*Total*
France	205,206,453	328,175,911	533,382,634
Britain	317,641,818	241,211,777	558,853,395
Belgium	45,035,003	45,278,431	90,313,434
Italy	15,805,757	34,722,408	50,528,165
Portugal	57,055,336	42,367,918	104,423,254
Serbia	260,078	–	260,078
Russia	44,973,518	8,286,803	53,260,321
Japan	629,587	77,713	707,300
Allies (total)	686,607,550	705,120,961	1,391,728,511
	Imports	*Exports*	*Total*
Germany	185,373,167	74,418,566	259,791,733
Austria	10,334,926	8,797,340	19,132,266
Turkey	–	5,761,019	5,761,019
Bulgaria	80,823	793	81,616
Central Powers (total)	195,788,916	88,977,718	284,766,634

Source: H. Cenamor Val, *Los españoles y la guerra: neutralidad o intervención*, Madrid, 1916, pp. 206–7.

After the outburst of criticism aroused by 'Fatal Neutralities', Romanones played down his pro-Allied feelings. Throughout 1915, feeling he was close to regaining political power, he insisted that Spain should never abandon her position of neutrality. Once Romanones became Prime Minister he tried to erase from everybody's memory his earlier pro-Allied views by claiming that his personal sympathies should not interfere with the interests of the state; yet he never gave up his previous convictions. The Count, during his troubled premiership, endeavoured to pursue an increasingly pro-Entente international policy but disguised this fact from public opinion. He used secret diplomatic channels as a favourite means to deal with the Western Powers. To his despair, his initiatives were received by evasive Anglo-French responses. Romanones could not go beyond certain limits. He could not contemplate the idea of breaking off diplomatic relations with Germany.

Therefore the Western Powers were not prepared to satisfy Spanish imperialist ambitions in exchange for mere promises of platonic friendship. Romanones's approaches to the Entente, however, triggered off a vicious campaign against his government orchestrated by the Central Powers with the help of their Spanish friends. Germany had important interests in the peninsula. They included economic investments, 70,000 nationals and over 40 vessels which had sought shelter in Spanish ports at the outbreak of the war. The presence of a pro-Allied Prime Minister in power was a pending threat to all these interests. It was imperative therefore to bring about his downfall. The result was to push Romanones more and more towards the Allied camp. By early 1917 the situation was such that the administration led by the Count was heading for a diplomatic rupture with the Central Powers.

When Romanones took office in December 1915 he quickly realized he had to dispel the prevailing impression that he intended to depart from neutrality. He therefore appointed Miguel Villanueva as Foreign Minister. Villanueva, *cacique* of Logroño and a leading personality in the rival faction of the Liberal party led by the Marquis of Alhucemas, was known for his Germanophile leanings. It was a smart attempt on Romanones's part to kill two birds with one stone: to show everybody he had abandoned his pro-Allied views and to win the support of the other main Liberal clique. When Urzaiz was sacked in February 1916 Villanueva became Minister of Finance, and after the general election of April 1916 he was awarded the influential post of Speaker of the Lower House of the Cortes. The Prime Minister then had the way clear to entrust foreign policy to his friend Amalio Gimeno.

Romanones continued to stress in official circles his total commitment to strict neutrality. On 16 March he spoke in Madrid to the Círculo Liberal, the elite policy-making group within the Liberal party. The Count told his audience: 'Spain remains and will remain neutral because this is her firm will . . . the present government, like Dato's will observe the strictest neutrality in its relations with the belligerents.'[1] This idea was repeated to a packed Cortes during the Crown Message on 10 May 1916. A month later, Romanones stood up again in Congress to point out that neutrality was not the monopoly of one party but the faithful interpretation of the unanimous opinion of the nation. The maverick Count even suggested he had been the first to support neutrality without any reservations when Dato had first proclaimed it two years earlier. What Romanones was clearly not prepared to do was to allow a public debate on neutrality. Thus when the fierce Republican Marcelino Domingo tried to bring up the issue in October, he was told that it was such a sensitive subject that it could not be discussed in parliament at that time. But Romanones promised that the deputies would be allowed to express their views before the end of the year. His call for 'patriotic' silence was promptly backed by Dato. In late December, with the issue being ignored and the Cortes about to be closed, Domingo and the other members of the Republican–Socialist minority voiced their disappointment and anger.[2]

Parliamentary passivity contrasted with feverish diplomatic activity. The Prime Minister's intention was to conduct foreign policy unseen by parliament. He relied mainly on diplomatic activities in Madrid, Paris and London which could not be scrutinized or commented upon by politicians or journalists. A Germanophile and ultra-conservative, Polo de Bernabé, and a neutral aristocrat, Alfonso Merry del Val, retained their posts as ambassadors to Berlin and London respectively, but Fernando León y Castillo, a former ambassador at Paris with good connections among French political elites, returned there and Fermín Calbetón, a close friend of Romanones, was sent to the Vatican.

León y Castillo and Polo de Bernabé defended two opposite foreign policies. The former totally shared Romanones's view that Spain should move towards the Western Bloc. In April 1916 he wrote:

> I am for a neutrality leaning towards the Allies . . . it is inconceivable for us to continue with the kind of neutrality that some want to impose upon us with threats of civil war . . . 'Fatal Neutralities' was not only an editorial, but is becoming a prophecy and if God does not protect us it could become a catastrophe.[3]

However, at the same time Polo de Bernabé was affirming: 'I am unhappy that Villanueva is no longer at the Foreign Office. The kind of strict neutrality pursued by him is exactly that which I personally identify with . . .'[4]

Despite all his declarations of strict neutrality, the Spanish Prime Minister had not abandoned the ideas expressed in his editorial 'Fatal Neutralities'. Yet Romanones knew he had to act with extreme caution so as not to arouse suspicions. Therefore he left Polo de Bernabé at Berlin and moved his man to Paris. Romanones's instructions were clear: Spain's destiny was inevitably linked to that of France and Britain. He informed León y Castillo that he was there with the full confidence of the government. His mission was to let the French authorities know that Spain was ruled by a friendly and supportive government, and then to obtain their consent for the transfer of Tangier from its existing international status to formal Spanish control. According to Romanones, Tangier was his main concern. The city was the key not only to the control of the Mediterranean but also to the final pacification of the Spanish Protectorate in Morocco.[5]

If the Count seriously believed that the French were prepared to agree with his plans for Tangier, he was either naive or had been misinformed. León y Castillo found in France a proud and stubborn nation determined to fight to the end. The cruel and bloody battle of Verdun was soon to reveal that resolution. Moreover, France's image of Spain was of a state conspicuous for its Germanophilia. The fact that the government was temporarily in friendly hands was meaningless as long as important institutions such as the church, army and court were making no effort to disguise their pro-German feelings. The Spanish ambassador at Paris was therefore not exactly met by a welcoming party. He despaired that while Portugal had made an intelligent move by throwing in her lot with the Allies, guaranteeing her interests in a future international order and ensuring her presence at the peace conference, Spain, whose economic and political destiny was inevitably linked to that of the Western Powers even if they were beaten in the war, continued to be disliked because of a neutrality which was playing into German hands. León y Castillo was thus pessimistic about the likelihood of France's acquiescing to a change in the status of Tangier. He suggested that time and money would have to be invested in order to win over French public opinion.[6]

León y Castillo, encouraged by Romanones, promptly raised the issue of Tangier with the French government. In fact, the account of his interview with the French Prime Minister, Aristide Briand, is not without its comic aspect. The Spanish ambassador in opening the conversation said he was a man too old and broken to be able to do much in the way of negotiation, to which Briand replied that the brave attempt which he had just made to take Tangier by storm was a most gratifying proof of youthful vigour. Briand went on to say that he did not think that now was a very suitable moment to discuss the question of Tangier. If France were suddenly to let it be known that she was prepared to acquiesce in a Spanish occupation of Tangier, without any corresponding concession on the part of the Spanish government, such an announcement would be interpreted as a sign that France was losing confidence in her ability to defeat Germany and was endeavouring to conciliate the neutral powers.[7] León y Castillo continued to approach leading French political figures such as Clemenceau, Pichon, Barthou and Frencinet, but his correspondence reveals the deadlock in which Spanish diplomacy found itself. A policy of nominal friendship, but empty hands in practice, would not obtain Tangier. The French were not prepared to discuss the question unless Spain adopted a new position. An alternative was to see whether Britain, the other major power guaranteeing the international status of Tangier, would be more willing to satisfy Spanish demands.[8]

The British proved to be almost as unresponsive as the French. During the first months of 1916 the Spanish embassy at London was bombarded with instructions. The ambassador Merry del Val was to seek support for Spanish claims over Tangier, to complain about the hostile attitude adopted by White, the British representative there, and to increase the commercial exchanges of coal and steel between the two countries. In June Romanones even wrote to Merry: 'We must be prepared for anything and aware of what they want from us, even intervention.'[9]

In fact, the British had not been overjoyed at the idea of a Romanones administration. They believed that unless Spain abandoned her official neutrality, a theoretically more friendly government might be a source of embarrassment more than anything else. Immediately after the fall of Dato, this feeling was expressed by the British ambassador in Madrid:

> I am not at all sure that a more openly friendly government may not be an embarrassment both for Spain and for ourselves. Mr. Dato held the balance well, officially and privately he was most friendly. Romanones may press for a price and try to raise the question of Tangier.[10]

The Foreign Secretary, Edward Grey, agreed with Briand that it was not an opportune moment to discuss Tangier. He recognized that it was a natural aspiration for Spain but insisted that no decision could be taken without French consent. Grey was not totally unsympathetic towards Spanish demands, believing that in order to keep Spain friendly some concessions might have to be made. Nevertheless, he also stressed that Spain should be asked something in return for that concession. Nobody wanted Tangier to be given up and Gibraltar was a sacrifice that Britain could not afford. Apart from that he did not know what else they could offer.[11]

In late March, at the request of Merry del Val, Grey agreed to discuss the question of Tangier in Paris with the French government. Grey wrote to Hardinge that he had stressed the need to keep Spain happy, but recognized that it was difficult for the French to withdraw from Tangier. Briand said that it was impossible to make such a concession as it would have the appearance of yielding to blackmail and would not be tolerated by French public opinion. Yet he did not preclude it from being considered at a more favourable time.[12]

After meeting Leon Geoffray, the French ambassador at Madrid, Hardinge concluded that the subject of an eventual transfer of Tangier to Spain would be postponed until the end of the war. In the meantime, with very little hesitation, the French replied that the cession of that city in the middle of the war would be regarded in France as a sign of weakness and as an attempt to draw Spain into the war on the side of the Allies. Furthermore, it might offend the Sultan of Morocco. Although a vassal of France he required rather delicate handling, as Turco-German emissaries were endeavouring to promote a Muslim movement against France and her Allies in Northern Africa. Moreover, it would be unwelcome to the French element in Morocco, and it was not certain that it would render the Spaniards more friendly in their attitude towards the European war. It appeared possible to Hardinge that those difficulties might be overcome by a secret understanding between France and Spain. In the event of a successful termination of the war, including the recovery by France of the two provinces lost to Germany in 1870, the French government would be willing to transfer Tangier to the Spanish zone, it being understood that until that event the Spanish government would maintain a benevolent attitude towards the Allies.[13]

In an attempt to win public support for a more benevolent neutrality towards the Allied cause, Romanones sought to enlist the aid of Antonio Maura. The veteran Conservative statesman was still the most respected and influential politician of the Spanish right and his voice was bound to have a decisive influence on those sectors of society identified with law and order, who were in fact the core of the Germanophile movement in Spain. Some of his followers were among the most noisy supporters of the Central Powers. Ultra-conservatives, Catholics and monarchists, these *Mauristas* loathed the idea of a victory for Republican France and for the political principles which that country represented. On 4 September 1916, Maura met Romanones and the king in Santander to discuss the international question and work together with them on the preparation of a major speech he was to deliver six days later at Berlanga.[14]

Maura's speech before a huge audience of his followers at Berlanga in September 1916 was the second of the three he delivered during the war. The first, at the Royal Theatre in Madrid in April 1915, had already revealed a veiled pro-Allied tendency. At Berlanga, Maura came very close to the international stance maintained by the Count. This was hardly surprising since they had exchanged ideas a few days earlier. The speech was typical of Maura: of great length, eloquent, verbose and abounding in allusions to abstract general principles. He dealt mainly with the war and foreign policy, making an important public declaration which emphasized a certain leaning on the part of Spain towards the Allied cause. Intervention in the European war was rejected, but a rapprochement with the Allies was defended as the logical conclusion drawn from history, economy and geography. Maura finally referred to Tangier as indispensable to Spanish expansion in Morocco and, bearing in mind the audience which he was addressing, claimed that Spain had the right to expect to be treated as a sister by the Entente. If, however, the general policy of England and France sought to weaken the influence and power of Spain, it would be the natural duty of Spanish statesmen after the war to reconsider their position and perhaps to look for support in a different political combination.[15]

Maura's speech stunned part of his habitual audience. The *Maurista* journal *La Acción* went out of its way to stress that Maura was still a staunch supporter of strict neutrality, but others described it as a betrayal. Romanones himself declared he was in total agreement with the ideas presented by the old Conservative leader. Republican leaders like Melquiades Alvarez and Alejandro Lerroux gratefully welcomed his views. Lerroux even argued in his journal *El Progreso* that after two years of war, Maura and he were in full agreement.[16]

Maura's tacit support for Romanones's foreign policy failed to produce the expected effect upon the Western diplomats. They were, if anything, dismissive and unimpressed. The British Foreign Office wrote: 'The Spanish government's attitude may now have been modified by the speech of Maura, though it seems more likely to be intended as a form of blackmail; a hint that Spain might help us in return for Gibraltar or Tangier.'[17] The French adopted a similar approach. The ambassador in Madrid thought that it would not affect the situation. Spain could only help the Allied cause if she was to serve them in some concrete and practical way, for instance, by the seizure of the interned German ships. Moreover, he described Maura's speech as 'an attempt to hedge and envelop in pompous and lengthy phrases, a statement which contained nothing new, whilst France was being asked to pay an unduly high price for words which had no real value'.[18]

A practical and immediate departure from the official strict neutrality was something that Romanones, in a country divided by philias, was unable to offer. The Liberal leader claimed in his memoirs that there were substantial offers to persuade him to join the Entente, especially during the meeting he held with the French Foreign Minister at San Sebastián in September 1916. However, Romanones maintained that when he realized that the general mood in the country was against a direct involvement in the conflict he refused to join the Allies and instead merely sought to work for a benevolent neutrality towards their cause.[19] In fact, he was withholding a good deal of the truth: as he was prepared to go much further than he suggests.

There is no evidence that at any time the Spanish government was under any kind of economic or political pressure to join the Entente. Surrounded by Allied countries who controlled the sea routes and depending for her economic survival on the trade with them, Spain would not have been able to withstand their combined force.

The story was very different in the case of the Central Powers. The relative passivity of the Western Powers contrasted with the ruthless determination and forceful methods of Germany and her friends to ensure that Spain never abandoned the position it had adopted at the outbreak of the war. Germany identified her cause with that of law and order. She found her most ardent supporters in the army, aristocracy, court and clergy. On 27 January 1916 leading representatives of all those institutions assembled at the German embassy in Madrid to celebrate the Kaiser's birthday and express their sympathy for Germany at that critical time.[20]

Germany's strategy in Spain began to change in the course of 1916. Knowing that the government of the country was in unfriendly hands, German agents embarked on an active and ambitious campaign of destabilization, infiltration and sabotage which went far beyond the diplomatic activities permissible for any country acting in neutral territory. There were three objectives: to gain control of public opinion, to damage the interests of the Allies and to bring down any hostile administration.

Control of public opinion, in particular the press, was an important German success. Both the Central and the Western Powers took advantage of the exorbitant rise in the price of paper to come to the financial rescue of different newspapers and thus managed to influence their editorials. In this practice the former always held the lead while the latter only reacted when the advantage enjoyed by the Central Powers had become evident. A secret British report in October 1917 noted the poverty and weakness of Anglo-French propaganda in Spain in comparison with that of the Central Powers. It confirmed that the substantial sums lavished by the latter on the Spanish press had paid off, as public opinion was to a large extent moulded by the German embassy.[21]

Despite the shortage of paper, Spanish journals devoted 50 per cent of their columns, if not more, to thorough coverage of the situation on the European battlefields. Massacres such as Verdun, the Somme and Gallipoli were meticulously described. Naturally, depending on the newspaper's leaning, these bloody events were portrayed as proof either of the invincibility of the mighty German armies or of the resolution and bravery of the Allies.

The primary objective of all the pro-German publications in Spain was to ensure the strict maintenance of neutrality. To that end Germany did not just seek to control that part of the right-wing media closest to her ideological position, but also invested heavily both in the Liberal press edited by rivals of Count Romanones and in the pro-neutral Anarcho-Syndicalist journals. It was obviously a covert operation in which these newspapers received large amounts of money and in return opposed any departure from tacit neutrality. Whereas right-wing newspapers accused any interventionist politician of treason to Spain, those on the left stressed the fact that the working class would be the section of society paying with their lives for the madness of entering into the 'imperialist war'. The right-wing press disguised its Germanophilia with slogans of patriotism and *Españolismo*. They were the defenders of the ultimate interests of the nation, seeking to prevent the country from sliding into a disastrous war and fighting for strict neutrality. Their effort was combined with that of the left, which continually accused the pro-Allied elements in Spain of being behind the orgy of exports which was tearing the country apart.

Virtually all the journals of the political right were in friendly hands or under direct German control: the most widely read were the monarchist *ABC*, the *Maurista La Acción*, the Carlist *El Correo Español*, the Catholic *El Debate* and *El Universo*, the Conservative *La Tribuna* and *La Nación*. The last two were practically owned by German capital. The Allies were favoured by *La Epoca*, the official newspaper of the Conservative party, and by Romanones's mouthpiece, *El Diario Universal*, as well as *El Liberal de Madrid*, *El Heraldo de Madrid*, *La Correspondencia de España* and *El Imparcial*. Germany, however, had influence over the main journals of the democratic faction of the Liberal party: the Marquis of Alhucemas's *La Mañana* and *El Día*, edited by Niceto Alcalá Zamora, future President of the Second Republic. In theory, all the main publications of the left backed the Allied cause. This was the case with Araquistáin's *España*, the Republican *El País* and *El Parlamentario*, Lerroux's *El Progreso* and the PSOE's newspaper, *El Socialista*. Nevertheless, German capital was behind the neutralist editorials of *Solidaridad Obrera*, organ of the CNT, and of the ultra-left Republican *España Nueva*, edited by the controversial Republican deputy Rodrigo Soriano.

The amount invested by Britain to control, or, at least influence, the Spanish press seems derisory when compared with that invested by Germany. In March 1917, Britain spent about 24,000 pesetas (see Table 4.2). In 1916 the German embassy had contributed 35,000 pesetas monthly just to the liberal newspaper *El Día*. The fact that the foreign policy of the Liberal Prime Minister could be lambasted by an influential liberal journal was regarded as a

Table 4.2 Britain's monthly expenditure on the Spanish press (pesetas)

La Correspondencia de España	8,500
El Imparcial	7,500
España	1,500
La Epoca	3,000
El Parlamentario	2,500
Los Bárbaros	500
Cantabria	500
Política	75
Total	24,075

Source: Crown copyright material in the Public Record Office reproduced by permission of the Controller of Her Majesty's Stationery Office. FO 185/1345, no.463 (Report in March 1917 from John Walters, correspondent of *The Times* and British director of propaganda in Spain).

worthy investment. Its editor, the leading Liberal deputy Alcalá Zamora, was in nominal charge of the editorials, but the Maneshmman brothers, two German agents, held actual control. Soon after, Austria literally bought *La Nación* and Germany began to sponsor the Republican newspaper *España Nueva*. Its editor, the Republican deputy Rodrigo Soriano, received 4,000 pesetas monthly. In 1916 alone, Germany spent 500,000 pesetas on activities related to manipulation and control of the Spanish press. Anarchists were often used to write neutralist editorials. A company called the Sociedad Civil de Estudios Económicos was set up in Madrid, Calle Campoamor 20, as a front to carry out these activities. The company was chaired by a Spaniard who had previously been employed at the Austrian embassy and a German, Gustavo Motschmann, was the go-between for the company and the Anarchists. By the end of the war, the Central Powers controlled over 500 local and national newspapers in Spain.[22]

Right up to the end of the war, the concerted and well-organized campaign carried out by the Germanophile press proved to be a formidable force. Any criticism of Germany – be it of innocent lives lost in a submarine attack or atrocities committed in the territories occupied by her – was rapidly depicted as warmongering and an open invitation to intervention. Even the sinking of Spanish vessels was justified. Ironically the owners of those vessels, accused of smuggling contraband and collaboration with one of the warring factions, were blamed for their own misfortune. After all, Germany was only fighting for her survival and she had to do so with all the methods available to her. In June 1916, before the submarine campaign had begun in earnest, one of the most vociferous Germanophile journals published a series of articles under the headline 'A Sensational Document'. It provided a complete list of Spanish companies producing material for the Entente and of Spanish ships contributing to their war effort by carrying cargo from one Allied port to another. In fact, it was almost a final warning to the Liberal government to put an end to contraband and profiteering and an advance justification of a possible change in the hitherto benevolent attitude adopted by Germany towards the Spanish merchant fleet. Furthermore, the articles were used as the proof that the main cause of the inflationary trend affecting Spain was the fact that her transport and basic products were being cynically used or exported abroad.[23]

By 1916 German influence in Spain was such that the nation was regarded in the Western chancelleries if not as a Germanophile country, at least as a doubtful friend. This was not only a result of the image given by a bellicose Germanophile press, but also by the dramatic intensification of German activities in the peninsula which went largely unpunished. There were flagrant cases of complicity between German agents and Spanish authorities, examples of infiltration into Anarchist groups and subsequent organization of strike action so as to disrupt industrial production and exports for the Allies, and finally unrestrained and vicious submarine attacks off the Spanish coasts.

In February 1916 the British Foreign Office received a secret report warning of the potential danger presented by the presence of between 70,000 and 80,000 German residents in Spain and confirming that the recent wave of strikes in Barcelona had been fomented by German agents for the purpose of stopping exports from this area reaching France.[24] In May, Vaughan, Secretary of the British Embassy in Madrid, wrote that it had been verified that German submarines were being furnished with many supplies in Spanish waters, particularly along the coast of Valencia where small vessels belonging to the rich tobacco smuggler Juan March were being used for that purpose. Also, a consignment of one million cartridges had been seized at Madrid railway station – which suggested that many others had got through. The belief was that its destination was Morocco to support the Moorish revolt against the French.[25] In June a serious incident occurred when, without previous notice, the German submarine U-35, supposedly responsible for several attacks on Allied convoys in the Mediterranean, arrived at Cartagena. An embarrassed Romanones had to face an avalanche of protests from Paris and London. The official version given by El Imparcial was that the vessel had brought a personal letter of gratitude from the Kaiser to king Alfonso for the excellent treatment given to those German officers who had surrendered to the Spanish authorities in Guinea after the loss of the colony of Cameroon. There were, however, suspicions that its real mission was to establish links with the crews of German ships interned in Spanish ports and to co-ordinate new actions with other submarines near the coast of Bilbao.[26]

During the next months French complaints mounted about submarine raids off the Spanish coasts and German money and arms reaching the rebel Moors in Morocco. In July, León y Castillo wrote to Romanones: 'What a pity! The French just want a proof of our friendship, and this is the spectacle we are providing.' Romanones was determined to show the Allies where his sympathies lay. In early August he decided to protest against the German treatment of civilians in occupied territories. On 27 August he briefed León y Castillo that the German government had been informed that no more visits would be allowed and that its submarines should stop using Spanish territorial waters.[27] On 1 September, the Spanish Prime Minister sent a note to the monarch expressing his belief that the country should adopt a more benevolent neutrality towards the Allies. Then, on the eve of his meeting with the French Foreign Minister, the Count told Colonel Tillon, the French Military Attaché, that he believed neutrality should not be a position of equidistance between the belligerent nations, but should be one of sympathy for France and England and that he was most desirous of giving evidence of this.[28]

Romanones's pro-Allied initiatives confirmed the worst suspicions of the Central Powers. Germany abandoned the carrot and henceforth used the stick. After September 1916 the number of submarine attacks and the amount of sabotage and spying activity shot up dramatically. They resulted in the division of the country into those who were prepared to defend neutrality at any price and thus justify any German action, and those who argued that such hostility should be answered by the immediate severing of diplomatic relations. The Prime Minister's attempts to check Germany's manoeuvres were unsuccessful. The odds against him were formidable. He was confronted by a very resourceful and well organized intelligence network which was backed by a powerful press lobby and could act at will with the complicity of authorities that in particular cases, like those of the colonies of Guinea and Morocco, reached scandalous dimensions. After December the battle between Romanones and Germany and her Spanish friends became war to the knife. There could be only two possible outcomes: either a final breach with the Central Powers or the end of Romanones's Premiership. The fact that the most ardent supporters of his foreign policy were Republicans and Socialists persuaded the bulk of the dynastic forces that his downfall was a price worth paying.

Like the other neutral nations Spain had seen her trade affected by the hostilities. Both sides tried to hurt each other by imposing an economic blockade to disrupt the other's supply lines. They drew up lists of products which they would not allow to reach an enemy port. Thus neutral vessels, if caught carrying forbidden cargo, could easily be accused of smuggling contraband and have their goods seized. Allied naval supremacy, from the very beginning of the conflict, meant that a desperate Germany had to resort increasingly to the use of U-boats instead of surface ships. In the first stages of the war, German submarines limited their role for the most part to searching neutral boats and destroying prohibited goods. Spanish vessels had often been detained by French or British warships and driven to an Allied port where they were fined if contraband was found. Crews and boats were promptly released once the fine was paid.[29] As the war dragged on, however, German U-boats began to sink any vessel navigating towards an Allied port. Friends of Germany argued that circumstances had imposed these methods upon her.

Yet for those on the receiving end the change of tactics made a serious impact, especially in terms of loss of lives and destruction of material.

German submarine action had been relatively moderate towards the Spanish merchant fleet. During the first two years of the war only eight Spanish ships had been sunk. After September 1916 that policy changed radically. In just one week during that month three Spanish boats – *Olazábal, Mayo* and *Luis Vives* – were sent to the bottom. Germany had decided to switch to bullying tactics. The idea was to show Romanones and those contemplating a departure from strict neutrality what they were risking. By April 1917 the toll had risen to 31 ships or 80,000 tons of much-needed marine transport.[30] A real battle of words was taking place in public opinion. The barbarism of the Teutonic war machine was constantly denounced in the Francophile journals which demanded strong measures to put an end to the disaster. Yet for the Germanophile press it was only the natural outcome of the conflict. They argued that Germany was within her rights to treat as enemies all those supplying the Allies with the means to continue the war.

Romanones also found obstinate resistance to his pro-Allied position in the colonies. Relations between the Spanish authorities in the Spanish possessions in Africa (Morocco, Guinea and Western Sahara) and the neighbouring French administration had never been particularly cordial. There had always been rivalry and probably also a certain degree of jealousy towards the more competent and successful French colonial system. The outbreak of the war in Europe caused even further deterioration of the already troubled relations. Admiration for the efficiency and discipline of the German army and pleasure at the setbacks of France were not strange to many Spanish officers, but it was almost the rule among those in the colonies. Thus they were more than happy to turn a blind eye to the activities of German agents.

An outrageous example of complicity took place in Spanish Guinea. In early 1916, facing an all-out Allied offensive, the German colonial army in the Cameroons retreated towards Spanish Guinea. In February, France and Britain advocated the internment of 60 German officers and several thousand native troops in the Spanish colony. The intention was that the German officers would shortly be sent to the peninsula to be held in Saragossa and the disarmed natives returned to their country.[31] Time passed and the operation kept being postponed.

In October the French ambassador Geoffray called to the attention of Amalio Gimeno, the Spanish Foreign Minister, the arrival at Fernando Poo, the capital of Spanish Guinea, of cases containing ammunition and rifles which had found their way to a camp of interned German officers. The German commandant had been heard to say that they would return in triumph to the Cameroons in a few months. The French ambassador requested that the German officers be immediately transported to the peninsula and the natives to the Cameroons. He also announced that French authorities on the nearby coast had received orders to divert to their ports all Spanish ships bound for Fernando Poo so that they might be searched for guns. Gimeno promised two vessels to convey the Germans to Spain.[32] Yet the Spanish government saw its plans thwarted by the close co-operation between the theoretically imprisoned German officers and the Spanish colonial authorities, particularly the governor, Angel Barrera, and the commandant in chief Manuel Giménez Pidal. Barrera had been aware of the presence of weapons at the German camp and had done nothing. Moreover, German and Spanish officers not only fraternized openly but even interchanged duties as if they belonged to the same army. On 28 October 1916 two French cruisers, *Surcouf* and *Astrea*, arrived in the colony with guns positioned and manned and did not leave before informing Barrera that the Allies would not consent to the presence of armed Germans near their former colony of the Cameroons. In December the British government communicated to the Spanish ambassador in London its dissatisfaction with the situation in Guinea. There was no doubt about the good intentions of the Spanish government, but neither the Navy Office nor Governor Barrera could be trusted.[33] The news that the removal operation had begun did not arrive until February 1917. The previous month a parade had been held in honour of the Kaiser with the participation of Spanish officers.[34] Yet Governor Barrera retained his post until March 1918.

Morocco, divided into a Spanish and a French Protectorate since 1912, represented the clearest example of rivalry and lack of collaboration between the two administrations. Both colonial powers had the tacit consent of the Sultan to establish their zones of influence but had run into the opposition of armed natives. They had been engaged in guerrilla warfare, but co-operation had been lacking. Instead, mistrust had been the general rule. Germany took advantage of this situation to create trouble for France in her North African possession.

In 1916, at the same time as Romanones was making his bid for Tangier, the French had been complaining about German agents in the Spanish zone actively encouraging, arming and financing a Moroccan rebellion. The German consulates at Tetuán, Larache and Melilla had become bases for spy networks whence German nationals like Bartels, Koppel and Richtels provided the rebel leaders, Abd-el Malek and Raisuli, with money and weapons to continue their raids into French territory.[35] It was impossible that the Spanish authorities did not know what was going on under their very noses. The Liberal Prime Minister despaired that the German manoeuvres were not only an abuse of the hospitality enjoyed by her nationals but a clear attempt to endanger both the pacification of Morocco and the relations between France and Spain. In fact, the zeal of the Spanish authorities in combating the German–Moorish links in the peninsula contrasted with the passivity of the colonial officers in Morocco. The police were active in the peninsula in wrecking the German initiative to make Mulay Haffid the new sultan of Morocco. Haffid, resident in Barcelona, was under the close surveillance of the Spanish intelligence services and Romanones pledged that if necessary he would be expelled from Spain. In November, one million pesetas intended for Raisuli and half a million for Abd-el Malek were intercepted, and thereafter orders were given for the arrest and expulsion of Koppel from the Spanish Protectorate.[36] But the smuggling of arms into the French zone continued without interruption and German officers became advisers to Abd-el Malek's troops. The malice or the weakness of the Spanish authorities was then openly demonstrated when High Commissioner Jordana demanded that the rebel leader Raisuli be appointed Grand Visir of Tetuán in February 1917. The French colonial office was enraged. Nevertheless, Spanish operations in Morocco had one major imperative: to prevent a high number of casualties in what was mostly regarded as an unpopular colonial adventure. Thus the official explanation for appointing such a controversial figure was that in order to pacify the Spanish zone the collaboration of influential native leaders was needed.[37]

British secret reports agreed with Romanones's memoirs in their description of the extent and nature of German operations in Spain. By late 1916, as well as her powerful press lobby and her activities in the colonies of Morocco, Guinea and to a lesser extent Western Sahara, Germany had established spy networks in Bilbao, Barcelona, Valencia, Málaga, Huelva and the Canary Islands. The objective was not only to spy on France but also to acquire information about shipping routes and to infiltrate Anarchist and revolutionary groups in Spain. These could then be easily manipulated to disrupt industrial production for the Allies.[38]

December 1916 represented a watershed in terms of the polarization of the country over the neutrality issue. It also brought about an open declaration of war between Romanones and the Germanophile forces in the country. On 12 December the Central Powers published a statement claiming that they were ready to negotiate peace. But they made no important concessions and the statement was marked by threats to resume the hostilities in an even more lethal manner if the Western Powers did not accept their overtures. Naturally the Entente rejected the German terms, alleging that they had not chosen war but that it had been thrust upon them. They were not prepared to stop until German military might had been crushed. The peace initiative was followed up by the United States President Woodrow Wilson, who on 18 December sent a note to both belligerents and neutrals in an attempt to see if there was any possibility of finding common ground to stop the carnage. But the gap was too great to be bridged.

In Spain the irreconcilability of the two positions was well documented. The pro-Allied press condemned the German approach, applauded the words of the Allied leaders and even accused Wilson of unwittingly acting as an honorary agent of Germany. By contrast, the Germanophile press praised the peace initiatives and argued that the pro-Allied elements in Spain were behaving like foreign agents, who were not only happy to see the slaughter continue on the European battlefields, but wanted to drag Spain into it as well.[39]

74

Various peace initiatives offered Spain the longed-for opportunity to play a mediating role in the conflict. No other country and no other head of state had worked so hard to fulfil that role. Alfonso had taken personal charge of establishing a diplomatic centre in Madrid to deal with both sides, gathering information on missing citizens and soldiers, acting on behalf of the population in occupied territories, advocating the repatriation of wounded or sick soldiers and performing a large variety of other altruistic services. Additionally, her position of neutrality had enabled Spain to take charge of the interests of some of the belligerent nations in hostile territories. Some outstanding examples by late 1916 were the protection of German interests in Portugal and Romania, those of Austria-Hungary in Italy and Portugal, of France in Germany, Turkey, Persia and occupied Belgium, of Russia in Germany, Austria-Hungary and occupied Belgium, of Britain in Austria-Hungary, etc.[40] The enthusiasm of the Spanish monarch for the peace initiatives was reported in full by the British ambassador:

> The king said that he hoped the Allies would wait for full particulars respecting the German proposals, before they summarily rejected all idea of negotiations. I think His Majesty meant to suggest that what Germany would begin by proposing might be materially modified in the course of discussion; and although the Spanish government would probably share the task of mediation with the United States, it is one which the king would naturally undertake with pride and interest, as likely to considerably increase the prestige of his country in world politics.[41]

A few days earlier the monarch had told his Prime Minister that this was a crucial moment which had to be exploited. He was going to use his attendance at the funeral of the late Austrian Emperor Franz Josef in Vienna to meet the rulers of the Central Powers and then on his return journey exchange views with the Allied leaders in Paris. From these meetings Alfonso expected to emerge as the arbiter of peace in Europe.[42]

At first Romanones toyed with the idea of the Spanish monarch initiating mediation between the belligerents. He tried to introduce the idea when he met the French ambassador, and was taken aback when the latter responded that there could be no question of the peace proposals being entertained. The French diplomat was categorical:

> For forty years we have lived under the German menace; we have never been able to take a step without being threatened by the iron fist; successive Spanish governments can testify to the brutal and insolent interference of German diplomacy at almost every stage of Franco-Spanish negotiations respecting our interests and spheres of influence in Morocco. At last the cup has overflowed; France has

been attacked without provocation by her enemy and her children have sacrificed themselves in thousands to ensure that this brutal attack shall never be repeated. Any compromise, any patched-up peace, such as that which the terms suggest, would provoke an outburst of universal indignation.[43]

In the course of that conversation, Romanones suggested that the services of a mediator, who might perhaps succeed in procuring rather more favourable conditions, could be a good solution, but the French ambassador told him emphatically that his idea would not be accepted by the French government. León y Castillo confirmed that impression a few days later. The Liberal leader acted accordingly and refused to endorse Wilson's initiative. Instead, on 28 December he published a statement protesting against the sinking of Spanish vessels and alleging that the destructive activities of submarines went beyond the rules of international law. He even clashed with the monarch when he opposed the latter's attendance at the funeral of the late Austrian emperor in Vienna and his wearing of an Austrian uniform at the private service which subsequently took place in Madrid.[44]

Romanones's behaviour convinced Germany that he was the main enemy of her cause in Spain. Until then a significant degree of hostility and suspicion had existed towards him; henceforth there was open war. In late December a vicious campaign began against the Liberal leader. The signal had been given by the Austrian ambassador, the Prince of Furstenberg, who in an interview on 26 December with *La Nación* had hinted that Count Romanones was behind contraband interests. A few days later the French intercepted a telegram in which the German ambassador, Prince Max of Ratibor, requested from Berlin more funds to support an anti-Romanones campaign.[45] For the following four months, savagely hostile editorials were published in the Germanophile press. The Prime Minister was singled out as a warmonger surreptitiously seeking to embroil the nation in the European conflagration. Comparisons were drawn between the Count and the interventionist Greek politician Venizelos. Spaniards were warned in apocalyptic tones that under the current premiership a national disaster was bound to occur sooner or later. All the Germanophile newspapers claimed that the post of Prime Minister was incompatible with the Count's private export interests. They suggested that he was actually using his privileged position to profit from selling products abroad and was therefore a smuggler of war contraband, placing Franco-British interests above the national interests of Spain. He was thus behind every malady affecting Spain, from workers' disturbances and inflation to food shortages and lack of transport. The press called on the government to resign and cease growing rich on the European tragedy and the miseries of the Spanish people.[46]

On 8 January, facing a divided party, social unrest and under heavy pressure from a hostile Germanophile press, a besieged Romanones decided to present his resignation so as to make a come-back reinforced by the confidence of the monarch. His manoeuvre was in fact entirely staged. Since he knew that he was still backed by a majority of Liberal deputies and had the goodwill of Eduardo Dato, the other *Turno* leader, it represented a pre-emptive move aimed at forestalling any possible challenge to his leadership. The king himself confided to the British ambassador that Romanones's departure had been a necessary piece of theatre to strengthen the Prime Minister's hand against Germanophile forces and rivals in the Liberal party.[47]

The hostile press was not silenced. They were enraged and quickly denounced the proceedings as further proof of the duplicity and bankruptcy of the existing administration. *La Acción* even argued that the monarch was becoming an unwitting accomplice in these wicked manoeuvres.[48] Yet Romanones still seemed to be in charge of the situation. The violence of the press attacks had failed to disturb the Count and if anything had strengthened his pro-Allied views.

On 9 January 1917, in a desperate attempt to disrupt the economy of the Allies, the Central Powers announced their intention of intensifying the submarine campaign from February onwards. Any neutral vessel heading towards any Allied port would be sunk. The German initiative provoked anger among the neutral nations. In early February the United States broke off diplomatic relations with Germany. *España*'s editor, Araquistáin, called the German initiative a declaration of war.[49] Romanones wrote to León y Castillo that were public opinion not so divided he would immediately adopt the American policy. For the moment he could not, but had to wait for the right psychological moment.[50]

Romanones once more appealed to the patriotism of the Cortes and pledged to work in close collaboration with them. This attitude was clearly revealed in his speech to parliament on 1 February: 'The decision of the Central Powers to use all possible means to stop all maritime traffic with France, Britain, Italy and the Eastern Mediterranean entails grave consequences for Spain. This government is resolved that the life of this country must not be disrupted and shall not be disrupted. This government is therefore determined to take such steps as may be appropriate in these circumstances.'[51] This firm position was confirmed in the note delivered to Germany and described by the French as as strong and dignified a protest as could be made by a neutral country. The most important point was the rejection as a legitimate method of warfare of the destructive course pursued by Germany and her allies, jeopardizing the economic life of Spain and endangering the lives of her citizens.[52]

Despite all his promises, the Prime Minister did not intend bringing up the issue in public debate. Instead he continued to rely on diplomatic channels. Thus, in response to the insistence of Catalan Republicans like Rodés and Domingo for a discussion of the international question and Morocco, the Prime Minister simply decided to suspend parliament on 26 February.[53] In fact, what nobody knew was that the Spanish ambassador at Paris had already established crucial contacts with the French government. León y Castillo met the French Foreign Minister, Jules Cambon, at the Quai d'Orsay and intimated that his country was willing to go to great lengths to grant direct assistance to the Allies. In reply to a request for a more precise statement, León y Castillo said that Spain might place all her natural resources at their command. This was far from impressive since the Allies were already in a position to draw raw materials and manufactured goods, as well as agrarian produce, from Spain, by virtue of the many purchases, contracts and orders that had been arranged. Cambon asked what Spain expected to obtain in return and was told that she desired Tangier, Gibraltar and a free hand in Portugal. The Spanish ambassador emphasized that Spain did not want to annex Portugal but just to link both peninsular countries by some sort of treaty or alliance. The French Foreign Minister insisted that Spain should intervene militarily even if only on a small scale, but León y Castillo responded that this was impossible for the present owing to the divisions in his country. Yet Spain would break off diplomatic relations with Germany, open her ports to the Allies, smash German espionage and contribute to the production of war material. Cambon then stated that he was in favour of granting the Spanish demands although he could not say anything about Gibraltar.[54]

Romanones was totally convinced that the only way to consolidate the status of the country among the great powers and to head off the increasingly troubled domestic situation was to depart from strict neutrality. German bullying tactics and the Americans' tough response seemed to bear out his view. Both León y Castillo and Calbetón advised the Count to follow the American lead and break off diplomatic relations with Germany. Calbetón even suggested that the continuance of neutrality was a stain on national honour and dignity.[55] But the Count was still waiting for the right moment to act. On 12 February the king's brother claimed that behind the back of the monarch and of all good Spaniards, Romanones had sealed a secret treaty with the French so that Spain would soon enter into the war on the side of the Allies.[56] On 16 February, an individual who was in fact a German sailor was arrested in Cartagena with two suitcases full of explosives. The Count wrote that there was enough dynamite to blow up all the fleets of the world and all the Spanish factories. He commented that it was not surprising that the Allies doubted the reliability of Spain when he could not control what was going on in many Spanish cities.[57]

In March, events in Russia proved decisive in intensifying the 'war of words' in the peninsula. The Tsar was overthrown and a provisional government installed. The end of autocracy in Russia and its replacement by a modern democratic republic filled the pro-Allied forces in Spain with joy. The despotism associated with Tsarism had been an embarrassment for the Western Powers, but now the new Russian regime, added to the entry of the United States into the war in early April, radically transformed a conflict of imperialist aims into a worldwide ideological struggle: democracy and freedom against aggression and militarism.

In Spain, Socialist and Republican journals insisted that the Russian Revolution had not been the reaction of people weary of war, but rather directed against a despotic and tyrannical political order whose leaders were seeking a compromise peace with their imperial counterparts in Germany and Austria. These journals became the most outspoken supporters of a diplomatic rupture with Germany and in some cases even advocated open intervention.[58]

The speed with which the Western Powers abandoned the Tsar to his fate and recognized the new regime in Russia sent waves of panic through the Spanish ruling circles. More than ever they were determined to stay out of the European nightmare. Nothing could be gained by joining a side which, it seemed to them, was closely identified with Republicanism. Yet Romanones, regardless of the radical changes in Russia, had already decided to depart from strict neutrality. The psychological moment he was waiting for arrived on 6 April when a German submarine sank the steamer *San Fulgencio*. The numbers of outrageous German attacks on the Spanish merchant fleet had increased dramatically since February. The glaring difference was that in this case, the *San Fulgencio* was outside the forbidden waters and heading towards Spain with a much-needed cargo of British coal.

Documentary evidence reveals that the events which took place during the two weeks following the *San Fulgencio* disaster could have changed the history of contemporary Spain. During that period the Prime Minister kept in close contact with Western diplomats so as to negotiate terms for a possible departure from neutrality. Simultaneously the debate between the pro-German and the pro-Allied press reached its peak. In the end, Romanones lost the battle. His position was opposed by the other monarchist leaders. Furthermore, the Allies, particularly Britain, turned out to be lukewarm towards the Count's move. Unlike France and the United States, Britain considered the price for the Spanish rupture with Germany to be too high. Furthermore, there was hardly any reason to meet Spain's demands if she was being forced by German brutality to embrace the Allied cause in any event.

The Prime Minister's correspondence with León y Castillo revealed the frenzied atmosphere of those two weeks. The latest German sinking, the entry of the United States and some Latin American republics into the war, and the internal situation in the peninsula were some of the factors that led to the Count's final resolution to throw in his lot with the Entente without wasting any more time. Yet he knew he was playing a deadly game in which the strength of the opposing forces was immense. On 14 April he wrote to León y Castillo:

> The crucial moment has arrived, the sinking of the *San Fulgencio* has been the final straw. The route I will take is already determined in the direction that you know and is a logical conclusion of the

conversations of last September . . . The note to Germany will be the first and fundamental step . . . But I am not overconfident . . . opinion does not follow me even within my own party . . . I do not know how I am going to play my cards yet . . . the struggle between the Germanophiles and myself is to the death.[59]

At the same time, intense diplomatic activity had been taking place behind the scenes. This had been primarily directed at procuring concessions from France. On 8 March the Permanent Under-Secretary of State for Foreign Affairs disclosed to the British War Cabinet information from Paris to the effect that Spain was making approaches with a view to joining the Allies.[60]

In early April, Vaughan, secretary at the British embassy in Madrid, relayed that the French ambassador, Geoffray, had held a long conversation with Count Romanones and discussed the position created by the entry of the United States and some Latin American countries into the war. The Spanish Prime Minister argued that if Spain maintained her present position she would certainly sink to the level of an insignificant power such as the Netherlands. Romanones had said that the moment had come when Spain could no longer remain neutral and that in the next day or so he would make a public declaration of policy to the effect that she must come into the war on the side of the Allies. If his advice was disregarded Romanones said he would resign. The Count was still confident he had the full confidence of the monarch, but added that his position was very difficult owing to the king's Austrian connections. At their next meeting Romanones asked the French ambassador if he could use his influence with the pro-Allied press to shift public opinion towards his position. Regarding Tangier, Geoffray declared that France had no authority to dispose of the city but agreed to use her influence with the interested parties to secure it for Spain. Vaughan gathered from the French diplomat that the French military authorities were very keen on Spain taking a positive course of action. An important gain would be the use of Spanish ports for Allied warships. Another consideration was that France would be relieved of considerable anxiety with regard to German intrigues in Morocco and thus might be able to release some of her troops there. Finally, another important point was that the French believed that if Spain broke off diplomatic relations with Germany the effect on morale would be enormous and would cause any South American states still wavering to do likewise.[61]

The United States, a newcomer to the subtleties of European diplomacy, was the only power to adopt an uncompromising position. Now that the Americans had decided to intervene in the war they thought that other neutrals should make their position clear, especially a country like Spain whose attitude could have an important impact on Latin America. The American ambassador, Joseph Willard, therefore attempted to force the issue.[62] Yet the United States was an exception. The other Allies, led by Britain, had concluded that it was inadvisable to bring direct pressure on the Spanish government.

The British line was not entirely motivated by pure altruism, but was the result of long and deep consideration of the advantages and disadvantages of possible Spanish intervention in the war. In January 1917, Jocelyn Grant, the military attaché in the British embassy at Madrid, completed a long and thorough investigation into the state of the Spanish army. He had established contacts throughout 1916 with artillery officers and members of the General Staff. He concluded that that state was pitiful. Grant observed that transport appeared to be lacking, equipment was very poor, there was an acute shortage of rifles and ammunition despite recent purchases in the United States, and there were hardly any modern aeroplanes or heavy artillery. It was therefore difficult to believe that the Spanish army would ever be in a condition to threaten anybody except possibly the Portuguese.[63]

Two months later, in a joint note concerning Spain's value as an ally, the General Staff and the Admiralty agreed with Grant on the poor shape of the Spanish army which they compared with that of Romania. Yet they stressed that Spain enjoyed some important advantages. She possessed some of the largest mineral resources in Europe. Furthermore, Spanish intervention could represent for the Entente an increase of half a million active troops and four million in the reserve, although they had very little combat experience and lacked competent senior officers. Nevertheless, Spain was not in direct contact with enemy territory; consequently there was no danger of her being overrun and troops could be safely trained before engaging in combat.[64]

The British Foreign Office was more negative in its conclusions. The entry of Spain into the war on the side of the Allies was regarded as a distinctly mixed blessing. They saw the disadvantages of her co-operation as outweighing the advantages. There were indeed some important ideological and economic contributions that Spain could offer. The decision of such an intensely Catholic country would necessarily influence the feelings of Catholics throughout Europe and America. Germany would lose her strong commercial position in Spain, which would mean important opportunities for British enterprise. Of more direct assistance was the fact that the peninsula would no longer be used as a possible source of supplies for the enemy and the interned German ships in Spanish ports would be freed to carry Allied trade. Yet the Foreign Office believed that the conditions which Spain was likely to impose in return for her assistance meant the disadvantages of her collaboration outweighed the advantages. The Spanish demanded Tangier, Gibraltar and a free hand in Portugal.

With regard to Tangier it was claimed that Spain was quite incapable of governing or developing the city efficiently. She was deemed unable to hold her own ground there and her rule spelt corruption and incompetence. Moreover, British diplomats feared that if France was to agree to Tangier now being Spanish, there was a perpetual future danger of France picking a quarrel with Spain in order to seize Tangier and even Spanish Morocco. This would nullify all the elaborate precautions taken in 1904 to exclude France from the northern coast of Morocco. As regards a possible exchange of Gibraltar for Ceuta, the British Foreign Office felt that the Spanish city would be worthless if certain surrounding hills which were at present included in the international zone of Tangier were not included in the deal. It would require the assent of France for them to be included in a British Ceuta. However, while the war in Europe lasted there was a chance of procuring French agreement without having to pay an exorbitant price. Later on that would probably be impossible. An interdepartmental committee, under the chairmanship of Lord Curzon, with naval, military and diplomatic representatives, was appointed in early April 1917 to report on the subject. Until that committee reached a conclusion any discussion on Gibraltar should be postponed. Finally, concerning Portugal, the solution of linking that country to Spain by some sort of treaty was not considered detrimental to British interests, for Portuguese misgovernment was a persistent source of anxiety. Nevertheless, it was also noted that however exasperating the Portuguese administration might be, there was no avoiding the fact that Portugal was Britain's oldest ally and therefore it would be a gross breach of faith to promise Spain a free hand in that country. Nor could the Allies, who were fighting for the rights of small nations, stand by and let conditions be imposed on Portugal, without themselves being pilloried in the eyes of the world. The Foreign Office was also disturbed that Spain might use the opportunity to divulge the assurances given by the former Foreign Secretary, Sir Edward Grey, to Alfonso XIII when he visited England in July 1913 that Britain would not oppose Spanish intervention in the neighbouring country. Such a revelation at that stage of the war could be disastrous. After considering all the pros and cons, the final conclusion reached by the Foreign Office was that on balance the advantage lay in Spain's remaining neutral.[65]

The final instructions to Vaughan were that the War Cabinet approved of Spain's moving towards the Allied camp, but no territorial promises should be made and in particular the subject of Gibraltar should not be mentioned. They encouraged the British Secretary to come up with suggestions.[66] He wrote back insisting that if the 'Tangier bait' was judiciously handled it might prove effective, and if this was not sufficient an offer could be made to extend Spanish Guinea northwards to include the coast opposite Fernando Poo and restore the Caroline Islands. Vaughan stressed that the note which the Spanish government was about to send to Germany would be crucial. He described the Spanish Prime Minister as a desperate and isolated politician who admitted that the continual sinkings of Spanish vessels and the prevention of external trade had put him in an impossible position, leaving him with the sole option of breaking off diplomatic relations with Germany. Yet he found himself the target of a vicious and unbearable Germanophile campaign and was continually asking the French Ambassador for help to win the battle for public opinion, as alone he could not trust the attitude of the army or the trend of domestic politics.[67]

The Count had reason to be worried. His foreign policy had been receiving overwhelming support from unwanted quarters. As well as Republican leaders, the Socialist Pablo Iglesias, in a plea as unexpected as it was passionate, had proclaimed in an editorial in his newspaper that the duty of the government was to break off diplomatic relations with Germany.[68] This could only contribute to the general paranoia among the ruling elites, who felt that the Allies had played an important role in the events in Russia. The Catholic *El Debate* even noted that the current British ambassador in Madrid had been in Portugal at the time of the revolution which brought about the downfall of the Braganza dynasty there.[69]

The Germanophile press hammered continually on the idea that there was an interventionist plot led by those who were trafficking with the wealth of the country against the will of the people who wanted neutrality and peace above all. War would mean only famine, ruin and dislocation. The pro-German newspapers even suggested that France and Britain were to blame for the sinking of Spanish vessels: German children were starving due to the Anglo-French blockade and Germany had therefore been forced to respond in kind. Some alleged that it had not been proved that the *San Fulgencio* had been sunk by a German submarine, others that Germany was entitled to sink her since she was transporting British coal. They were largely successful in giving an impression of patriotism and impartiality as they claimed that they stood for the best for the country: namely, peace and neutrality in the European conflict. In contrast, the belligerent editorials in the pro-Allied press appeared to many to be part of a foreign-sponsored campaign which could well cost the lives of thousands of Spaniards.[70]

Romanones's strategy suffered a serious set-back when nearly all the main dynastic leaders spoke against the departure from strict neutrality. In his own party, the other Liberal leader, the Marquis of Alhucemas, and the Speaker of the Lower Chamber, Miguel Villanueva, declared that the continuance of neutrality was essential for the life of the country. The Conservative leaders Dato and Maura also expressed similar ideas. The only exception was Joaquín Sánchez de Toca, a former Speaker of the Upper House and several times Conservative minister, who argued that it was not Spain but Germany who had broken neutrality. The two final shattering blows arrived first with the publication of a series of editorials in the officers' newspaper *La Correspondencia Militar*, which (in a clear allusion to the United States) warned against joining forces with those who in 1898 had taken advantage of the weakness of Spain to steal her last colonies; and then when the monarch himself, in a speech to the troops in Leganés (Madrid), confirmed that the intention of Spain was to remain neutral.[71]

A depressed Romanones confessed on 18 April to the ambassador at Vienna: 'Public opinion is every day more hostile to any protest against Germany's behaviour . . . behaviour that it even tries to justify . . . this feeling is shared by many members of my party.'[72] In the Liberal leader's private papers there is a draft version of the note which should have been delivered to Germany. The Count writes that in September 1916 he had briefed the monarch on his intentions to move towards the Allied camp. Then there is a complete list of the most infamous outrages committed by Germany, ranging from espionage to attacks on the merchant fleet. Romanones concludes that Germany should be notified without delay that the next sinking would mean the rupture of diplomatic relations. German interests in Spain would then be taken over in order to compensate for the country's losses. An active policy would be adopted against German agents abusing Spanish hospitality and relations with the Allies would be strengthened.[73]

The Prime Minister's plan seems to have been to send a forceful message to Germany demanding an explanation for the sinking of Spanish ships. If as expected she refused to modify her submarine blockade, he would resign and make his policy a question of confidence, and so his return to power would mean an immediate rupture of relations. In fact, the note was never sent. On 19 April the king entrusted the Marquis of Alhucemas with the formation of a new Liberal cabinet. The same day another Spanish vessel, *Tom*, heading towards Spanish territorial waters, was sunk. The Germanophile press finally collected the big prize, the head of the Prime Minister. To add insult to injury, one of them pictured the Count in a cartoon with his heart pierced by a sword labelled 'neutral press'.[74]

Romanones's interventionist policy brought about his downfall. In April 1917 he met the opposition of the Restoration's ruling elites. Court, upper classes, church and king had always been ideologically closer to the Central Powers than to the Allies. The revolution in Russia confirmed their belief that the country could not take the risk of intervening in a major conflict. They concluded that with a restless working class, a reformist Catalan bourgeoisie and an unhappy officer class, it was madness even to consider entry into a war for which, after all, Spain was neither militarily nor economically prepared. Romanones, as the leading *Turno* politician committed to more active intervention, was forced to resign. Henceforth strict neutrality would be maintained to the end, regardless of the price in terms of lives and national honour.

5

THE GATHERING STORM
The Praetorian insurrection

The year 1917 proved to be a watershed in Europe. The Russian Revolution in March and the entry of the United States into the war a month later transformed a conflict between two imperialist blocs into an all-out ideological clash. By then all the European ruling elites' hopes of silencing domestic opposition by obtaining a quick and decisive victory in the battlefield had vanished. In fact, the Great War accelerated the demise of the old regimes. It heralded the arrival of a new era: one of mass politics and ideological militancy. The American President, Woodrow Wilson, was regarded by many as the best hope for the foundation of a new democratic world order. The proclamation of his fourteen points in January 1918 seemed to justify those hopes. Freedom of navigation and trade, the abolition of secret diplomacy, self-determination for national minorities and the foundation of a League of Nations to guarantee peace were some of the ideas put forward by the new American diplomacy. However, running parallel to the political offensive initiated by Wilson lay the reality of social distress and economic hardship which could hardly be resolved by his altruistic principles.

Mounting domestic tensions in Europe triggered a tide of violence which cut the continent off for ever from the old world before July 1914. In 1917 mutinies among French troops after the failure of the bloody Nivelle offensive, the increase of labour militancy in Britain, antiwar demonstrations and creation of workers' councils in Germany, food riots and the erection of barricades in northern Italy and the triumph of the Bolshevik bid for power in Russia revealed to the different governing elites how their hegemony had been effectively eroded. From now on, they would have to face the political awakening of the masses and their demands for social and economic reform. Furthermore, the consolidation of Bolshevism in Russia and the appeal of Lenin's ideas among the dispossessed and despairing masses triggered off a period of political unrest and class struggle which surpassed in intensity that initiated in 1789.

The crisis which rocked the foundations of the Spanish regime was the regional version of the general crisis which was engulfing the other European states. The Romanones cabinet was to a large extent responsible for unleashing the chain of events which led to the torrid summer of 1917. Nevertheless, it was only an acceleration of the decline of the ruling order which had begun in 1898. The elitist regime of notables could not adapt to a changing world characterized by popular mobilization, economic transformation and social expectations. The first sign of the latent crisis was the re-emergence of the divisions within the governing Liberal party.

The dynastic parties of the Restoration period were characterized by internal factionalism. Their artificial foundations and lack of a coherent programme prevented the development of proper organization or discipline. Each party was led by several notables who through kickbacks, patronage and nepotism had managed to muster a sizeable number of loyal deputies. The leader was generally the one with the greatest following and influence. In the event of an unresolved dispute, it was commonly accepted that the politician appointed by the monarch to form a government would be the leader of the party.

Until his death in 1903 the Liberals were led by Práxedes Mateo Sagasta. A pragmatic man and skilful orator, he had agreed in 1876 that his party would alternate in power with the other dynastic group, the Conservatives led by Antonio Cánovas. Under these two statesmen, the so-called *Turno Pacífico* was consolidated and enjoyed its most successful period. Sagasta was Prime Minister five times. A master in the art of electoral manipulation, under his leadership corruption and *amiguismo* flourished. He avoided any serious challenge to his position by permitting cronies to plunder the state. Not without reason was he nicknamed the 'old shepherd'. Finding a successor to his post proved to be a difficult matter. Several bigwigs representing different factions claimed the inheritance and no-one seemed to have the upper hand until Alfonso XIII threw his weight behind José Canalejas, the young and promising star of the Liberal-Democratic faction, in 1910. Canalejas's assassination two years later paved the way for a new era of party in-fighting. The shrewd Count Romanones emerged triumphant after the leader of Canalejas's faction, Manuel García Prieto, Marquis of Alhucemas, reluctantly accepted the Count's leadership.

García Prieto had been rewarded with the title of Marquis of Alhucemas for his role (as Foreign Minister in 1912) in the conclusion of the treaty with France which divided Morocco into two protectorates. He was an amiable and kind man, whose political methods seemed honourable by comparison with Romanones's manoeuvres. As son-in-law of the former Liberal Prime Minister, Eugenio Montero Ríos, and member of the board of several leading banks, he had risen rapidly to the top of the party. Yet he was a weak politician, easily dominated by other party notables and not the strong person to lead the country through a difficult period. His weakness would prove fatal to the constitutional order in 1923.

On 19 April 1917 the Marquis was entrusted by the monarch with the task of creating a new Liberal cabinet. Four of Romanones's ministers, including Santiago Alba who stayed on at the Treasury, remained in office.

Alhucemas's plan was to diffuse the tension in foreign affairs that had characterized the last months of the Count's time in office. Consequently he immediately published a statement pledging to maintain the same strict neutrality
as had been upheld by his predecessors in office while adhering faithfully to
all the treaties to which Spain was a party. He also undertook to return the
country to normality by restoring the constitutional guarantees which had
been suspended by Romanones in March as a result of the UGT–CNT manifesto, and to adopt urgent measures to deal with the *crisis de subsistencias*.[1] On
22 April constitutional guarantees were duly restored, the Socialist Casa del
Pueblo was re-opened and a few days later the useless Junta de Subsistencias
was abolished. It was too little too late. The new government had hardly got
onto its feet when a tide of unresolved ideological and socio-economic problems swept it away. Alhucemas found himself presiding over the disintegration of his party and the polarization of politics. His administration lasted
only 53 days.

The international question became a thorn in the flesh of the new government. Until early June 1917 the neutrality debate remained a crucial issue.
Romanones's pro-Allied position had been the main cause of his downfall.
His replacement by Alhucemas had been greeted with enthusiasm and anger
by the pro-German and pro-Entente press respectively. The French media
described it as a victory for the German ambassador, Prince Max of Ratibor,
and his campaign.[2] The Allied chancelleries regarded the new administration
as pro-German. Several facts supported that impression: the Alhucemas cabinet refused to ratify an agreement with Britain for the export of coal; several
interventionist meetings were banned; submarine activities in Spanish waters
increased; German conditions for the return of Spanish ships in British ports
were accepted. Moreover, the diplomatic note sent to Germany in protest at
the sinking of the *San Fulgencio* and other Spanish vessels was deemed extremely mild: the government proclaimed its inescapable duty to protest
against the overbearing attitude of Germany and her methods of aggression
against a weaker state, but towards the end the note changed dramatically in
tone. Instead of the ultimatum that Romanones would have delivered,
Alhucemas stated his belief that Germany would welcome the neutrality of
Spain and would in future refrain from attacking any more Spanish vessels.[3]

Even as the note was en route to Berlin, the Spanish steamer *Triana* was
torpedoed near the coast of Alicante. The impunity and the boldness of submarine outrages peaked in early May when in a single day two French, one
Greek and three Norwegian ships were sunk in Spanish territorial waters in
the Cantabrian sea. The French authorities warned the Spanish government
that unless decisive measures were rapidly taken to safeguard naval traffic in
its waters, France would take over that responsibility. On 25 May it was
announced that two Spanish warships had been sent to the Cantabrian coast.[4]

It is hardly surprising that the Allies considered the Alhucemas cabinet
as a German success, especially when it was contrasted with the direction

followed by its predecessor. It would be wrong, however, to describe it as a pro-German government. Alhucemas was careful enough not to include Miguel Villanueva and Niceto Alcalá Zamora in his administration. Villanueva, Speaker of the Lower Chamber of parliament and former Foreign Minister, and Alcalá Zamora, a former minister and editor of the German-financed *El Día*, were the two most openly Germanophile members of the Liberal party. Indeed, only one minister, Julio Burrell, in charge of education under Romanones and now at the Interior Ministry under Alhucemas, shared similar views. It is perhaps more accurate to suggest that the international issue was the excuse sought by different party notables to get rid of Romanones and his subterfuges. Thus the position of the new cabinet represented a return to a more balanced neutrality that, taking into account the Germanophile campaign against Romanones and his pro-Allied line, might easily be regarded as a triumph for the German cause in Spain.

Yet Romanones was not a man to leave quietly. His resignation message was as shocking as it was unexpected. At four o'clock on the day of his fall, the Count handed a statement to the press in which he explained the causes of his departure from office:

> It is my absolute belief that the defence of Spanish lives and interests cannot be fulfilled with efficiency within the limitations of our present international policy . . . it imposes upon me the duty as leader and patriot to write this document and submit my unconditional resignation . . .
>
> I have always believed that the only international policy which could enhance the position of Spain in the world was the one initiated in 1902 . . . The outbreak of the war interrupted that policy, but it cannot and must not be changed . . . The evolution of events has confirmed my belief . . . a few weeks ago in the Cortes when discussing the German submarine campaign I declared that the life of our country would not be interrupted, now I declare that it is in serious danger of being interrupted . . .
>
> . . . another consideration . . . Spain aspires to the leadership of the moral confederation of all the nations of our blood . . . This cannot be accomplished if, at this decisive moment, Spain and her sisters appear divorced . . .
>
> I cannot honestly be in charge of the government of this country without matching my convictions with my actions . . . I loyally recognize that a great part of public opinion, including members of my own party, do not share my ideas . . . It is therefore impossible for one who deeply feels his position as a liberal and bears the responsibilities of government in a democracy, to rule against public opinion. I do not share that opinion but faced by its opposition I surrender . . .[5]

Romanones's message was an exercise in subtlety. Despite all his attempts to disguise it, he confirmed that notwithstanding all his professions of neutrality he had never believed in it. He revealed the factional dissent that had existed in his own party. This was hardly a surprise. The fact that four ministers remained in government confirmed the impression that the cabinet had been split by the Count's decision to send an ultimatum to Germany. Four had been loyal to their Prime Minister and resigned with him, four had opposed him and had stayed in office with Alhucemas. Yet to all those who could read between the lines the note constituted clear evidence that Romanones had not resigned but had been dismissed by the Crown.

Nobody who knew the political mechanisms of the Restoration system could believe that Romanones had resigned due to the hostility of public opinion. There was no real democracy in Spain. Elections did not return governments, rather governments made elections. The monarch was the pivot of the whole process, as it was he who appointed a Prime Minister who then enjoyed total autonomy to rig the ballot. Government crises were not produced by movements of opinion, rather they originated at the top and were resolved inevitably with the active involvement of the Crown. It was, moreover, entirely normal for a Prime Minister to remain in office without a clear majority in the Cortes and with hostile factions in his own party as long as he possessed the confidence of the king. Consequently Romanones had been forced to stand down by the only person with the power to make him, Alfonso XIII. The British military attaché, Jocelyn Grant, shared that view. On 5 May, after meeting the king, he wrote that he was convinced that the Spanish monarch, under the influence of an almost entirely Germanophile court and the information provided by Colonel Kalle, the German military attaché, had decided to withdraw his support from Romanones when the latter declared in favour of sending an ultimatum.[6]

The statement had a poisonous effect on an already polarized society. The pro-Allied press fully endorsed Romanones's position on foreign policy. *España* and *El Socialista* denounced the activities of German agents who had managed to bring down the former Liberal cabinet with the support of reactionary politicians and the monarch. They warned the king that by becoming the last barrier against the country taking a pro-Allied line, he was preventing the triumph of democracy in Spain and risking his throne.[7] The Germanophile newspapers were furious. The most important Catholic journal, *El Debate*, compared Romanones's resignation message to leaving a bomb under the armchair of one's heir. It argued that the Count had no right to publish a memorandum which might provoke diplomatic complications, neither had he any right to compromise the monarch who had favoured him in the past with his confidence. He had committed a political disloyalty in confessing that during his premiership he had been conspiring against that neutrality of which, on coming to power, he had declared himself to be the staunchest defender. The Austrian-financed *La Nación* called it a monument of perfidy.

The Carlist *El Correo Español* described it as a legacy of suicide. Even the neutralist newspaper of the Conservative party, *La Epoca*, called it a crushing legacy for his successor and an invitation to civil war.

In the spring of 1917 the debate around the international question reached its peak, momentarily overtaking the *crisis de subsistencias* as the main issue on the agenda and acquiring a frightening dimension. In this context, the manifesto issued by the Reformist Party was very significant. In April 1917, this group for the first time abandoned its usual caution and went out of its way to demand the rupture of diplomatic relations with Germany. In the Reformist manifesto Romanones's resignation message was praised and called a clear vision of the future. At this critical moment, when Spain was on the verge of separation from her sister nations of the Latin world and her economic life was under attack, the maintenance of neutrality was labelled the most shameful surrender of dignity and honour. The Great War had become a struggle of ideas, liberty being defended by the Western Powers and autocracy by the Central Powers. It would therefore be preferable for Spain to be on the side of a vanquished France and England rather than with a victorious Germany and Austria.[8] The Germanophile reply appeared in the right-wing *ABC* two days later. The Conservative newspaper said that millions of Spaniards would prefer a thousand times a civil war rather than passively and selfishly collaborating in the ruin of Spain. The *Maurista La Acción* equated *Lerrouxismo*, *Romanonismo* and Reformism. They were all one and the same, part of a foreign-orchestrated campaign whose objective was to drag Spain into the conflict. It exhorted Spaniards to be prepared to counteract this wicked manoeuvre.[9]

The debate around the neutrality issue also raged inside the labour movement. The Socialist leader Pablo Iglesias made clear his views and those of his party in *El Socialista* on 28 April when he noted that the question could no longer be postponed: the moment had arrived to break off diplomatic relations with Germany. Mariano García Cortés, former editor of the paper, was still permitted to voice the opinion of the minority of the PSOE which was opposed to workers taking sides in a capitalist war. Yet in the same pages Luis Araquistáin responded that Socialism should be in the vanguard of the struggle for democracy. Thus there could be no peace without first crushing German militarism.[10]

At the same time the CNT organ, *Solidaridad Obrera*, was arguing that intervention would play into the hands of those interests represented in Spain by shipowners, profiteers and, with a clear allusion to Lerroux, a few sham Republican politicians.[11] The Anarcho-Syndicalists were extremely careful not to write anything which might offend the Socialists and damage their unity pact, so the Catalan and most important branch of the CNT, the Confederación Regional del Trabajo (CRT), decided to send an obscure militant, José Burrobio, to Madrid with the task of informing the Socialists of the risks which they were incurring for the labour alliance by pressing ahead with their interventionist stance. His trip was a waste of time. When on 17 May he met the National Committee of the UGT he was told by Largo Caballero that Socialists would continue to express their opinions regardless of the CNT's objections.[12]

The international question therefore became a growing obstacle for the successful continuance of the alliance between the two workers' organizations. In the second half of May they were adopting opposing positions. On the one hand, the National Committee of the CNT published an article which, while stressing the belief that labour unity should be preserved above anything else, criticized the Socialists for abandoning internationalism. On the other hand, the UGT–PSOE confirmed its commitment to the pro-Allied camp. The PSOE's Madrid branch rejected García Cortés's motion condemning capitalism rather than Germany as the cause of the war and his call for an end to the alliance with the Republicans. Instead they endorsed a proposal demanding rupture with Germany and support for the existing commitments with the Republicans. In a meeting of the UGT's National Committee, Pablo Iglesias went even further. He suggested that the trade union should follow the party's lead and stage a debate on the neutrality issue. The veteran leader added that Socialists should offer their total support to any administration prepared to break off diplomatic relations with the Central Powers, although this should not jeopardize their right to oppose the government over domestic policy. It was finally agreed to summon an extraordinary congress to discuss the international issue on 1 July.[13]

In fact, the course of events was to prevent that congress taking place and to shift the focus of attention away from the international question to the domestic situation. The Socialist leadership was determined to go ahead with its pro-Allied campaign and seemed to value its alliance with the Republican parties more than that with its Anarcho-Syndicalist counterparts. Iglesias and the others had never had much enthusiasm for joining forces with the CNT. They had only agreed to do so as a result of pressure from below and on the condition that they played a leading role. Thus they did not appear greatly concerned that, as a consequence of their pro-Allied stance, the labour pact might be endangered. It was in the hands of the CNT's National Committee to take a final decision. In 1917 both the CRT and the CNT were still controlled by Syndicalists like Salvador Seguí whose main objective was the strengthening of the organization and of trade union activity and who were prepared to collaborate with the Socialists. Yet their position was beginning to be undermined by a more purist and combative Anarchist sector that profoundly rejected any links with the reformists of the UGT. It is thus difficult to conclude that if the more pragmatic Syndicalist leaders had been prepared to follow the Socialist lead, if only for the sake of workers' unity, they would have managed to overcome the opposition of the more radical Anarchists.

In the spring of 1917 the divide between the two Spains was at its widest. In the middle, a bewildered Alhucemas continued to behave as if nothing was happening. In the space of one month two mass gatherings took place in

Madrid's bull-ring. The first on 29 April was addressed by Antonio Maura and mainly rallied Germanophile members of the *Maurista* movement and people of conservative leanings. The response came on 27 May when the most outstanding Republican and pro-Allied elements spoke to their followers. Symbolically enough, the second gathering was financed by Count Romanones.[14] Although representing opposite ideologies, both groups could claim to possess a real mass following on either the right or the left of the political spectrum. Moreover, they had something in common: their hostility towards and rejection of the existing status quo.

Maura's speech was once again misinterpreted by his followers. Indeed it could be viewed as an endorsement of the official neutrality, but as in his two previous speeches he refused to take an openly anti-Entente line as many *Mauristas* would have liked. He declared that no politician would dare to drag the country into the European war. Overlooking the many German outrages against the Spanish merchant fleet, he even claimed that Spain had received no offence from Germany. Yet Maura insisted once more that Spain's cultural and economic affinities inevitably linked her destiny with that of the Western Powers. Referring to the contentious issues of Gibraltar and Tangier, he suggested that Britain and France had not behaved decently towards Spain in the past and that now was the ideal time to correct that and consolidate the friendship between the three.[15]

Maura's speech was badly received by the French press, which described it as a monument of spite and rancour and the opinion of the leader of a party whose pro-German sympathies had long been known.[16] But the veteran Conservative leader had something different in mind. He believed that he had not made an anti-Allied speech but rather reminded the Allies of Spanish claims and the price they would have to pay for Spain to join them. However, the principal target of his message was neither the Entente nor his own followers, but the Crown. Maura's address was a clear bid for office after eight years of political ostracism. It was a balancing act in which he tried to present himself as the apostle of national salvation in this moment of extreme national polarization. According to Maura, the gravity of the international conflict and the bankruptcy of the two ruling dynastic parties were leaving the nation defenceless. He was offering himself as the best solution remaining in a monarchist camp plagued by petty squabbles and personal rivalries.

Maura's scheme backfired. He hardly pleased anyone. The Germanophile press underlined the commitment of the old statesman to neutrality. Nevertheless, those who examined his words carefully soon found flagrant contradictions in them. *La Epoca* asked how it was possible to maintain neutrality and at the same time move closer to the Western camp. *La Correspondencia de España* welcomed the pro-Allied words of the *caudillo* of a mostly Germanophile party but wondered why the Allies should give away Gibraltar and Tangier for nothing. *España* and *El Liberal* agreed in calling the speech a 'decoy' in which Maura had sought to side with no-one and had failed with everyone.[17]

One month later, all the heavy-weights of Republicanism rallied their followers in the same bull-ring. The most popular were the Republican politicians Alejandro Lerroux and Melquiades Alvarez, the famous philosopher and novelist Miguel de Unamuno, the editor of the Republican *El País* Roberto Castrovido and the Galician Republican journalist Alvaro de Albornoz. The Socialists declined to take part but expressed their support. It was clearly an emotive gathering, featuring white banners on which the names of all the Spanish vessels sunk by Germany appeared painted in red. Above all it was a spectacle in which Republicanism and the Allied cause were inextricably linked. All the orators declared that owing to German conduct neutrality was not a valid position. They were all enthusiastic about the course of the war: the fall of the old order in Russia in March and American intervention in April. Those defending neutrality were accused of opposing progress and attempting to keep the country feeble, backward and decrepit. According to the Republican speakers, only by joining forces with the democracies could Spain become a democracy herself and take an active part in the construction of a new world order. The high point of the event was when Melquiades Alvarez virtually gave the monarchy a final ultimatum: either Alfonso XIII ceased to obstruct a more pro-Allied line or the regime would undergo the same fate as those in Greece and Russia. The meeting was closed with the reading of three conclusions: first, Spain could no longer remain isolated and indifferent in the face of the international strife; secondly, for the sake of her own interests, Spain's international policy must incline to the side of the Allies; and thirdly, in view of the outrages committed by Germany against her neutrality, Spain in order to defend her dignity must break off diplomatic relations with that country regardless of the consequences.[18]

Although, not surprisingly, Romanones's mouthpiece, *El Diario Universal*, called the event an example of mobilization and citizenship, the pro-Allied gathering seemed to identify the cause of the Allies with that of Republicans and Socialists in Spain. The occasion was not wasted by the pro-German press, which accused the Western Powers of encouraging revolution. There were even hints that British ambassador Hardinge's mission in Spain was to organize an insurrection against the regime as Sir George Buchanan, his counterpart in Petrograd, had done a few months earlier.[19] Hardinge, a Conservative and monarchist, was appalled. Since the outbreak of the war he had been embarrassed by the fact that the forces ranged against the regime were also the most supportive and friendly towards the Entente. After the pro-Allied gathering he feared that Republicans were using the debate on Spanish neutrality as a pretext for an attack on the throne. In early June he wrote:

> It would be very unfortunate if the sympathies of our friends on the extreme left should succeed in identifying the Allied governments and their cause with the domestic aims of Republicanism . . . We are in danger of losing the good will of many influential classes and

politicians now well disposed to us if the Germans can succeed in persuading them that our victory will imply the triumph here as in Russia of those forces of Socialism and anarchy . . . to counteract that effect I have published a letter in *La Epoca*.[20]

In that article, entitled 'A diplomatist friendly to the Allies', Hardinge did his best to dispel any idea that the Allies were behind subversion and insurrection in Spain. His message was clear. The British ambassador pointed out that of the eleven Allied countries seven were monarchies, so it was wrong to identify their cause with that of Republicanism. Moreover, it would not be to the Allies' advantage to promote a revolution in Spain which might well end in civil war. The chief service that Spain rendered to the Western Powers was the sale of her products, especially minerals. A revolutionary strike and the ensuing closing of the mines at Peñarroya or Río Tinto would therefore be the last thing that the Entente would wish to happen. The conclusion was that they wanted an orderly and prosperous Spain and not one torn apart by internal strife.[21] A month later and in line with the intention of presenting a moderate image in Spain the British suspended their financial aid to the left-wing magazine *España*. The magazine would be rescued by the French, who did not share the political scruples of their allies.

The international problem probably gave Alhucemas more than one sleepless night. The hostility between German and Allied supporters was getting out of hand. After the Republican gathering, the Prime Minister decided to ban any future public demonstration in which the war was to be discussed. Yet the German submarines continued their criminal activities. In late May two more Spanish vessels, *Patricio* and *Erega*, were sunk near Spanish waters. There were clashes outside the German consulate in Saragossa. The fatal blow to the government, however, came from a different quarter: the military barracks.

A few weeks before the fall of the Romanones administration, the Minister of War, General Luque, had ordered the Captain General of Barcelona, General Echague, to ensure the dissolution of the Juntas de Defensa. Echague subsequently reported that he had successfully completed his task. In fact, the officers' trade unions, although officially dissolved, continued their activities clandestinely and probably with the knowledge of a sympathetic Echague.

The Spanish ruling class in general and Alfonso in particular were terrified by the outcome of the Russian Revolution. The state of shock in which the monarch found himself in the spring of 1917 was perfectly revealed in his conversations with foreign diplomats. Over and over Alfonso warned the British and French ambassadors of the dangers looming in the future if the revolution in Russia was not nipped in the bud. He was particularly devastated by the fact that the Tsar had been deserted by the nobility and the imperial army.[22] Observing the increasing polarization and radicalization of Spain, the last thing that Alfonso could permit was the existence of military trade unions whose leaders talked about ending royal favouritism and cleansing the army. The image of the Russian soviets of workers and soldiers was clearly in his mind. In this state of frenzied panic the king put pressure on his new Minister of War, General Aguilera, to make sure that once and for all the Juntas were disbanded. Romanones confirmed Alfonso's concern in his memoirs:

> His Majesty had a real obsession with the Juntas and, badly advised, believed that with energetic measures such as arrests and court martials the problem could be solved. A docile Aguilera, lacking political expertise, was prepared to carry out his orders to the last detail.[23]

Alfonso and his government could hardly have suspected the degree of organization and solidarity that the Juntas had attained. Confronting them head on was to prove a mistake. Such was the impact of the officers' rebellion on a discontented and troubled society that the international issue, which had dominated the agenda for the last year, was now left aside and would not re-emerge with intensity until the summer of 1918.

On 25 May, Colonel Benito Márquez and the other leaders of the Central Junta at Barcelona were summoned by General Alfau and ordered to disband the movement within 24 hours. When the following day they refused, an unhappy Alfau was left with no alternative but to arrest them for insubordination. Immediately a new Provisional Junta was set up in Barcelona and officers in all the peninsular garrisons, in a symbolic act of solidarity with the leading *junteros* in Barcelona, presented themselves to their Commanders for imprisonment. A hesitant Alfau was recalled to Madrid and replaced as Captain General of Catalonia by the more energetic General José Marina.[24] It was too late to quell the determination and immense strength of the officers. The local Juntas at Valladolid and Saragossa cabled Barcelona enquiring whether they should detain the train carrying Marina to his destination. When Marina arrived in Barcelona on 30 May he found himself totally isolated in a hostile atmosphere with no-one prepared to obey his orders – which, according to Márquez, were to shoot the leaders of the rebellion.[25] An increasingly worried king had simultaneously sent his friend the Commandant of Artillery, Foronda, to Barcelona on a conciliatory mission to calm the situation. The press in Madrid still had hardly any idea of what was occurring in the Catalan capital.

The first day of June 1917 was later hailed by army officers as a glorious page in modern history and regarded by Márquez as potentially the beginning of a new Spain.[26] Events were to prove that it represented in the long term a decisive step towards the military dictatorship which seized power in September 1923. On 1 June the *junteros* delivered a devastating blow to the authority of the government when they circulated two manifestos. The first was a long and tedious exposition of the aims of the Juntas. They argued in regenerationist rhetoric that the military problem was just a part of the greater problem affecting the nation. They accused the ruling oligarchy of serving only the interests of *caciques* and of leading Spain to moral decline and economic ruin. They insisted they were not motivated by political leanings or objectives. According to the *junteros*, in the army there were followers of nearly all the political parties and equally there were Francophiles and Germanophiles. Yet as a united body representing the corps, the Juntas de Defensa were above parties and divisions and their aim was simply to work for the regeneration of the country.[27] The desire for change, renovation and the cleansing of politics was shared by most Spaniards. Thus the manifesto was bound to be welcomed in all political quarters but those of the governing elites. There was, however, a latent danger. The army was indicating its rejection of politics and once more taking over the role of defender of the 'sacred values' of the nation. Nevertheless, in June 1917 it was still too early to tell which side the army would take, that of reform and democratization or that of regeneration from above and authoritarianism.

More shocking was the second manifesto. In all but name it was an ultimatum. The language was extremely respectful and marked throughout by allusions to patriotism and to the sacrifices undergone by the army. But according to the statement, discontent in the armed corps could no longer be contained. That discontent sprang from three sources: first, low morale owing to internal dissatisfaction and poor military organization; secondly, professional dissatisfaction at the lack of equipment; and thirdly, economic hardship caused by the officers' low pay. Additionally, there existed much favouritism and injustice in the selection and promotion procedure. The officers had therefore been forced to create the Juntas de Defensa to seek redress for all their grievances. The response of the authorities had been to meet the fairness of their demands with the arrest of their leaders. Before resorting to other methods, the Juntas gave the government a twelve-hour deadline to release those in prison and allow them to return to their posts, to give guarantees of no future reprisals and to recognize the existence of the Juntas by approving their statutes. Although claiming no political objectives, the officers made blatant threats that unless their conditions were promptly met the cabinet would be faced with a military insurrection.[28]

The ultimatum of 1 June was no bluff. It amounted to a full-scale coup with action organized for the following day. The regional Juntas had received instructions from the Central Junta at Barcelona to take over the military governorships and main army headquarters of their regions on 2 June at 3 p.m. Command would then be offered to the two most senior generals, and, if no general accepted, two senior colonels would be put in charge.[29] There was a rumour that Lerroux, always keen on fishing in troubled waters, was organizing a force to storm the prison and release the *junteros*. Moreover, General Marina had already realized that the Juntas, despite all their regenerationist language, were not an antimonarchist movement, let alone revolutionary, but a product of military discontent. If the officers were well treated and their demands satisfied, then their potential threat could be diffused. So in an abrupt about-face the Captain General of Catalonia became their spokesman and had little difficulty in persuading a bewildered Alhucemas to release the leading *junteros*.

The officers' victory had been complete. Confronted with the threat of a *pronunciamiento* (military coup), the political elites backed down. The authority of the Liberal cabinet and of the political system had been shattered, even though there was a clumsy attempt at concealment. The news spread by the government indicated total normality. Nothing had taken place in Barcelona. It was all reduced to a purely military matter which had been successfully resolved by General Marina with the release of certain officers in that garrison.[30] The façade proved useless. *La Correspondencia Militar*, which had become the Juntas' mouthpiece, could not be silenced. Whereas Alhucemas, the Minister of the Interior, Julio Burrell, and the Minister of War, General Aguilera, continued to insist that nothing extraordinary was happening, editorials in that newspaper boasted about the glorious feat achieved by the officers and described it as a death warrant for the still-existing 'Empire of oligarchy and *caciquismo*'.[31] The dimension of the government's shameful defeat was common knowledge on 5 June when *La Epoca* published the ultimatum of 1 June.

The *junteros'* leaders and their trade unions were functioning although the cabinet still claimed that they did not exist. Their confidence was such that Colonel Márquez after being released from prison had declared that they did not owe their freedom to anybody but themselves.[32] When they insisted on their statutes being recognized, Marina agreed without consultation. It was a staggering blow to the remaining prestige of the administration. Alhucemas had been prepared to negotiate and gradually accept parts of the statutes, but not to be presented with a fait accompli. Marina's position was backed by the king, who had already realized that the Juntas, far from being a threat, could be manipulated. Alfonso had been brought up as a soldier king and had always found himself more comfortable among officers than among politicians. Events in Russia also helped persuade him that the future of the Crown largely rested on the support of the army. Thus on 9 June the Marquis of Alhucemas presented the resignation of his government.

After 24 hours of consultation with all the main dynastic personalities, the king decided to recall Alhucemas and ask him to remain in power. Nevertheless, the Marquis confirmed his resignation. Romanones described the dilemma that the government had to face. On the one hand, to fight against the army would be rash, but alternatively, to submit to its demands was an unequivocal sign of weakness and inferiority.[33] The Count neglected to add that he had sent a letter to Alhucemas stating his resolution to oppose any government that acted to endanger the sovereignty of civil authority.[34] It is difficult to predict what the Marquis would have done, but probably he would have attempted to negotiate with the officers. Before the fall of his government he had already approved the first article of their statutes and had nothing to lose by adopting a gradual approach. The damage to his authority had already been done and the best solution would have been to promise the officers recognition of their statutes but gain some time in the bargaining process so as to save face. Alhucemas had been deprived of that option when it was rejected by Count Romanones, still the nominal leader of the Liberal party.

Many Liberals were infuriated by Romanones's behaviour, especially when the very same Romanones who was so meticulous about the preservation of civil authority – and had thus provoked the fall of the Alhucemas administration – wasted no time in informing the new Prime Minister, the Conservative Dato, of his total support although the latter had pledged to recognize the Juntas' statutes.[35] To add insult to injury, *La Correspondencia Militar* argued that the officers were not to blame for the fall of the government. They had nothing in particular against the Alhucemas cabinet and if anyone had caused its collapse it was Romanones. One day he had been the staunchest defender of the constitution (to justify his lack of support for the cabinet) and the next he had abandoned it to back Dato.

Romanones's move looked to many Liberals like a stab in the back. They felt that an end should be put to the Count's trickery. Romanones had always known that not being in charge of a Liberal government was a risk to his leadership of the party. In 1913 he had plotted with the king and leading Conservative figures to avoid being replaced by a rival Liberal administration. The Count's scheme in 1913 had brought about the end of the leadership of Maura and the formation of a cabinet headed by Eduardo Dato which led to the split of the Conservative party between *Mauristas* and *Idóneos*. In that way, the *Turno* was re-created with Romanones still in control of his party and Dato heading the other dynastic formation. Romanones's move in June 1917 seemed a replay of that carried out in 1913. Yet passions were now running high. The Count had concealed his pro-Allied policies from many of his colleagues and placed Spain on the brink of entering the war. Since April 1917 he had been continually creating trouble for the government. His resignation statement and his contribution to the interventionist gathering had not been forgotten. Therefore more than a few Liberals regarded Romanones's stance during the June crisis as almost an act of treason.

Realizing that internal dissent was still growing and that a challenge to his position was about to take place, the resourceful Count tried a risky manoeuvre. He voluntarily resigned the leadership. But his real object was to force those working to undermine his authority to call off their offensive or to show their hand prematurely. Thus on 23 June a beleaguered Romanones wrote to the Presidents of both chambers of Parliament and senior members of the Liberal party, Miguel Villanueva and Alejandro Groizard, announcing his decision to give up the leadership of the Liberal party. He stressed in that letter that it had been an honour to preside over the party, but the time for renewal had arrived. In order to avoid divisions he was willing to sacrifice his post and recommended the establishment of a directorate to take over.[36]

The last thing the Count had in mind was to pack up and go. His move had been a pre-emptive strike to avoid losing more ground and support. Hidden within the unselfish and generous language of his letter was the suggestion that he was prepared to continue in his job if that was the decision of the party. Thus he was not withdrawing his candidacy for the post of Liberal leader, he was just forcing the hand of his rivals. And indeed, they did not waste time. Villanueva and Groizard quickly rejected the idea of a directorate and began to lobby the party to accept the Marquis of Alhucemas as leader. On 27 June, Romanones's counter-attack began in earnest when, after receiving a letter signed by Groizard and Villanueva asking for his endorsement of Alhucemas's bid for leadership, he refused to give it. The excuse put forward by the Count was extremely weak and could barely disguise his real motive, his intention to cling to power at any price. Having observed that many of his former friends and collaborators had rushed to join the Alhucemas camp, Romanones alleged that he could not surrender his position until the 'secret' differences with his former supporters had been resolved.[37]

With this attitude, Romanones contributed decisively to splitting the party. During the following days the spectacle presented by the Liberal notables, fully covered by the national press, was pitiful. It was a grotesque show in which they exchanged insults and blamed each other for the chaotic situation. Romanones was accused of being behind contraband interests and on the pay-roll of foreign powers. Alhucemas was described as a political mediocrity who was trying to use his former leader as scapegoat for the glaring mistakes of his administration.[38] The majority of the Liberal barons, such as Villanueva, Alcalá Zamora and Santiago Alba, showed remarkable zeal in their support of Alhucemas. It was evident to them, as faction leaders, that the weak Marquis would be much easier to manipulate than the maverick Count.

In early July two rival Liberal assemblies took place. One was organized by those still loyal to the leadership of Romanones and rallied 63 senators and 55 deputies. The other backed Alhucemas and was supported by 99 senators and 135 deputies. The Liberal party, as a united and coherent force, was dead.[39] The crisis of that political group revealed the bankruptcy and decline of the whole system. The country was divided by the international question, tormented by the *crisis de subsistencias* and faced with the unresolved Catalan, labour and military issues. At the same time, the artificiality and hollowness of the *Turno* was being revealed in full by the disintegration of the Liberal party. Spain was desperately searching for solutions and the party responded with a sad display of mean rivalries and old-fashioned disputes. It was a pathetic struggle between discredited politicians squabbling over influence and patronage. With both dynastic parties suffering internal schisms, the *Turno Pacífico* was nearing its end.

6

TWO PARLIAMENTS IN ONE COUNTRY

The revolution from above

The military rebellion of 1 June 1917 had marked a decisive moment in the history of the constitutional monarchy. The latent tensions in Restoration society could no longer be contained and all the forces of revolution and reaction in the country exploded.[1] The First World War, by bringing about socio-economic changes, political mobilization and ideological awareness, had thus accelerated the disintegration of the outdated Canovite settlement.

On the one side there were the king and the governing classes, the former fighting to preserve both authority and throne, while the latter struggled to maintain their monopoly of power. On the other, there was the challenge from all those left out of the *Turno Pacífico* who sought to change the political alignment. The most important were the following: the *Mauristas* as the main group on the right of the political spectrum, representing the Catholic and Conservative middle classes; the Lliga Regionalista, the party of the Catalan industrial bourgeoisie; Republican groups who stood for the commercial and progressive middle classes and the petty bourgeoisie; and the working classes forming part of either the Socialist UGT–PSOE or the Anarcho-Syndicalist CNT. Finally, there was the army organized into Juntas de Defensa. It was evident to everybody that the stance taken by the military would be crucial. A coalition of political forces assured of the neutrality, if not the active support, of the officers would certainly produce the collapse of the ruling order. Therefore the energies of both government and opposition were from the very beginning largely devoted to wooing the officers to their cause.

The success of the military disobedience effectively initiated the subordination of the political life of the nation to the requirements of the officers.[2] Yet their antioligarchical language, lack of political connections and insistence that they had no ambitions to govern raised the hopes of all those opposed to the ruling system. They saw it as the signal to step up their activities.

Anarchy and indiscipline appeared to be the order of the day. The regime seemed on the point of collapse. The number of strikes rose dramatically: building workers in Bilbao and Saragossa, dockers and miners in Carthagena, bakers in San Sebastián, metal workers in Vitoria. The example of the officers was soon imitated by others. The corporatist revolt spread to the bureaucracy and the civil service where Juntas began to be set up overnight. They were followed by similar organizations of non-commissioned officers who announced their solidarity with their officers, but stressed their determination to seek redress for their economic grievances and to obtain the fulfilment of past promises of promotion. Otherwise they warned that discipline might break down and chiefs and officers would be held responsible.[3] The moderate liberal newspaper *El Heraldo de Madrid* described the situation in apocalyptic terms as final evidence that the revolution had begun in Spain, and warned that the governing elites were still feigning blindness and deafness while the revolution gained momentum.[4]

Political groups did not waste the opportunity to take advantage of the existing political vacuum. Maura declared that the importance of the manifesto issued by the Juntas on 1 June was understood by every citizen except the 'blind and deaf men' who ruled the country with the misguided support of the monarch.[5] Republicans and Socialists believed that the long-expected revolution was around the corner. On 5 June they agreed to establish a provisional government formed by Alejandro Lerroux for the Radicals, Melquiades Alvarez for the Reformists, Pablo Iglesias for the Socialist Party and Francisco Largo Caballero for the UGT. The acting chairman was Melquiades Alvarez, who had no difficulty in convincing the others that their objective ought to be the summoning of a Constituent Cortes which would accomplish a peaceful political revolution. The masses should be restrained and only called out to take part in a general strike should the army try to forestall their plans through a coup.[6] Misgivings about the possible attitude of the army were clearly expressed by the Madrid branch of the PSOE. On 8 June it issued a note blaming the regime for the present situation and warning the government to defend the prerogatives of civil power.[7] Yet in general, confidence was very high. Pablo Iglesias wrote that the army had shown by its defiance that it no longer supported the regime and therefore that the struggle of others was justified.[8] On 9 June the Catalan Regionalists Francesc Cambó and Raimón d'Abadal wrote to the government demanding in the name of constitutional legality the immediate opening of the Cortes. The same day Cambó declared in *La Veu de Catalunya* that the Juntas' demands were just and that it was sad for a country when only those prepared to use force could obtain redress for their grievances. The Catalan leader also hinted that he was prepared to work within the framework of a federal republic.

Two days after the resignation of Alhucemas, the king decided to entrust the Conservative leader, Eduardo Dato, with the task of forming a new government. This solution was not well received. In theory, Alfonso was merely abiding by the constitution. Yet these were not normal times. The king, impervious to the reality of social unrest, military revolt and the spread of discontent to civilian sectors, opted for the continuity of the *Turno* fiction. There was a clear desire everywhere for the political renovation of the country, and the return of Dato with nearly the same cabinet which had proved its incompetence two years earlier was bound to be regarded as a blatant challenge to public opinion.

The monarch's decision was viewed by the Left as an indication that the regime was beyond any possibility of reform. Revolution was not only desirable but inevitable. The left-wing press agreed on their assessment of the crisis. *El Liberal* and *El País* noted that the king could change politicians but not the underlying reality. *El Socialista* pointed out that the crisis of the regime was a fact. The moment had arrived for Republicans and Socialists to bring down the monarchy. In similar terms *España* suggested that the king had failed to respond to the warning given to him in the bull-ring and therefore the throne was about to follow the same fate as those in Greece and Russia. Even the normally austere Melquiades Alvarez declared:

> We are seeing the success of a military rebellion . . . such a gap exists between society and state that the healthy elements of society welcome the stance of the Juntas. This is the natural product of the existing oligarchical regime . . . If Spain wants to be saved, people and army have to co-operate in bringing about a revolution whose main objective must be the creation of a new regime whose legitimacy must rest on the will of the nation.[9]

Right-wing journals, with the obvious exception of *La Epoca*, mouthpiece of the Conservative party, were critical of the monarch's solution. Both *El Imparcial* and *ABC* expressed their disbelief that at such a critical moment the king had not sought to assemble new men and instead had relied on a figure of the past like Dato. The Catholic *El Debate* spoke of royal blindness and warned that Spain might well be watching the last chapter of a decrepit political order. The *Mauristas* were outraged. It was rumoured that Maura was so confident of his return to power that he had already drawn up his list of ministers. On learning that Dato and not he had been appointed Prime Minister, the veteran statesman declared that he wanted to be freed from all future responsibilities. The country was asking for a complete change and the crown had unfortunately responded by giving a vote of confidence to the 'causes of the evil'.[10] The royal decision was a bombshell in *Maurista* circles. During the first days of June, *La Acción* had been recommending prudence and patience, but once Dato took over, the *Maurista* newspaper agreed with the others that the king, by backing the farce of the *Turno*, had taken a step which amounted to political suicide. *Mauristas* demonstrated outside the Palace. The monarch was insulted by the *Maurista* circle in Madrid, where one of the most determined militants, Francisco Salcedo Bermejillo, destroyed a portrait of him. The antimonarchist reaction among *Mauristas* was such that in an editorial *El Socialista* wondered whether Maura and his followers were prepared now to abandon the monarchy.[11]

Francesc Cambó and his colleagues of the Lliga Regionalista emerged amidst the reigning chaos as the leading force able to co-ordinate the disparate interests of the pro-renovation forces and create a political alternative to the *Turno*. Yet the party of the Catalan industrial bourgeoisie was anything but revolutionary. It did not necessarily seek the destruction of the monarchy, but rather a substantial realignment of politics by wresting power from the ruling financial and agrarian oligarchy. In fact, Cambó orchestrated an offensive whose ultimate end was to carry out a political revolution in order to pre-empt a deeper social revolt. He regarded the blind maintenance of the discredited Canovite political framework as the gravest danger for a peaceful transition to a modern democratic order. The Catalan leader would even claim that to become a revolutionary was the most conservative thing to do.[12] In fact, his plans were not that different from Maura's idea of a 'revolution from above' or Melquiades Alvarez's calls for the democratization of the regime.

The Catalanist offensive, which rapidly won the support of Republicans and Socialists, began with the publication on 14 June in Barcelona of a manifesto to the country signed by all the Lliga's deputies and senators. In that document they argued that Spain was not ruled by real political parties. Elections were a fiction. The results were rigged in Madrid by those appointed by the monarch. The Regionalists added that the situation had changed. Hitherto political crises had always been resolved at the royal palace, but the impact of the army's indiscipline had put an end to the continuity of that charade. The government, faced with an ultimatum, had backed down and conceded defeat. In any democratic country a *pronunciamiento* of that kind would have been received with revulsion and hostility. In Spain, on the contrary, the Juntas had found sympathy since their inception. This was because they represented sincerity in the midst of so many fictions and deceits. From this general analysis, the Catalanists concluded that the nation was going through a key moment in its history. The solution to the crisis had to be based on total constitutional reform following federalist lines. They called on public opinion to abandon passivity so that real political parties with mass support could satisfy the demands of the electorate.[13]

Cambó then undertook an intensive campaign of mobilization, travelling to the capital and meeting the leaders of nearly all the political groups. When the Minister of the Interior refused to open the Cortes, his lieutenant Abadal called for a gathering of all the Catalan senators and deputies at the City Hall in Barcelona on 5 July to discuss what urgent measures should be adopted to resolve the chaotic situation of the country. Republicans and Socialists threw their support behind the Lliga's move. They had confirmed on 16 June their determination to collaborate in the overthrowing of the ruling order. Notwithstanding all their revolutionary language, they were reformists who abhorred violent solutions and lacked any real practical plans. Thus Cambó's initiative was accepted enthusiastically, for it gave them a chance to continue their activity against the regime in co-operation with others without the need to resort to more forceful methods.

The meeting of 5 July represented an outstanding victory for the Lliga, now the undisputed leading group of the pro-renovation forces. The success was total as 59 out of 60 parliamentarians attended the gathering, although 13 Monarchists soon withdrew. Three motions were presented. One proposed by the Monarchists was abandoned. Another put forward by Francesc Macià, a retired colonel close to separatist positions, was also dropped. The third, supported by Regionalists, Liberals, Republicans and Reformists, was voted for unanimously. In fact, it was merely an endorsement of the tactful approach devised by the Lliga. The motion underlined the Catalan desire for Home Rule which could be extended to other regions. It concluded by demanding the immediate opening of parliament in the form of a Constituent Assembly which would deal with the organization of the state and with military and socio-economic questions. In the event of another refusal from the government, all Spanish parliamentarians were summoned to attend an assembly in Barcelona on 19 July.[14] The Lliga had achieved what it desired. The federalist principle had been accepted and the form of the regime was left for a Constituent Assembly to decide. Cambó wrote in his memoirs: 'The others were a bunch of fools, lacking organization or ideas. From the first moment, I had them eating out of my hand.'[15] Yet to be certain of victory, Cambó knew he needed the participation of *Mauristas* and Juntas. Without them, his initiative could easily be interpreted as revolutionary or separatist.

Despite all their efforts, Cambó and his partners failed to win the backing of the Juntas. The insurrection of the officers had stirred all those seeking to challenge the political status quo. They were obviously taken in by the regenerationist language with which the *junteros* adorned their declarations. Events were to show that this appreciation was mistaken. The Juntas' movement was above all an outburst in defence of the corporative interests of the army. Economic and structural demands had priority, the rest was merely rhetoric. The army certainly did not feel any particular affection for the governing elites. On the contrary, they believed they had been let down by the ruling politicians. Suffering from low pay and an unfair system of promotion, they saw themselves as the 'poor relation' of the power bloc. Thus they sought to improve their situation. Nevertheless, they were never a movement directed against the monarchy. Theirs had been a revolution without revolutionaries.[16]

The Spanish army had always seen itself as the last bulwark in defence of the sacred values of the nation. Those endeavouring to break up the country or to disrupt public order, the Catalanists and leftists, had been the army's historical enemies. It was therefore unthinkable that, despite all their organized protest, officers would be prepared to join forces with them to overthrow the regime. Only a blunt and clumsy response by the government would force them to adopt that position. An editorial on 9 June in *El Ejército Español* was eloquent on the point. It warned both Republicans and Socialists not to use flattery in an attempt to win over the army for their political aims. Moreover, the spread of the corporatist movement to the non-commissioned officers and fear that ordinary soldiers could get involved also confirmed the anti-revolutionary stance of the officers. Pamphlets such as those entitled *Soldados* and signed by the Catalan Republican Marcelino Domingo, calling on the troops to follow the example of their officers and set up their own Juntas, only served to enforce the anti-Republicanism of the army.[17]

There was however in the summer of 1917 a strong possibility that bourgeoisie, proletariat and army might join forces. This possibility was to a large extent dependent upon the response of Antonio Maura. He could have become the link between the deputies and the armed services. As a deeply conservative and Catholic politician and staunch critic of the existing system, Maura could have been the guarantee that the Assembly movement was neither threatening the unity of the country nor endangering law and order. In fact, in the summer of 1917 Maura and the *Maurista* movement were in the privileged position of determining the destiny of the country. Their political group could have tipped the balance either way. Yet even while many *Mauristas* were eager to join others in the task of overthrowing Dato and the despised *Turno*, the opposition of their leader was to be total. Gabriel Maura wrote that if at this crucial moment his father had adopted a different line, a considerable part of the right would have been prepared to abandon the monarchy. Indeed, it does not seem an exaggeration to contend that rejection of the ruling order had reached such levels in 1917 that even the traditionally monarchist Catholic middle classes would have been prepared to support any moderate solution to get rid of the artificial Canovite formula.[18]

Maura's agreement was sought both by the Juntas and the Assembly but his response to all the approaches was characterized not only by absolute refusal but even by contempt. In fact, notwithstanding all his passionate attacks on the *Turno*, the old Conservative leader was a devout monarchist who rejected any position which might endanger the throne.[19] He regarded himself as a visionary, a national saviour and not as a revolutionary leader who might assist others in illegal manoeuvres. In 1917 he presented himself as a monarchist bulwark against the threats of military rebellion and civil revolution. He kept waiting for a signal from the king that never came. His passivity not only benefited the government but also contributed to the destruction of *Maurismo* as a renovating force. The crisis of 1917 also revealed the internal contradictions within the *Maurista* movement, between the right-wingers who supported an authoritarian solution backed by the Juntas and those who wanted to join forces with the democratic alternative offered by the Assembly.[20]

Lacking political contacts and certain of their strength, the Juntas looked for someone to represent their interests in the political arena. In their eyes nobody could fill that role better than Antonio Maura, a decent right-wing politician with charisma and real mass following who since 1913 had become one of the leading voices calling for dignity in political methods and the end of oligarchical rule. As early as 6 June 1917, two captains of the regiment Los Cazadores de Estella wrote to Maura suggesting that he was the man the nation needed at that critical moment. They offered him their total support and maintained that the garrison in Barcelona was not breaking discipline, but acting with real patriotism and seeking to save Spain.[21] Gustavo Peyrá, the Catalan *Maurista* well known for his hatred of the Lliga, became the mediator between the Juntas de Defensa and Maura. Peyrá, a leading exponent of right-wing *Maurismo*, kept his chief informed about the officers' resolutions and tried continually to persuade him to seize power with their aid. On 20 June Peyrá informed Maura that he had established contact with Márquez and another leading *juntero,* who had expressed their discontent with Dato and guaranteed the unity and determination of the officers to back a new administration headed by him. Two days later Gabriel Maura informed his father, then resting in the summer resort of Solozarno, that he had met Peyrá who had confirmed that the Juntas were virtually exercising a dictatorship in the country and were pressing the crown for a Maura solution. According to Peyrá, if 'the Chief' had finally taken a decision he should inform him as soon as possible by sending him a note or a letter to the Hotel Roma in Madrid under the code-name Pepe.[22]

Maura was a Liberal above all. He believed in the constitutional order and the supremacy of civil government. The last thing he had in mind was to become the representative of a military lobby. Thus he wrote to Peyrá making crystal clear his opposition to any initiative unless offered to him through the legally established channels. He added that his own philosophy barred him from adopting the Juntas' proposed strategy to gain power. Maura was still hoping for a last-minute call from the Palace, but he was not prepared to apply pressure himself or let others do so.[23] Peyrá kept insisting that the Juntas, although disillusioned by Maura's attitude, still appreciated his patriotic stand and believed he was the right politician to lead the country. He tried to convince Maura by suggesting that in the hands of the *Turno* politicians, the country was on the verge of disaster. Peyrá argued that the officers were neither rebels nor antimonarchists, they just loathed Dato and the oligarchy as much as the *Mauristas* did. They did not want to get involved in politics but as good patriots they wanted Spain to be ruled by a honest politician. Peyrá also warned that if a military dictatorship had not yet been established it was only due to the lack of a general with enough prestige to take over.[24] All was in vain. Maura informed his son Gabriel that he refused to have any contact or even discussion with the *junteros*. He described the Juntas as 'engendro monstruoso de añeja depravación' ('a monstrous freak of ancient depravity') and added that he had refused to receive a messenger from the Central Junta at Barcelona, who had been left waiting in heavy rain.[25]

At the same time, there was immense pressure from other leading *Mauristas* to persuade their leader to throw in his lot with the Assembly. It was all in vain. Maura's refusal proved decisive in paralysing many of his followers, who regarded Cambó's initiative as the practical example of the very revolution from above preached by Maura. Maura's sons, Miguel and Gabriel, kept their father well informed of the events in the country. They drew a picture of unrest, chaos and disintegration. Spain was being torn apart and her future was in the hands of the clumsy Dato. Miguel, in particular, insisted that his father should join others like Cambó who were working for solutions to end the intolerable situation.[26]

With the organization of the Assembly in July, Maura was besieged by an impressive number of requests for advice as well as arguments in favour of Cambó's alternative as the only valid and peaceful solution for the renovation of politics. On 4 July the *Maurista* Centre at Chamberí in Madrid wrote to their leader suggesting that power could no longer remain in such incompetent hands as Dato's and indicating that if *Maurismo* found itself without guidance at such a crucial stage, the energy and strength of the movement would inevitably fade away. Alfonso Nadal, an influential Catalanist, wrote twice on behalf of Cambó to Maura advocating the attendance of *Mauristas* at the gathering of deputies in Barcelona. On 6 July, Nadal sent a copy of previous correspondence between himself and Cambó in which the latter argued that Catalan public opinion was united behind the Assembly because it represented the most significant attempt to modernize political life. On 11 July he referred to a past meeting with the leading *Maurista* Angel Ossorio in which both had fully agreed that for important reasons the *Mauristas* should take part in the Assembly. Otherwise there was a danger that revolutionary elements could take advantage of the current military indiscipline or that Republicans could give the Assembly a more leftist character. Ossorio himself wrote to Maura, confessing that he was filled with pessimism and arguing that the *Mauristas* should collaborate with the Catalan leader in providing an appropriate leadership for the Assembly. On 10 and 11 July, Cambó sent Gabriel Maura a copy of the conclusions reached on 5 July and invited him to Barcelona. Cambó begged him to re-consider the significance of the moment and stressed that the presence of *Mauristas* would prove that his initiative was neither exclusive nor seditious.[27]

Maura's response was similar to that given to the Juntas. He refused to associate either himself or any of his followers with any subversive scheme. On 6 July he told his son Gabriel that he was prepared neither to join an initiative which was not openly sanctioned by the crown nor to co-operate with those political forces that in 1909 had subscribed to the 'Maura No!' campaign. He described the Assembly as a 'depressing symptom, a *zoco profesional* [professional flea market] which is now trying to constitute itself into a Cortes and from which only hypocrisy and shame can be expected'.[28] Thus the veteran leader showed his commitment to old-fashioned legalism.

He believed that the best policy was one of caution and prudence. Consequently his plan was to stay on the fence waiting for the final disintegration of the *Turno* in expectation that the king, faced with a revolutionary avalanche, would then have to resort to his services.[29] In the meantime he endeavoured to cool the ardent impetuosity of his followers. Ironically, Maura did not realize that by this attitude he was undermining the strength of his movement while doing a great service to the existing government.

Maura's advice was therefore for calm. On 7 July in his reply to the *Maurista* Centre at Chamberí he suggested that current events were merely proof of what he had been preaching for years. He claimed that nothing had occurred that would make him change his mind and abandon his passivity. A few days later he wrote to Ossorio recognizing that public opinion wanted to put an end to the disastrous status quo. However, he was not going to support any subversive strategy and would not advise anyone else to do so. The same argument was repeated continually to all those seeking his advice. Maura continued to point out that he was not surprised that those who wanted to change the ruling system and who found legal paths closed might turn to alternative routes. Yet his position was clear: his record and political philosophy vetoed his attendance at the gathering of deputies in Barcelona. Simultaneously Gabriel Maura informed Cambó's lieutenant Abadal that although they held many views in common he had to decline the invitation to take part in the Assembly as he could not join something deemed illegal by the government.[30]

Maura's opposition to the Assembly helped to isolate this initiative from the Juntas and clearly played into the hands of the cabinet. On 10 July, Peyrá confirmed that where Cambó, Lerroux and Marcelino Domingo were, the officers would not be.[31] Five days later, a satisfied *La Epoca* published a statement in which the *junteros* confirmed their refusal to intervene in politics and their determination to obey the orders of the government. Yet Dato could not be unaware that he was walking a tight-rope.

On taking office, the Conservative administration had to contemplate the prospect of the existing order falling apart. It was not clear whether Dato was the right man to save the regime from collapse. Unlike Maura, known for his forceful style and personal charisma, Dato was regarded as a grey and dull politician, a compromiser and a court lackey and therefore not the ideal person to take tough decisions. Yet he was to prove more resourceful than others expected. He tried to maintain his usual easy-going image and allowed his Minister of the Interior and right-hand man, José Sánchez Guerra, to personify the ugly face of the government. The Dato–Sánchez Guerra partnership could not ignore the threat posed by a possible collaboration of bourgeoisie, proletariat and army. The government's main objective was therefore to prevent at any price the sealing of that alliance. The strategy was very simple. All sorts of methods and measures, no matter how despicable they might be, were undertaken in order to set the different groups against each other. Any behaviour, from coercion to deceit, was admissible as long as it led to the isolation and discredit of the parliamentarian forces. At the same time, a variety of concessions were granted to appease the Juntas and confirm them as the main bulwark of the established order.[32]

After the requisite promises to maintain strict neutrality and devote special attention to national defence and economic matters, Dato's first real acts in power sought to please the Juntas. Thus he rapidly approved their statutes and carried through some reprisals demanded by the officers. Among others, two former Ministers of War and some generals close to the monarch's entourage, such as His Majesty's master of horse, the Marquis of Viana, were sent to the reserve. However, the Juntas continued with their antioligarchical language. On 25 June they issued a manifesto in which the ruling oligarchy was blamed for all the evils of the country. The military re-affirmed their apolitical character but they also stressed their determination to regenerate the nation.[33] The following day *El Liberal* published an interview with General Alfau, the former Captain General of Catalonia, which constituted a serious blow to the prestige of the crown. Alfau revealed that the order given to him to dissolve the Juntas had been signed by the Minister of War, General Aguilera, without the previous approval or knowledge of the cabinet. He was hinting that the decision had been taken as a result of pressure brought by the king. Alfau declared that he was entirely in favour of the Juntas, as they were working to destroy the centres of corruption and would not stop until the health of the nation had been restored.

The Prime Minister did not delay his response. That same day he ordered the suspension of constitutional guarantees and introduced tight censorship, banning the publication of news regarding fundamental issues such as Juntas, movements of troops, strikes, exports, neutrality and international events. The country was no longer to be informed of anything which might be embarrassing for the government. On 2 July a royal decree increased the defence budget to provide salary increases of 25 cents daily for the troops in the peninsula and 15 cents for those in Africa. The king's military household was re-organized with the introduction of a limit of four years' tenure for any officer and the dismissal of some of its members.[34]

Dato was prepared to go to scandalous lengths to win the favour of the Juntas. On 10 July it was made public that behind the back of his Minister of War, General Fernando Primo de Rivera, the Prime Minister had sent a letter via the civil governor of Barcelona, Leopoldo Matos, to the Central Junta. Dato enquired about their demands (and promised to meet them through royal decrees), asked for the names of the generals who should go to the reserve, and asked whether, if they were not happy with Primo de Rivera, they would be willing to accept a civilian as Minister of War. The officers replied that they had already made clear many times what objectives they had and which generals should be sent to the reserve. They also stated that they did not mind who was Minister of War as long as that person fulfilled his duty. As soon as news of the manoeuvre became public a wave of contempt and derision ensued. Dato denied everything but it was confirmed by the Juntas. General Primo de Rivera wrote to the Prime Minister expressing his discomfort and his readiness to resign. A scapegoat had to be found and Governor Matos accepted the role. He travelled to Madrid and explained to the Minister that it had all been his own initiative. Primo de Rivera did not resign and the affair was rapidly covered up.[35]

Dato tried to put a brave face on what was a staggering surrender of the prerogatives of a civil government and a shameful exercise in the flattery and appeasement of the army. He was aware that an impressive grouping of political forces were mounting an offensive to overthrow the political system. If he were to succeed in crushing that challenge he needed to be able to rely on the repressive forces of the state. He was prepared to pay the price even if this meant damaging the prestige of the government. His scheme paid off. The officers turned down by Maura, who obviously did not share Dato's disregard for civil authority, pledged on 15 July to back the administration.

The introduction of censorship and the suspension of constitutional guarantees marked the beginning of the government's offensive. Those measures were justified as necessary steps to prevent agitators from attacking the fundamental pillars of the state and portraying Spain abroad as a country torn by chaos and anarchy.[36] The Minister of the Interior issued instructions to the civil governors warning them to be aware of any subversive movement. Lists were to be drawn up of the leading suspicious characters in every province so that governors could arrest them when the time was ripe.[37]

It became evident, after the meeting of Catalan parliamentarians on 5 July, that the main danger came from that quarter. Two days later a delegation from Barcelona, formed by the Republican Giner de los Ríos, the Carlist Marquis of Minarao and the Regionalist Abadal, travelled to Madrid and presented the conclusions of that meeting. Dato responded the following morning, accusing the Catalan representatives of organizing a seditious movement. He declared that only the government with the backing of the crown was entitled to summon, suspend or dissolve the Cortes. He concluded his statement by appealing to the wisdom and patriotism of the parliamentarians to renounce their plans – failing which the government was prepared to act with composure but with resolution.[38]

Dato's approach was typical of his soft and compromising style. He tried to be firm and conciliatory at the same time. His accusation that the parliamentarians' demands were illegal and seditious was certainly accurate. However, his treatment of the equally illegal, and probably more violent, revolt of the officers had been very different. Dato's stance seemed a confirmation of Cambó's words that in Spain only those who were backed by force could find redress for their grievances.

Government and parliamentarians were engaged in a test of wills with neither side prepared to back down. On 12 July the latter protested at the government's response to their demands. They pointed out that it was ironic that those who were appealing to public opinion and constitutional formalities were at the same time imposing unprecedented censorship to prevent opinion from being freely expressed. By such behaviour the government had made a fiction of the constitution and the Cortes. Dato again answered in his traditional style. He suggested that the parliamentarians were abandoning the courtesy and moderation that should regulate relations between men of honour, and stressed the government's determination not to allow gatherings which could disrupt public order. Once more he appealed to their patriotism and advised them to call off the Assembly.[39]

The general atmosphere between the meeting of 5 July and the gathering of deputies in Barcelona two weeks later was frenetic. Different witnesses noted that no other event in living memory had raised such high hopes and expectations. *El Heraldo de Madrid* confessed that despite its traditional opposition to the Catalanist moves, this time they had devised an initiative which should be followed by the rest of Spain.[40] Cambó was the soul of the entire enterprise.[41] On 10 July he wrote to Colonel Márquez, the Chairman of the Central Junta at Barcelona, in an attempt to lay the ghost of separatism. He emphatically denied that Catalonia was seeking independence. According to Cambó, that would be a terrible mistake which would only lead to the region becoming a French department. In fact, the Catalan leader claimed that Catalonia, the only region in the country to overturn the electoral sham orchestrated by the ruling oligarchy, should lead Spain in this critical moment. Thus they shared the same objective pursued by the army, namely the construction of a greater Spain.[42] His appeal went unheard. Márquez later recognized that the officers had made a mistake by not throwing their support behind the Assembly. Traditional prejudices in an institution dominated by Andalusian and Castillian officers made them believe it was an antimonarchist and separatist initiative.[43]

Cambó was more successful in winning over the proletariat. The PSOE's National Committee agreed that Pablo Iglesias should attend the gathering of parliamentarians in Barcelona.[44] However, the reception was much colder in Anarcho-Syndicalist quarters. The CNT rightly considered Cambó's initiative to be a manoeuvre to stave off a revolution from below. On 17 July, they reluctantly agreed to collaborate with the others. Yet the programme published in *Solidaridad Obrera*, which included demands for the abolition of diplomacy and customs barriers and power to the trade unions to veto any law passed by parliament, revealed how far the Anarcho-Syndicalists were ideologically from the ideas of the other political forces.[45]

The government was not prepared to let Cambó and his partners proceed with their scheme unhindered. Its reaction fluctuated between panic and defiance. Any method was permissible to discredit the Assembly. A campaign of misinformation, harassment and threats was carried out without interruption. Censorship was rigorously applied. Catalanist and Republican newspapers such as *El Progreso*, *La Veu de Catalunya*, *La Lucha* and *La Publicidad* were banned. Republicans and Regionalists in turn resorted to changing the names of the journals and the town of publication, issuing clandestine editions and distributing leaflets in the streets. Incendiary pamphlets, purporting to emanate from the parliamentarians, were falsified by the government and handed out by *agents provocateurs* in order to frighten the Catalan middle classes. By contrast Republican and Regionalist pamphlets stressed the seriousness of the movement and insisted on people behaving with discipline and composure. Cambó even argued that the authorities should fulfil their duty to crush a movement which was seditious. However, history would not forgive them if they were instead suppressing an initiative which was backed by public opinion and sought the regeneration of Spain.[46]

The government managed to erect a *cordon sanitaire* between Catalonia and the rest of the peninsula. The Catalan initiative was isolated and portrayed as a separatist plot. Cambó was described as its architect, and traditional enemies of the monarchy like Lerroux and Iglesias as his accomplices. Sometimes the opposite view was promulgated. The revolutionaries had gained the upper hand and the Catalanists were collaborating in exchange for the independence of their region. Other practices employed by the government were the bribery of deputies, the threat to suspend the Cortes on 17 July and thereby remove the political immunity of its members, the close surveillance of leading Republican and Catalanist politicians and the reinforcement of the local garrisons with fresh troops.

On the eve of the Assembly the national press was forced to report that this initiative was a farce and everything was under control.[47] The cabinet was divided between those like Sánchez Guerra, who advocated the use of tough measures, and others, such as the Minister of Justice, the moderate Manuel Burgos y Mazo, who believed that the best tactic was to let the affair pass off as of little consequence. It was rumoured that Dato had threatened to arrest and send all the deputies to the Spanish colony of Fernando Poo in Africa and had told General Marina that no bullet should be spared when the order to fire was given.[48]

In the meantime the monarch had not remained quiet. The overthrow of the Russian and Greek monarchies and the revolutionary atmosphere did not allow him to be at ease. After his U-turn during the Juntas affair, he began to speak in public about their patriotism. They were soon received and flattered by the king.[49] The most senior officer, General Weyler, was sent on a tour around the peninsula to inform the *junteros* of Alfonso's readiness to support them and meet all their demands.[50] The king often sent his aides-de-camp to the Gran Peña of Madrid, the officers' social club in the capital, to ascertain the moods of the army. He asked them not to take steps against the new Minister of War, Fernando Primo de Rivera, who had not been well received by them and who, due to his old age, was dubbed 'the mummy'.[51]

The king, aware of the crisis of legitimacy of the ruling political system, intended to bypass government and find his own solutions. Ensuring the loyalty of the army was essential for the security of the throne, yet the danger was not entirely deflected as long as the political offensive remained. In public he continued to back Dato, but the sovereign's confidence in his ministers was limited and should the survival of the monarchy require it, the government could be sacrificed. Alfonso's plan was to approach the moderate elements in the opposition and offer concessions in order to detach them from their more revolutionary partners.

On 28 June the king met Gumersindo de Azcárate, the aged Republican President of the Institute of Social Reforms, who with Melquiades Alvarez led the Reformist party. Alfonso tried to win Azcárate's support to persuade the Reformists to desist from their revolutionary intentions. The king even suggested he was willing to pass by royal decree some of the fundamental demands of the labour movement. But Azcárate was of little help. He did not have enough influence or power to change the line adopted by his party. The Reformists were now bound with the other Republican groups. Thus the veteran Republican leader told Alfonso that it was too late. The king was devastated. Talking to his friend, the engineer Domingo de Orueta, he claimed that he had seriously thought about abdicating but the royal family, in particular the Queen Mother, had compelled him to renounce the idea.[52]

The king's second choice was to approach the Catalan Regionalists. There he proved to be more successful. What emerged from the secret conversations between monarch and Catalanists has to be regarded as crucial if the events of 1917 are examined carefully. In fact, the king shared some common concerns with Cambó. Both were deeply worried that the situation might get out of control and were therefore anxious to have room to manoeuvre.

On 12 July the king met Alfonso Nadal, one of Cambó's trusted lieutenants. The monarch disclosed that he was sure that the *Mauristas* would not attend the gathering at Barcelona. He also revealed that he was prepared to grant the Catalanists some concessions, including two or three portfolios in a new coalition government, if the latter gave up the idea of summoning the Assembly. Alfonso confessed that he was not pleased with the way Dato was conducting affairs and complained he was not being fully briefed. He described the political situation as 'a fetid pond' and recognized that should the Assembly take place it would probably be better if the right was well represented, otherwise the left could control the agenda.[53]

A few days later, probably at the request of the king, a meeting was arranged between several officers, Cambó and two priests. Márquez later wrote how he met Cambó for lunch at the Convento Pompeya in Barcelona. They were accompanied by two other officers, the Captains Herrero and Villar, and two priests, Father Planas and Father Ruperto, who represented the monarch. Father Ruperto is described by Márquez as a mysterious character who lived in luxury in a room with two telephones. Ruperto announced that all sorts of concessions could be made as long as the Assembly never took place. Cambó responded that a cancellation was not feasible at this late stage. Then Ruperto suggested a plan that could please everyone. The Assembly would be held not at the town hall but at a secret location. There the deputies should be able to pass their resolutions while the civil governor was trying to find them. By using censorship the government could later claim that the meeting had never taken place, while the parliamentarians could argue the opposite. It is extremely suspicious that the actual course of the Assembly seems to have followed that scheme. It appears to bear out the allegations of the Socialist Andrés Saborit that every single detail of that meeting had been worked out in advance by Cambó and the monarch.[54] The government was apparently at no time aware of what was being plotted behind its back. The Conservative cabinet would never have agreed to resign and give way to a coalition government in which the Catalanists were well represented.

On the morning of 19 July, Barcelona was a city occupied by a hostile army. There were 30,000 soldiers patrolling the streets and four warships in the harbour. Catalanist and Republican manifestos had been published calling for restraint and warning the people not to follow any provocative slogans which would be spread by *agents provocateurs*. Shops were to remain closed between 3 and 6 p.m.[55] The whole affair started ludicrously and was to end in the same way. Yet it is impossible to deny the far-reaching consequences and transcendent importance of the event. Indeed some of the vicissitudes were worthy of a thriller.

It began with several taxi chases in which the deputies were tailed by the police. Once their pursuers had been shaken off they met secretly to discuss the agenda of the day at the home of Josep Bertrand i Musitu, one of the Lliga's leading politicians. Then the parliamentarians convened for lunch at the Casino del Parque, whose restaurant had been hired under the pretext of a wedding party, and from there they walked to the Palacio del Gobernador del Parque de la Ciudadela. Lluis Durán i Ventosa, Mayor of Barcelona and Secretary of the Lliga, received up-to-the-minute information from Cambó on the development of events. Due to the secrecy and uncertainty surrounding the meeting, Ventosa acted as the outside link between the parliamentarians and the press.[56] There was a total of 55 deputies and 13 senators, 46 of them from Catalonia. The Assembly was presided over by the Radical Giner de los Ríos and the Regionalist Abadal. The ceremony was symbolically initiated by shouts of 'Viva Catalunya!' from the Spanish deputies to which their Catalan counterparts responded with 'Viva España!' A proposal previously discussed and accepted by all the groups was passed. That motion described the government as an affront to parliament, a provocation to Spain and Catalonia and an obstacle to the renovation of the country. It noted that unless the crisis initiated by the military revolt of 1 June led to a thorough reform of the political life of the country that action would become a mere display of indiscipline. In conclusion, they demanded the summoning of a Constituent Cortes after general elections organized by a national government representing the will of the nation. Three sub-committees were created: one to study constitutional reform and municipal autonomy, the second to deal with the issues of national defence, education and administration of justice and the last to examine socio-economic problems. At that moment, the Assembly was broken up by the appearance of the police commanded by Governor Matos. When the president of the Assembly, Abadal, answered that he would not order the dissolution of the gathering and would yield only to force, Matos, by placing his hand on the shoulder of Abadal, signalled the arrest of every parliamentarian. They were released from custody outside the building.[57]

The whole affair appeared to have closely followed the script worked out by Father Ruperto, the enigmatic priest who, according to Márquez, spoke on behalf of the king. Indeed, a buoyant Sánchez Guerra informed the journalists in Madrid that the Assembly had not taken place. The timely intervention of the Governor had prevented the adoption and transmission of any resolutions and had broken up the gathering before it had time to transact any business.[58] A cheerful and confident Dato told the British Ambassador that the Catalan movement had been suppressed in such a fashion as would render it ridiculous. The Prime Minister added that no arrest was intended as it might arouse public sympathy for the Assembly or make the parliamentarians heroes. The aim of the government, to prevent the reformers from meeting in order for them to become objects not so much of sympathy as of ridicule, had been achieved. According to the Conservative leader: 'The bubble of the Barcelona revolution had been pricked as soon as its leaders saw the government was in earnest . . . now the plan is to dissolve the present Cortes in August and organize elections in September to give a good working majority to my party.'[59] He was soon to regret his words.

Gustavo Peyrá believed that the government had gained the upper hand. He wrote to his chief, Maura, suggesting that if anybody could claim victory it was the cabinet. Peyrá observed that the Assembly had been a charade. Governor Matos had been aware of the conclusions of the Assembly hours before the parliamentarians gathered. The Catalan *Maurista* also pointed out that the officers were tired of recent events: first, the disclosure of Matos's deal with the Juntas and the ensuing denial of the government and second, the 'hide and seek' game of the Assembly.[60] The *Maurista* newspaper *La Acción*, probably using Peyrá's account, declared that what others had regarded as a historic day had actually been a 'hysterical day'. That journal begged that no more such ridiculous actions should ever take place. Everything had developed according to the script with Regionalists and Republicans eager to see the event cancelled and Dato now able to claim that he was a national hero. *La Acción* warned that while the deputies were easily overcome by a simple touch on the shoulder, something else was going to be needed to overcome the nation.[61]

The government was soon to lose the battle for public opinion. If its objective had been to discredit the Assembly and disrupt its activities, it actually achieved the opposite effect. The prestige of the cabinet sank even lower and the position of the parliamentarians gained widespread support. It was likely that Cambó had arranged the affair with the monarch through Father Ruperto so that events should not get out of his control. That plan would not necessarily conflict with the objectives of the Lliga. The Regionalists wanted a Constituent Assembly to change the political structure of the country peacefully, not a storming of the Bastille.[62] Yet the transcendental importance of the Assembly cannot be denied. It constituted the most important attempt in the history of the Restoration monarchy to effect a political modernization and genuine democratization of the system by peaceful means. A variety of forces, including the industrial bourgeoisie, the commercial and professional middle classes, the petty bourgeoisie and the urban proletariat momentarily came together to try to put an end to the monopoly of power enjoyed by the financial and landowning oligarchy.[63] The Assembly was designed to reflect the new socio-economic reality brought about by the Great War and was proof that the old system, composed of private dishonesty and public make-believe, could no longer be tolerated.

Until early August the Assembly gained daily in strength while the government's strategy backfired. Dato and Sánchez Guerra overplayed their hand. They kept denying that the parliamentarians had time to pass any resolutions; as soon as the deputies returned to their places of origin, and despite the tight censorship, the truth began to come out. For instance, the maverick deputy for Almadén who had attended the Assembly, Cánovas Cervantes, was also editor of the newspaper *La Tribuna*. In a front page article on 21 July that journal accused the government of lying. All the national press, with the exception of *La Epoca* and *ABC*, described the version put forward by the government as final proof of the bankruptcy, falseness and immorality of a group of professional politicians who had to resort to deceit and misinformation. Even *La Acción* changed its line dramatically and in tune with the other newspapers called Sánchez Guerra a liar. The *Maurista* newspaper argued that the government was desperately trying to cling to power by using and abusing censorship. How low was 'Dato el equilibrado' prepared to sink? Spain had had enough of deceit.[64]

On 26 July virtually all the national press representatives decided to boycott the official news and signed a document calling for the end of arbitrary censorship and the abuse of governmental prerogatives. A few days later, a no longer cheerful Sánchez Guerra met a delegation of the press and announced that he was prepared to lift censorship. Yet the administration could not take the risk of allowing total and unrestricted freedom of expression. Thus in what can be regarded as an exercise in cynicism and effrontery, the Minister of the Interior added: 'Now you gentlemen will be your own censors while I limit myself to the role of supervising your judgement.' Unsurprisingly, the experiment did not work and strict censorship was re-imposed in early August.[65]

Simultaneously, the parliamentarians had continued their campaign. On 21 July the Regionalists published a statement in which they confirmed that the Assembly had indeed taken place despite all the government's provocations, and called on other Spanish deputies to join an initiative designed to build a new Spain. This was followed by a meeting of representatives of all the antigovernmental political groups on 27 July. They declared themselves pleased with the welcome that the Assembly had in the country. Deputies distributed themselves between the three sub-committees – socio-economic, constitutional and administrative – appointed by the Assembly and announced their determination to report with their conclusions at a new meeting to be held in Oviedo on 16 August.[66] More threatening for the survival of the government was the impact that the Assembly had on *Mauristas* and Juntas.

Many leading *Maurista*s considered that the parliamentarians' programme coincided with their own ideas and, believing they should take part in the next meeting at Oviedo, increased their pressure on Maura. As early as 21 July, Cesar Silió, a veteran Catalan *Maurista*, provided 'the Chief' with information that contradicted Peyrá. He alleged that the version of the Assembly given by the government was 'fantastic'. Important conclusions had been passed and practically all Catalonia supported the initiative.[67] A few days later Gabriel Maura concurred with that view. He added that even the officers were for a Constituent Cortes and a national government. In fact, the only factor that damaged the image of the Assembly was the people who had taken part.[68] More resolute were the positions adopted by Maura's other son Miguel and by Angel Ossorio. Miguel stated his conviction that the Assembly had been a total success and a defeat for the government. He agreed with Cambó that the country was in favour of this kind of peaceful revolution, which was indeed necessary to avoid a social insurrection. Miguel bitterly commented: 'It is difficult and even dangerous not to attend a second meeting of the Assembly. It is going to appear as if, having attacked the *Turno* for years, we Mauristas are going to make its survival possible by our abstention.'[69]

On 7 August, Ossorio expressed a similar view. He wrote to Maura arguing that the latter's abstentionism had given a major boost to the *Turno*. Ossorio insisted that their collaboration would represent the end of the system. He also pointed out:

> This is the moment to choose between on the one hand, the Assembly and those fighting against the existing state of affairs and on the other, the *Turno*, the king and the oligarchies. Besides, it is incongruous that after preaching the urgency of change, we are fearful at the moment of truth . . . The Assembly is therefore the best way to end the status quo. There are only two other solutions: a Maura

administration or a revolution. The first is not forthcoming and the second is becoming each day more desirable.[70]

Maura was still reluctant to act. He continued preaching caution. He recognized that the parliamentarians had passed conclusions which were also pursued by the *Mauristas*, but he was utterly opposed to political schemes which had the active support of antimonarchist elements and could thus endanger the survival of the crown. He still scornfully described the Assembly as the 'Parlamento Codorniu'. By naming the Assembly after this famous sparkling wine produced in Barcelona, Maura seemed to be implying that it was all 'bubbles'.[71]

Yet after the events of 19 July it was doubtful whether Maura's old-fashioned legalism could long contain the calls for action from some of his more restive supporters. The situation had reached such a climax that it was difficult to believe that the Catholic middle classes would continue to reject an initiative which in the safe hands of the Catalan industrial bourgeoisie could free Spain from the despised and obsolete grip of the landowning oligarchy. In reply to Ossorio an increasingly isolated Maura stated that he would never lose his faith in the monarchy or legality. It was therefore impossible for him to collaborate in a movement which could lead to the ousting of the monarch and which included many political groups which had been fighting him for years under the slogan 'Maura No!' Yet he realized that his position was becoming untenable even within his own movement. So he was prepared to stand aside. 'If the Assembly succeeds and then puts into practice some of the ideas preached by me for so many years I have no objection to getting out of the way.'[72]

The government was receiving equally menacing signals from the officers' quarters. There were rumours that Colonel Márquez was losing prestige among his fellow *junteros*. The others had not been pleased to learn that he had had secret meetings with Cambó.[73] Nevertheless, the antioligarchical rhetoric of the Juntas continued in earnest. In early August, Father Planas was sent to Santander, where the monarch was on holiday, to deliver a document in which the officers stated their position. Once more they emphasized that they were behind crown and country. They described the *Turno* parties as a collection of ambitious, incompetent intriguers who had brought the country to the verge of irreversible ruin. They encouraged the king to head the revolution desired by Spain. New men and new methods based on morality, equity and justice were needed. They supported the idea of a Constituent Cortes after general elections had been held under a National Government. They even had a list of possible men who could form part of that cabinet. The post of Prime Minister was left vacant for the king to select. General Marvá, a military man who according to Saborit was liked by the working classes, was suggested as possible Minister of the Interior as guarantee of the purity of the suffrage; a relatively obscure General Borbón was to be in charge of the Ministry of

War; Cambó was to take over Public Works; Santiago Alba, the Foreign Office; Urzaiz, the ostracized former Chancellor under the Romanones cabinet, was to return to his former post; Melquiades Alvarez was to go to Justice, and two intellectuals, Ramón y Cajal and Torres Quevedo, were to be in charge of Education and Labour respectively.[74]

The Dato cabinet panicked. The Juntas, despite all their assurances of backing the ruling order, had not abandoned their attacks on the *Turno*. Furthermore, they were becoming more and more involved in politics. The programme endorsed by them was extremely close to that of the Assembly. Both rejected the existing status quo and demanded the formation of a National Government to summon a Constituent Cortes. The list of possible ministers included only two dynastic politicians. One of them, Santiago Alba, was on the left wing of the *Turno*, and the other, Urzaiz, having been fired from his post had since become one of the *Turno*'s most outstanding critics. Francesc Cambó and Melquiades Alvarez, two leading personalities behind the Assembly initiative, were brought into the government. The others were either officers or else had no political connections. On 1 August the Socialist journal published sensational news: an approach by Count Romanones to the PSOE to form a coalition government had been rebuffed. The desperation of the dynastic leaders had reached a critical level.

7

THE HOT AUGUST OF 1917

The revolution from below

As the carnage and devastation continued unabated on the battlefields, living standards and shortages worsened everywhere in Europe. America's decision to enter the war opened up the prospect of a clear swing in the Allies' favour. But on the Eastern Front, the Russian army disintegrated after its last ill-fated offensive. The popularity of the Provisional Government there was waning as the Bolshevik slogan of 'Peace, Bread and Land' seemed to be in tune with the wishes of the masses. In July, widespread riots erupted in the capital Petrograd and were only suppressed by rushing troops from the front. Soldiers' mutinies and desertions, food riots and workers' militancy multiplied across Europe. It seemed that the end of the old order of 1914 was in sight.

In Spain revolution also appeared imminent by the summer of 1917. The ruling classes were gripped by panic. Many believed that the liberal monarchy would be swept away, like Tsarism in Russia earlier in the year. Nevertheless, the parliamentarians' leadership conferred upon the revolutionary movement a nature closer to Paris in July 1789 than to the spontaneous and popular mass uprising of Petrograd in March 1917. The government had its back to the wall. Running out of time and losing authority by the day, it could not permit a second meeting of the parliamentarians to be held in Oviedo on 16 August. The prospect of a political gathering in which the bourgeoisie, middle classes and proletariat could offer a political settlement which basically satisfied the desires of *Mauristas* and officers was a nightmare. Realizing the contradictory interests and objectives of the opposition, the Dato administration took a risky gamble. The plan was to provoke the labour movement into an ill-timed strike so as to scare the bourgeoisie and use the army to quell the disturbances. Thus the government could claim to be the saviour of Spain and the guarantor of law and order.[1]

A transport strike, beginning on 19 July in Valencia and coinciding with the Assembly in Barcelona, provided the administration with the tool to crack the formidable alliance organized against it. The struggle between railway workers and the Companía del Norte had been going on since the summer of 1916. In July of that year the former had obtained an important victory, but all indications were that the company was biding its time and

120

waiting for the right moment to exact its revenge. In April 1917 *El Socialista* began to accuse the company of not fulfilling the terms of the settlement and seeking to provoke a new clash with its employees.[2] The transport strike of July 1917 gave the company that opportunity. In the polarized atmosphere of the summer of 1917 the dispute soon degenerated into a violent confrontation. The strike paralysed 70 per cent of transport in Valencia, with dockers coming out in sympathy. On 21 July the Captain General of that region, General Tovar, declared a state of emergency. A few days later the situation had been normalized but at the price of two dead, several wounded and many arrests. General Tovar, eager to soothe matters, released all prisoners and was willing to negotiate with the workers. However, the Compañía del Norte refused to re-hire 36 workers of the local branch of the Railway Union sacked during the conflict. Here the government found an issue which could lead to its showdown with the labour movement. Soon the conflict began to escalate. On 2 August the National Railway Trade Union announced that unless those employees laid off were allowed to return to their posts all its members would strike on 10 August. The company refused to back down and the trade union had to fulfil its threat. This was the moment in which the leaders of the UGT and the PSOE decided to link this offensive to the general strike which had been planned since March.

The general strike initiated on 13 August was a disaster from the start. The stoppage was a success only in the industrial centres of Madrid, Barcelona, Valencia, Vizcaya, Guipúzcoa and Asturias. It had little, if any, impact on central, western and southern Spain, with the exception of mining concerns like Río Tinto, Cartagena, Peñarroya and Linares-La Carolina. The revolution thus remained a purely urban revolt confined to Madrid and a few industrial spots in the north and the east and was barely noticed in the rest of the country. There was hardly any response in the two Castiles or Extremadura, with the exception of Santander (at that time part of old Castile), and in Andalusia it was basically limited to parts of Granada, Huelva, Córdoba and Seville. Its failure to establish any links with the countryside eased the task of the authorities in putting it down. The Catholic trade unions published a manifesto condemning the movement and expressed their readiness to continue working, while young monarchists volunteered their assistance to run the public services and act as honorary policemen. The final key factor that sealed the fate of the general strike was the fact that the army remained united and loyal to the government and left no crack through which the revolutionaries could bring the regime down. So the events of March in Petrograd were not to be repeated in Spain. A state of war was quickly declared and the army placed in charge of public order.

The workers managed during the first day to bring Madrid to a standstill. Bricklayers, bakers and printers responded as one man to the call to strike. Pickets made sure that shops and bars remained closed. The following days pitched battles ensued when strikers tried to halt transport in the capital.

Trams were heavily protected by troops. Workers threw stones and were answered by volleys of bullets. Machine guns were used against demonstrators in the proletarian districts of Cuatro Caminos, Ventas and La Guindalera. It was a merciless slaughter which left dozens of casualties even though women and children often acted as shields for the workers. On the night of 14 August the police arrested the strike committee in the house of a Socialist couple, José Ortega and Juana Sanabria, whose address was, ironically, 12 Calle del Desengaño (Disillusion Street). A second strike committee was also captured the following day. The movement was deprived of leadership. By 16 August the revolt was over in the capital. Nevertheless, that day also saw a mutiny in the Cárcel Modelo, the local prison, crushed mercilessly. Suspiciously enough, seven leading militants were among the casualties. Witnesses would say later that they had been executed once the mutiny had been put down. Catalonia with 37 dead registered the highest number of casualties. There the strike had been effectively organized by the Anarcho-Syndicalists. The stoppage was total in the capital and in neighbouring towns. Unlike the UGT, the CNT militants were willing to use more violent tactics. Thus barricades were soon put up and snipers harassed the soldiers. The latter responded with appalling ferocity. Some quarters of Barcelona were only taken after days of street fighting and shootings, and in places like Sabadell the workers' headquarters were reduced to rubble by artillery fire. On 16 August the journalist and Republican deputy Marcelino Domingo was arrested. By then the CNT leadership had also been captured or was in hiding. Bilbao also suffered a high level of casualties. With moderate Socialists like the journalist and efficient orator Indalecio Prieto in charge there, the workers conducted an essentially non-violent protest. But they were met by fierce brutality with soldiers firing upon the population at random. In the mines of Río Tinto ten workers were gunned down by the troops. There were also violent clashes in the province of Alicante. In Yecla three people, including a Socialist councillor, were killed. In other provinces like Valencia, Guipúzcoa and Saragossa the toll was lower. By 18 August the government could boast that the revolution had been crushed. The moment of panic was over. It was time for speeches, medals and rewards. The leaders of the revolutionary movement had been captured, were in hiding or had fled abroad. Yet the miners in Asturias were able to hold out on their own for seventeen more days. It was useless, however, and they finally had to surrender. The working class leaders were forced to conclude that they could not match the repressive might of the state. The official figures released by the authorities confirmed a total of 71 dead, 200 wounded and 2,000 arrested. The reality was probably two or three times these numbers.[3]

An analysis of the failure of the revolutionary movement of August 1917 reveals some important facts. First, the initiative during the events belonged at all times to the government which, by means of provocation and deceit, managed to outmanoeuvre the labour movement; secondly, the internal contradictions of the basically moderate Socialist organization pushed by circumstances to lead a revolution became glaring; and thirdly, the final decision to go ahead with the revolutionary strike was encouraged by the overconfidence of the Socialist leadership, who believed that both bourgeoisie and army were behind their initiative.

The Dato cabinet used and abused a social conflict to break the always uneasy alliance between bourgeoisie and proletariat and to win the Juntas to the cause of law and order. There had been a threat of a general strike since March 1917, but the Socialist leadership only very reluctantly, and after exhausting all the alternatives, decided to play that card in August.

In June a provisional committee had been set up by Republicans and Socialists. In the event of launching a general strike to overthrow the regime, plans had been made to divide the leadership geographically. A sick Pablo Iglesias, seconded by some leading Socialists (Julián Besteiro, Francisco Largo Caballero, Andrés Saborit and Manuel Cordero) was to be in charge of Madrid, Castile and Vizcaya. The Reformist Melquiades Alvarez, backed by the leaders of the Asturian Socialist miners, Teodomiro Menéndez and Manuel Llaneza, and the Anarcho-Syndicalists Eleuterio Quintanilla and José María Martínez, was to lead the movement in Asturias and León; and finally the Radical Alejandro Lerroux, supported by the CNT leadership, was to organize matters in Catalonia, Valencia and Andalusia.[4] Those plans were rapidly shelved when Cambó produced his own initiative. Most Republicans and Socialists were delighted to back the peaceful political revolution envisaged by the Catalan leader. At the same time, the government was busy spreading rumours that a railway strike and a revolution were imminent. Orders were given to the local authorities to take appropriate measures such as the surveillance and arrest of the leading suspicious elements.[5]

By the time of the Assembly, all the revolutionary initiatives had been postponed. A strike committee had been formed by Francisco Largo Caballero and Daniel Anguiano for the UGT and Julián Besteiro, Andrés Saborit and the only leading woman in the Socialist movement, Virginia González, for the PSOE.[6] Its mission was limited to the mobilization of the working class – but only if the Assembly was repressed and the parliamentarians arrested. Thus the outbreak of the transport strike in Valencia came as a total and unwelcome surprise to them. They certainly had no involvement.

The origins of that episode remain highly controversial. There are two hypotheses. First, it was instigated by *agents provocateurs* under the instructions of the government. Blame is placed on the secretary of the Railway Trade Union, Ramón Cordoncillo, who was a relative of Julio Amado, the Conservative deputy and editor of the Juntas' mouthpiece, *La Correspondencia Militar*. It has been suggested that he provoked the Valencia railway workers into taking precipitate action. Certainly, his role during the August events was more than suspicious. He was accused of not following instructions and permitting several railways to continue operating. Cordoncillo was later expelled from the Socialist ranks. The second explanation of events seems more plausible. Félix Azzati, a local leading Republican with Jacobin leanings, feeling overconfident that the regime was about to fall, prompted the railway workers to make their move. When Azzati arrived in Barcelona he was reprimanded by Pablo Iglesias and Melquiades Alvarez.[7] Whether *agents provocateurs* or local Republicans were behind the July transport strike in Valencia has never been determined. Nevertheless, the importance of that dispute cannot be questioned as it was the first step towards the general strike in August.

If the role of the government in July remains obscure, there is hardly any doubt that it provoked the revolutionary events of August.[8] The Socialists were outmanoeuvred and outwitted by a besieged and discredited cabinet. Daniel Anguiano, member of the strike committee and President of the Railway Trade Union, would declare a year later:

> Who could benefit from a general strike then? . . . We did not want it . . . We were prepared to accept all kinds of compromises . . . We intended to avoid it until the last moment . . . but Dato wanted to discredit the labour movement and to justify the repression of a general strike which he himself was provoking so as to consolidate his position in power, obtain the decree of dissolution of Cortes and maintain the fiction of the *Turno*.[9]

Largo Caballero, the influential trade union leader and also a member of the strike committee, added:

> The general strike did not take place because we wanted it but because of the attitude of the government towards the railworkers. Our strategy was to avoid a conflict . . . We had kept all the administrations informed of our plans and resolutions since May 1916 . . .[10]

There is sufficient documentary evidence to show that the Socialist leaders tried to halt the tide of events until the last minute; but they would discover that the intransigence of the Compañía del Norte was not only upheld but inspired by the government. The tragedy was that the Socialists' inability to control the situation allowed the government to regain the initiative which it had lost in July and set an agenda that ended in a bloodbath. Unlike the Bolsheviks in Russia, who, realizing that the opportune moment to launch their offensive had not yet arrived, managed to hold back the masses, the Spanish Socialists let themselves be dragged forward by the course of events. Lenin's party would re-emerge three months later stronger than ever. By contrast, in Spain the Dato administration, presented with the chance to nip the insurrection in the bud, did not hesitate. With its total control of censorship the government could spread all sorts of rumours and fantasies and even claim to be the saviour of public order.[11]

Initially a compromise seemed to be within reach. Viscount Eza, the aged landowner in charge of Public Works, seemed to be working for conciliation. When he met for the first time a workers' delegation presided over by Daniel Anguiano, Eza declared that he would not allow the company to carry out reprisals or dismissals. That was the critical moment at which the Minister of the Interior, Sánchez Guerra, stepped in, backed the intransigence of the company, made any agreement impossible and thereby let the dispute slide towards a final clash. The railworkers, pressed by the UGT, were prepared to postpone the strike scheduled for 10 August to allow time to find a compromise. The Compañía del Norte agreed to meet the trade union representatives, but refused to discuss the re-employment of the sacked workers which was in fact the basic cause of the dispute. Furthermore, the government accused the workers of breaking off the dialogue by postponing the strike but not cancelling it altogether. That essentially amounted to an ultimatum: the government demanded that the Railway Trade Union surrender unconditionally or otherwise fulfil its threat and launch the strike on the scheduled date of 10 August. As late as 9 August the trade union had expressed its willingness to accept the dismissal of its militants if the company was prepared to give an explanation. The workers could not concede more. It was all in vain. Guerra and Dato had made up their minds. They were prepared to 'take on the strike'. Even while negotiations continued, the Minister of the Interior was already giving instructions for the event as if he knew for certain that the strike was to take place.[12]

Until it was banned on 12 August *El Socialista* repeatedly argued that the railworkers were being pushed to strike against their will. *La Tribuna* commented on the situation on 10 August as follows:

> We deplore a government whose attitude is provoking a serious social conflict. This is the same government that when faced by the powerful {a clear allusion to the Juntas} showed its weakness. The workers have recoiled from the strike and the government has pitched them into it.

The railway workers could not back down and decided to go ahead with the strike. It was a difficult choice that was finally voted by a majority of just one. The decision forced the hand of the PSOE and UGT National Executives. For the sake of solidarity they decided to bring forward the date of the general strike to coincide with that of the railworkers. This decision was opposed by Pablo Iglesias, who from his sickbed argued that the Socialists should carry out a solidarity action but not a revolutionary strike. Yet for once his advice went unheard. The Socialists believed that if the railworkers went ahead on their own their organization, built up so painfully, would be destroyed and the whole Socialist labour movement would suffer the consequences.[13]

Their decision played into the hands of the government. Once the strike began it was easy for Sánchez Guerra, in control of the media, to describe the Socialist leaders as blood-thirsty revolutionaries or even, at the moment of their arrest, to present them in a ridiculous fashion. The Minister of the Interior spread the news that some had been found under beds and others in a wardrobe. Moreover, in a further attempt to discredit the revolutionary movement, it was alleged that thousands of pesetas and much foreign currency had been discovered among their belongings. Nothing could be further from the truth. Yet any slander to discredit their enemies were acceptable to Dato and Guerra.[14]

At such a historic moment the Socialists failed to become the dominant force among all those fighting against the regime. They were caught between two parallel offensives. On the one hand, the UGT had had an alliance with the CNT since July 1916, and on the other, they were collaborating with Republicans and Regionalists in the Assembly. The former alliance definitely had a more radical and revolutionary character than the latter. The Socialist leaders vacillated, as they felt more comfortable supporting the parliamentarians than co-operating with the Anarcho-Syndicalists. Nevertheless, they could not forget that the pact with the CNT was a response to pressures from below. Thus a breach with the CNT as a result of the extreme moderation of the Socialists could cause a significant loss of militants flooding to the more revolutionary rival organization.

The Socialists believed that their duty was to help the bourgeoisie carry out its revolution. According to the Socialists, a backward country like Spain did not have the necessary conditions for a Socialist take-over. Hence they were to limit themselves to backing the middle classes' objective of setting up a modern democratic republic with an advanced programme of social reforms to satisfy the workers. Consoled by a Marxian vision of inevitable historical stages, they were resigned to the fact that for some time the prominent role had to be played by the capitalist bourgeoisie.[15] As late as 2 August, a jubilant Pablo Iglesias was writing in *El Socialista* that all the important social forces in the country (bourgeoisie, middle classes, intelligentsia and proletariat) concurred in demanding the overthrow of the regime and the establishment of a democratic republic.[16]

During the summer of 1917 differences between the two workers' organizations became evident. Whereas the CNT envisioned a heroic insurrection in which the proletariat with the aid of bombs and pistols would topple the regime in one or two days of street fighting, the UGT was planning a massive, solidly organized strike movement and working beyond purely trade union level, conducting negotiations with the other parties.[17] Suspicion and mistrust between Socialists and Anarcho-Syndicalists was never totally overcome. The former kept advising restraint while the latter favoured action. Angel Pestaña, the leading member of the Catalan branch of the CNT, noted how since March 1917 his organization had been working feverishly for an

uprising, spending every last peseta in acquiring weapons, while the Socialists were deaf to their plans. Then in July, Pablo Iglesias infuriated the
Syndicalists when during his visit to Barcelona to attend the Assembly he
tried to dampen their revolutionary intentions. Iglesias even told them: 'For
you manual workers it is easy to defend violent methods, but for us intellectuals, it is different.'

The old PSOE leader could not have been very successful in his mission for
another 'manual worker', Largo Caballero, was sent to Barcelona four days
later to persuade the CNT to call off any hasty move. According to Pestaña,
Largo defended the Socialist position with dignity, but his face could not
hide his fear. Largo had met clandestinely a group of fully armed Syndicalists
at Valvidriera, in the mountains outside the Catalan capital. For several hours
the Socialist councillor, accustomed to bureaucratic tasks and office meetings,
had to put up with revolutionaries who never ceased brandishing their weapons and shouting anti-UGT slogans.[18]

For the UGT–PSOE leadership in Madrid the Lliga was an important partner in the political revolution to topple the system. For the CRT, however,
the Lliga, representing the interests of the industrial bourgeoisie, was the
enemy. It was thus not surprising that they were more than reluctant to
collaborate with the Regionalists and subordinate their activities to someone
like Lerroux, whom they quite rightly regarded as a demagogue without any
ideological convictions.

The unresolved transport dispute was a devastating shock for the Socialists. They were no longer merely seconding the other political forces but had
been suddenly pushed by circumstances into leading the offensive. It was to
be their baptism of fire as a leading force in opposition; it was a role for which
they were not prepared.[19] They were moderate, prudent and reformist politicians and trade unionists who had to transform themselves overnight into
revolutionaries. The ideological contradictions of the Spanish Marxists were
to imperil all the revolutionary hopes of their nation. They felt caught in the
vanguard of an insurrectionary process which was not of their own making
and were afraid to assume the role of protagonists. In the end they chose the
worst of both worlds. Trapped between the moderation of their parliamentarian partners and the impulsiveness of Syndicalists and some Republicans,
they backed an intermediate solution. They realized that a sudden ill-timed
general strike could lead to an abrupt end to all the revolutionary illusions,
and yet they did not halt that process. They tried to please both radicals and
moderates. They accepted leadership of the revolution, but at the same time
attempted to make it as peaceful as possible and to limit its goals to the
political programme voted by the parliamentarians.

Once more the man in charge of drawing up the manifesto for the general
strike was the revisionist Julián Besteiro. The document was remarkable
for its moderation. It was an appeal to both workers and the nation. It was
a purely political statement with no mention of any social demands. The

proletariat had endured months of harassment and injustices with fortitude, but the dogmatic position of the administration in the railway dispute pushed the workers into an unwanted strike. The manifesto stressed that it was not only the labour movement but also the Juntas and Assembly that had demanded the political transformation of the regime as the only solution to regenerate the country. Apart from their antimonarchist tone, the objectives sought by the Socialists were exactly the same as those of the Assembly; namely, the creation of a provisional government to stage fair and clean elections for a Constituent Cortes. The manifesto was accompanied by a series of instructions in which workers were told to avoid clashes with the authorities and to greet soldiers as fellow working men.[20]

Thus the Spanish Marxists went out of their way to make sure the bourgeoisie did not become alarmed by their action. In fact, the final goal was to facilitate a conquest of power by the liberal bourgeoisie.[21] Social and economic reforms were therefore ignored and the programme of the bourgeoisie accepted. It was a political and, as far as the Socialists could control it, a peaceful movement. There was obviously no way in which they could supervise the propaganda and the activities of the Anarcho-Syndicalists and some Republicans whose violent rhetoric often clashed with the Socialist plans.[22] Statements made later by the members of the strike committee were astonishing with regard to the moderation of the Socialist objectives and tactics.

> A peaceful strike, but political, we do not deny that. We could not leave the workers' organizations abandoned and defenceless with each one pursuing a different goal . . . We were therefore forced to lead them in a general strike . . .
> . . . when we declared the strike our objectives were those of the Assembly of parliamentarians . . . and it never had the violent character of the Juntas when an ultimatum of 12 hours was given.
> . . . our ideal was to change the regime, but our desire was to make this possible through peaceful means.[23]

> the manifesto and the instructions given by the strike committee were all peaceful . . . advising the workers not to resort to violence . . . in the meantime the Minister of the Interior was lying to the public and turning the army against the people . . .
> . . . What did the proletariat ask in August? . . . Just what the Juntas had demanded on 1 June but in a more peaceful way: a Constituent Cortes and a government to represent the will of the country.[24]

> I carried weapons and ammunition to Bilbao. But when I heard the instructions, those like me, who had carried weapons and ammunition, made sure that where the weapons had been stored, ammunition

could not be found and used by elements who later could not be controlled.[25]

The August movement had been after all a revolutionary attempt. It had been a serious bid to overthrow the oligarchy by illegal and extra-constitutional means.[26] However, it is difficult to see how a revolution could have succeeded when the revolutionaries lacked weapons. Indeed many witnesses would later describe the August days as a shooting gallery in which the troops fired relentlessly on the unarmed crowds.[27]

The Socialists' historical record shows they had always been against any kind of revolutionary adventure. The events of August 1917 constituted a departure from their normal cautious position. They starved their followers of weapons not only to assure the bourgeoisie of their moderate intentions but also because they were totally convinced that they were bound to succeed. They believed that their initiative could not fail as it seemed to have the support of the bourgeoisie and at least the neutrality of the officers. Had the Juntas and Assembly not expressed their willingness to overthrow the corrupt ruling governing elites and regenerate Spain? Once the government had made a solution for the railway conflict impossible and the railway workers had voted for strike action, the Socialist leadership cast away its usual prudence and, blinded by the regenerationist atmosphere of 1917, decided to declare a general strike. They believed that it was their necessary contribution to the political renovation of the country. The mastermind of the operation, Julián Besteiro, would latter comment bitterly:

> If we had thought that there was no possibility of victory we would not have voted for the strike. There could not be victory in a general strike with a political character if there was not a section of the bourgeoisie prepared to take over, or if the army was united against the people and ready to crush the rebellion . . .
> . . . the act of 1 June had an inevitable impact . . . It represented a moment of jubilation . . . We were naive enough to believe the revolution had already been accomplished . . . [28]

The labour movement in Spain paid dearly for the optimism and excessive confidence of its leaders. They were carried away by their own dreams.[29] Their ideological subordination to the bourgeoisie and their misinterpretation of the officers' attitude struck a deadly blow against all the revolutionary illusions. It also put an end to the dream of a united workers' movement. The moderate Socialist leadership decided to abandon revolutionary activity and return to reformist and legalist tactics. The CNT re-affirmed its apolitical leanings and its reliance on direct action.

Hopes that the army would refuse to defend the regime quickly disappeared. The peasant soldiers obeyed the orders of their officers, who in turn ignored all their antioligarchical language of the previous two months and followed the instructions of their generals. The Spanish troops had not been affected by the atrocities, carnage and weariness of the war. Rumours, spread by the government, that foreign gold was behind the disturbances and that the triumph of the revolution would lead to participation in the armed conflict removed the last hesitations among the troops. Most of them felt that it was better to shoot fellow workers in Spain than to dig trenches in France.[30]

The military response was if anything shocking in its unexpected brutality. The army acted once more as the praetorian guard of the regime, the last bulwark of law and order. General Echague, the Captain General of Madrid, drowned workers' protests in blood and transformed the mutiny at the *Cárcel Modelo* into a massacre.[31] In Barcelona, the city of origin of the Juntas, the officers did not hesitate to obey the orders of General Marina. Artillery was often used to subdue the revolutionary zeal of the Anarcho-Syndicalists. In order to prevent sniper fire, Marina commanded that windows and shutters should remain open and soldiers were instructed to shoot at those houses which had not complied.[32] Despite Socialist efforts to stage a peaceful protest in Bilbao, General Souza was no more merciful there. He announced that all those caught with weapons would be summarily executed and that soldiers would respond to any aggression in kind. Strikers were unfairly blamed for an unfortunate accident: the derailment of a train which caused many casualties. Reprisals were savage. The city was occupied by troops who for days kept shooting at any moving target. Children and elderly people were the main victims of the indiscriminate slaughter.[33] But first prize for violent repression went to General Burguete in Asturias. Burguete hitherto had been regarded as an intelligent and sophisticated officer. On the first day of the strike he published a manifesto promising to fight the revolutionaries to the death. Burguete encouraged the use of a train, nicknamed the 'train of death', to patrol the province. From its windows, soldiers shot at random on the unarmed and terrified population. In a new manifesto on 17 August he described as 'wild beasts' those miners still resisting in the mountains and vowed to hunt them down. Hundreds were tortured and many shot as he fulfilled his promise.[34]

Right-wing *Mauristas* quickly abandoned their opposition to the government and declared that the duty of every good citizen was to fight those encouraging social disorder. Some of them volunteered to act as honorary policemen.[35] With a few exceptions, Republicans adopted a passive role. Melquiades Alvarez collaborated with the Socialists in Asturias and even gave shelter to Manuel Llaneza, the miners' leader whose life would be in serious danger if he were captured by General Burguete's troops.[36] Lerroux confirmed his moral bankruptcy and his ability to disappear as soon as trouble arose. In his hide-out he met a CNT delegation who informed him of the fighting behind the barricades in the streets. He was horrified when they asked him for weapons to continue the struggle. The CNT then sought to collaborate with Marcelino Domingo and the separatist Francesc Maciá, while Lerroux stayed in hiding to see whether the revolution was successful. If so, he would demand to become President of the Republic. When it became clear that the authorities had gained the upper hand, the Radical leader bribed a police superintendent and fled to France.[37]

The attitude of the industrial bourgeoisie towards the revolutionary movement was ambivalent. Cambó and his friends were not happy with a move which could well mean that the initiative was slipping from their grasp. For the Lliga, the Assembly had always been an exercise in high politics in which the proletariat had to play a subordinate role. The Lliga was not necessarily antimonarchist. On the contrary, it was happy to seek a political accommodation within the regime. The objective was simply to end once and for all the monopoly of government enjoyed by the centralist landowning oligarchy and definitely not to subvert the social order. In that scheme, the proletariat was one more bargaining factor with which to persuade the king to accept the Assembly programme. The August revolution could endanger all that. It is more than obvious that the Lliga was not enthusiastic about the prospect of trigger-happy Anarchists taking to the streets in Barcelona. However, disowning an initiative which was being made on its behalf would have been a political error. If the revolution had succeeded Cambó would have become the leader of the moderate forces in the new political order. He was aware of what was being prepared and would not have wasted time in demanding his share of the spoils.[38] The strategy was to wait on events without making any specific commitments. Thus the Catalanists hastened to disassociate themselves from the strike, but, expecting to collect the fruits if successful, they did not condemn it either. The Catalan bourgeoisie had behaved very differently during the Tragic Week of 1909 when its newspaper, *La Veu de Catalunya*, had even encouraged the citizens to inform the police about the leading agitators. During the first moments of confusion there were rumours that the Assembly was throwing in its lot with the strike and delegating Lerroux to co-ordinate the offensive. That was rapidly denied in a statement signed by the leading Republican and Catalanist politicians on 14 August. Yet in that document blame for the grave situation was placed on the government's refusal to listen to public opinion. That intransigence had provoked a violent protest from the people.[39] However, the following day Cambó's lieutenant, Abadal, wrote in *La Veu* that it was ridiculous to accuse the Lliga of being behind the general strike. On 16 August, all the Catalanist leaders appeared before a judge to deny any allegations that they were involved in the revolution. The strike had been virtually crushed and therefore it was time for Cambó to make statements on behalf of law and order.

The August revolution was purely a domestic affair. No foreign state was involved in its preparation. Yet the Allies were accused of being behind the events in order to push Spain into the war on their side. Almost all Republicans and Socialists strongly supported the Allied cause and had the general strike succeeded the nation would probably have moved closer to the Western Powers. Nevertheless, at no time were they encouraged or financially backed to overthrow the regime. On the contrary, extremely conservative diplomats like the British ambassador, Arthur Hardinge, continually went out of their way to prove their good intentions to the Dato administration.

As the situation became more and more radicalized, Hardinge avoided seeing any of the representatives of the left but was informed by the Portuguese ambassador, who obviously did not share his scruples, of the strides made by the revolutionary movement. He regretted that his Portuguese colleague seemed to be in personal sympathy with them. Yet their mutual scepticism about political change in Spain was fully revealed when in conversation both agreed that Lerroux was unprincipled and venal and Melquiades Alvarez was a well-meaning idealist who after a revolution would be swept away by mobs and military tyrants.[40]

The Western Powers were the main foreign investors in Spain. They owned many of the economic resources of the nation, particularly mines, and were the main recipients of Catalan and Basque industrial production. Thus they preferred the existing status quo to the prospect of economic disruption and social turmoil which might be produced by a revolution staged by the pro-Allied forces in Spain. Furthermore, the example of Russia, torn apart by political militancy and in military chaos after the fall of Tsarism, persuaded the British and French governments not to encourage initiatives which could lead to similar situations. They had nothing to gain from civil disturbance in Spain. That was the message that Hardinge tried to pass to his hosts on several occasions with little success. Following his reports, twice in July a representative of the British cabinet stated in parliament that it was not its policy to force Spain or any other neutral country into the war.[41] Simultaneously, Hardinge was being advised by E. A. Unthorff, manager of the London and Westminster Bank, that gold was entering Spain but only due to profitable financial circumstances produced by the war. He denied categorically that the gold was being introduced to support civil unrest.[42]

Fear and paranoia that the Entente was behind a revolution gripped the Spanish rulers. The Germanophile press wasted no time in exploiting the situation and spread rumours that unrest was being funded by foreign gold. The alleged objective was to blackmail Spain into the war by threatening her with domestic revolution if she continued to remain neutral. According to these rumours, Catalanists, Socialists and Republicans were in close contact with their French counterparts so as to launch a revolution in Spain. The Embassy at Paris was continually bombarded with instructions from the Spanish government to put pressure on the French to end the unfriendly press campaign being conducted in France. León y Castillo confirmed the hostility of certain newspapers towards the Spanish regime, but also noted that it was not officially sanctioned by the French administration whose publications were behaving with courtesy and moderation. It was absurd to demand that the French government silence those newspapers which in fact were only showing their support for the most ardent friends of the Entente in Spain. León y Castillo suggested that the Spanish Socialist Antonio Fabra Ribas, a former member of the PSOE's National Executive now resident in Paris, could be at the centre of the intrigue and vowed to keep him under surveillance.[43] The paranoia sometimes appeared ridiculous. For instance, Dato commented that the railworkers were floating on French money, travelling everywhere by car and drinking champagne.[44]

In fact, the revolutionary events in the summer of 1917 constituted a serious setback for the Allied diplomatic campaign in Spain. Rumours and suspicions that the Entente was working to produce disturbances which might force the nation to enter the war on their side were constant. Hardinge even met Dato and his Foreign Minister, the Marquis of Lema, and offered his services for investigating the truth of any such stories.[45] It was to no avail. Lema, a known Allied supporter, even suggested that his former pro-Entente position had been rendered very difficult as a consequence of the current incidents. Additionally, the king, who since the events in Russia in March had been shifting towards the German camp, now thought his worst fears confirmed. On several occasions he declared that British and French radicals were behind the revolutionary conspiracies in his country.[46]

During the general strike the Minister of the Interior, through his tight control of the press, tried to hint that foreign agents were behind the unrest. Sánchez Guerra could thus present the government not only as the defender of law and order but also as the saviour of a nation under attack from an international conspiracy.[47] The calumny that the members of the strike committee had been found with millions in foreign currency was believed in many quarters, not least among many officers and provincial authorities. Some, like the civil governor of Huelva, Eusebio de Salas, or the notorious General Burguete in Asturias, proclaimed publicly that foreign gold was behind the disturbances.[48] Thus the authorities did not hesitate to repress what they regarded as a foreign plot with extreme brutality. Yet it could never be proved that the Western Powers had any link whatsoever with the events of that summer. *La Acción* presented as proof of their complicity some editorials in French left-wing newspapers like *La Victoire* and *L'Humanité* which regretted the failure of the revolution and argued that those who had taken part were the pro-Allied forces in Spain.[49] This did not prove anything which was not already known. Republicans and Socialists had always backed the Allied cause, and it was not a secret that a Republican regime dominated by them would sooner or later side with the Entente in the European conflict. Furthermore, it was normal for the French left to side with its Spanish counterparts. Yet this was far from showing any official involvement by the Western governments. In fact, only one diplomat, Monsieur Gilliard, the French Consul at Corunna, was expelled from Spain and even he was allowed to return when the French government guaranteed that those 'revolutionaries' who had escaped to France, in particular Lerroux and Maciá, would stay well clear of the border.[50]

The damage to the Allied image within Spanish ruling circles was done despite the lack of evidence. The king himself could not restrain his temper. When he met the French ambassador for the first time after the crushing of the general strike, Alfonso accused France of supplying gold and encouraging the revolutionary movement in Spain. Taken by surprise the ambassador, Leon Geoffray, replied with dignity that in France, a country of 40 million people, there might be a certain number of persons who would be willing to participate in revolutionary plots against Spain but that was not proof of the complicity of the French government.[51] The Central Powers had won an important propaganda coup. More than ever they could now claim to be the true friends of Spain and her monarchy. Thus for almost another year they would be able to carry on undisturbed with their subversive activities against the Allies both in the peninsula and in Morocco.

8

THE END OF AN ERA

The collapse of the *Turno Pacífico* and the search for a new political settlement

The collapse of the general strike constituted the failure of political reform from below. Yet if the Canovite system resisted that attack, its governing elites found it impossible to put back the clock of history. The first ever political initiative led by the Socialists heralded the arrival of mass politics and social mobilization. The old-fashioned Liberalism represented by the dynastic parties owed its survival to the military. Henceforth the permanence of the liberal monarchy would rest on the goodwill of the repressive forces of the state. The army had stopped the revolution but who was going to stop the army?

The victory of the Conservative government was short-lived. The Dato administration was soon to realize that it was living on borrowed time. Quashing the general strike had offered a temporary respite, yet once the revolutionary spasm of August was over, the government found itself back in the situation of July: isolated, discredited and loathed by nearly all the social and political forces of the country.

All the attempts made by the government to link the Assembly with the revolutionary movement failed. The bourgeoisie under the leadership of Cambó returned to the attack, resuming its activities. On 30 August, Cambó declared to *El Heraldo de Madrid* that the general strike had been a foolish action which had only served to delay and obstruct the offensive mounted in July. He denied having supported or encouraged the movement and even added that a general strike was an old-fashioned political method which was always bound to fail. Cambó was seeking to distance himself from his 'embarrassing' and now defeated partners on the left and also stress the moderation and seriousness of his alternative.

The Catalan leader was singled out by the cabinet as the mastermind of the antigovernmental offensive and the main political threat to their continuity in office. From the Conservative organ *La Epoca*, Cambó and his plans were continually criticized or ridiculed. His initiative was described as a recipe for civil war, and he was portrayed as a skilful but unprincipled politician who had tried to exploit the unsophisticated working classes. Now that they

135

were no longer of any use to him, the government alleged that he cynically called the August events senseless and dubbed as fools the very people who he had once encouraged.[1]

Cambó retorted by calling the *Turno* 'an orthopaedic device' and starting a tour through northern Spain. There he met members of the Basque Nationalist Party and Melquiades Alvarez. He also made contact with the leaders of the Liberal party, Alhucemas, Romanones and Alba.[2] On 27 September he wrote to Maura and tried to persuade the veteran statesman once more to join forces with him. Cambó suggested that both were working for the same ends. He insisted that a radical change from above was urgent. If the king kept on relying on the discredited dynastic parties, it would not be long before a real revolution, different from the 'grotesque adventure' of August, would take place. Cambó added that the situation was so grave that it imposed duties upon all of them, but particularly on someone with the charisma and prestige of Antonio Maura. A disaster would occur if they remained passive and Dato obtained the decree of dissolution of the Cortes which he needed to call new elections and continue the political fiction.[3] The Catalan leader was only re-iterating his belief that an unreformed oligarchic political system would lead sooner or later to a violent revolution. A conservative like Cambó was of course aware of this danger and eager to avoid a repetition of the chaotic situation then engulfing Russia.

As in July, Cambó's appeal to the veteran Conservative leader went unheard. Maura's orthodox legalism and reluctance to take an active stand was ironically one of the strongest assets of the government. He agreed with Cambó on the need to reform the system from above, but refused once more to endorse any project which could endanger the safety of the regime. He continued to present himself as the only dynastic leader with a real mass following in the country who could offer a popular solution in a moment of political and military unrest. It was short-sightedness or naivety on Maura's part not to realize that, although he loyally distanced himself and his movement from any active renovating tendency in the country, the monarch was not prepared to back him against the dynastic parties; especially since Maura, as a result of his own refusal, was not an alternative who could count on the support of either the Juntas or the Assembly.[4] Moreover, the king, always jealous of his central and paramount position in the state, was happier to deal with people like Dato or Romanones than with Maura. The latter's strong personality and style made him much more difficult to manipulate. On 4 October, Alfonso confided to the Foreign Minister Marquis of Lema: 'With Maura there will come a moment when it will be him or the monarchy. I had enough of him after what he did in 1909 and 1913.'[5]

The only pleasure left to Maura was to see the fulfilment of his prediction that the *Turno* was about to crumble. He had chosen, however, the position of passive spectator rather than that of a leading protagonist. The information he received in September from his sons, Gabriel and Miguel, during his holiday at the village of Solozarno in Santander seemed to confirm his prophecy. The conclusion they drew was that Dato's days in power were numbered. The Prime Minister was a political corpse who was doomed to fall as soon as the state of war was lifted and constitutional guarantees restored. They noted that Dato was still working to fix the next general election and had even offered a safe seat in Tenerife to Delgado Barreto, the right-wing editor of *La Acción*, in exchange for a truce. Barreto had naturally declined. Both brothers pointed out that the government was isolated and despised by everyone, Liberals, Republicans and Juntas. The officers' anger with the cabinet kept growing. They were tired of economic shortages and fed up with the moral bankruptcy of the Dato administration.[6]

Once again, the main threat to the existence of the government came from military quarters. Dato was aware that the military issue was still a thorn in his side. His strategy was to continue with his policy of appeasement in order to deflect the attacks and win a substantial number of the officers over so that with the army divided it would be politically harmless.[7] It did not work.

By unleashing the might of the army against the workers, Dato had unconsciously sealed the fate of his government and of the constitutional monarchy. The Prime Minister was the first to be shocked by the ferocity displayed by the troops. The armed services normally loathed the idea of being called out to police the streets. But once they had been given the task they did not want to be told how to do their job. For them putting down a revolt was just a military operation in which the workers were treated as enemies who deserved no mercy. On 12 August the Captain General of Madrid, General Echague, had already advised the Prime Minister that his soldiers would obey orders. The general also hinted that the job would be carried to its final consequences without political interference.[8]

The members of the government were appalled by the number of casualties. They were oligarchical politicians who, although eager to cling to power regardless, were by no means blood-thirsty. Dato appeared as a panic-stricken leader responsible for an out-of-control army massacring people in the streets. Members of the strike committee were captured and threatened with immediate execution. For weeks, they were held incommunicado before being told that they would be tried by a military court. Additionally, in flagrant violation of the constitution and by orders of the Captain General of Barcelona, General Marina, the parliamentary deputy Marcelino Domingo was arrested. The publication of his pamphlet appealing to the troops to join the workers had aroused the anger of the officers. He suffered all sorts of physical and verbal abuse and only the personal intervention of Colonel Márquez, who rushed to the military barracks, saved him from death. Finally, for his own safety, Domingo was sent to a prison ship and placed under the custody of the navy. Dato was either too weak or too frightened to stand up to the officers. He had to condone their actions while at the same time dealing with the growing protests of the politicians. Romanones himself wrote to Dato about the Domingo affair, demanding respect for the constitution. The Speaker of Congress, Villanueva, defended with praiseworthy energy the rights of Marcelino Domingo and won the support of several influential deputies. According to the law, a member of parliament could only be tried by the Supreme Court. Dato tried to evade the question and Marcelino Domingo was finally released without charge in October.[9]

The Juntas were soon to discover that the popularity they had enjoyed in June had evaporated after the brutal repression of the August movement. To add insult to injury, they realized that they had been used by the government to put down a rebellion which it had itself provoked. The officers turned their anger on the administration. A reward for 'past services' of 71 million pesetas, granted by the government on 21 August to increase defence expenditure, was not enough to appease them. They returned to their anti-oligarchical and regenerationist rhetoric. On 7 September the Central Junta at Barcelona issued a document to all the members in the provinces. The operation of putting down the rebellion was praised, but strong words were reserved for the Dato ministry, whose lack of foresight had turned a peaceful strike into a revolutionary movement. In a clear allusion to the government, they suggested that certain malicious politicians were trying to blame the army for the subsequent repression in order to build a wall between the armed services and the people. To re-build their popular image, the military demanded from the government the lifting of martial law, the re-establishment of constitutional guarantees and the acceptance of responsibility for the repression. Finally, in what amounted to a dire warning, they stated that it was their duty to intervene more actively in politics so as to impose justice and morality upon politicians.[10]

In fact, the army's decision to take a more active role in politics was nothing new. The novelty was that for the first time they had proclaimed it officially. The Juntas had reached important conclusions before being interrupted by the general strike. On 9 August they had decided to act against those generals considered enemies of their organization. Eight were singled out: Alfau, Luque, Figueras, Aguilera, Primo de Rivera, Carbó, Bazán and Riera. The following day they introduced first- and second-class sanctions to deal with them. Second-class sanctions, applied to the first four blacklisted generals, meant that no officer would consent to be their assistant. First-class sanctions would apply to the last four generals, who would be given respectful advice to change their methods and practices. Then on 11 August the Juntas decided they must have at least one representative in each region to stand for deputy or senator in the next general election. In September this process of increasing intervention and activism was stepped up. On 14 September they re-affirmed their goal of maintaining the system of promotion by strict seniority. Three days later a crucial decision was taken: it was now the officers' duty to participate more actively in politics so as to set the standards for public morality. The Juntas also decided to send letters announcing their resolutions to the Prime Minister, the Speakers of both chambers, the leaders of the political minorities, the Ministers of the Interior and War, the most important newspapers and if necessary to the monarch. On 21 September an overwhelming majority of *junteros* endorsed that conclusion and General Marina was designated as their representative to mediate with politicians.[11]

The confirmation of the Juntas' entry into the political arena was a shattering blow for the government's hopes of normalization and a dire warning for the constitutional system. Although Dato denied it when interviewed by the press, the officers had plunged the country into a deep crisis with no apparent solution. The Prime Minister rushed to San Sebastián to see the king. He managed to convince the monarch that with caution and concessions the army's threat could be dissipated. Thus a smiling Dato told the journalists that everything was under control. He had the confidence of the king and his purpose was to stay in office and celebrate local and general elections in November 1917 and January 1918 respectively. He cynically added that if the population was not happy with his conduct of government they could vote against the government – as if nobody knew that elections were fixed by the Minister of the Interior. Back in Madrid, Dato met General Marina and confronted him with the fact that he was supported by the monarchy. A statement was then released for the press. Dato, in his most flagrant display of hypocrisy and flattery to date, stated that the army was a patriotic and disciplined institution always prepared to fulfil its duty and obey the law. It was therefore understandable that the officers should be annoyed by the unfounded rumours and fantasies of recent days.[12]

The government was making a gross miscalculation if it was attempting to win time to neutralize the *junteros'* attacks by flattery and the distortion of the reality. The officers had intercepted a cable from Sánchez Guerra to the civil governors advising them to let the Juntas carry on with their activities. In the meantime they were to find out the names and political tendencies of the leading *junteros* until the moment arrived to turn against them.[13] The officers became more determined than ever to overthrow the Dato cabinet. Furthermore, the strategy of flattery no longer produced the results expected. On the contrary, it only provoked disgust among the officer corps.[14]

The government was to become a victim of its own game of misinformation. It insisted that everything was normal and, obviously well informed by Marina of the wishes of the Juntas, that there was no way in which the state of war could be maintained. Thus on 7 October it was lifted and thereafter constitutional guarantees were restored. Immediately an avalanche of criticism came from all quarters. It was a deafening clamour against the administration, without parallel in the history of the Restoration monarchy.

On 29 September the trial began against those accused of having led the revolutionary movement in August. On 4 October, the four members of the strike committee were found guilty of rebellion and sentenced to life imprisonment. Three other militants were sentenced to eight years and one day, two others to two years, four months and one day, and the only two women charged were acquitted. The occasion was used by Julián Besteiro, who spoke on behalf of himself and the three others accused, to blame the government for provoking the general strike. One of the military lawyers, the captain of infantry Julio Mangada, pursued that line of defence and found himself facing fifteen days under arrest.[15] After almost two months of suspension, *El Socialista* returned to the streets on 9 October and continually hammered home the view that the strike in August was not what the Socialists had wanted but what the government had forced upon them. A resolution was adopted to work for an amnesty for their comrades in prison and to concentrate on the next local elections in which the four members of the strike committee would be standing as councillors in Madrid. On 25 October, the Socialists voted unanimously to end all participation in official bodies as long as Dato remained in power.[16] That measure had been adopted before, against Maura in 1909 after the Catalan 'Tragic Week'. Now for a second time an essentially reformist organization boycotted a politician and cut all channels of communication with the state.

In October, Cambó re-affirmed his position as leader of the anti-*Turno* offensive. He was once more the engine behind the organization of the second meeting of the Assembly. On 15 October 77 parliamentarians met in Madrid. The government, now unable to ban the Assembly owing to the restoration of constitutional guarantees, including freedom of association, had to watch the show from the sidelines. The Assembly's sub-committee for constitutional reform presented its conclusions, which were duly approved. Those initiatives, if put into practice, could represent a real transformation of the political structure of the country and the establishment of a genuine constitutional monarchy. They significantly limited the prerogatives of governments and of the monarchy itself. Article 17, which enabled an administration to suspend constitutional guarantees, was to be reformed. It was agreed that any such suspension should not exceed 15 days and that within that period parliament should be consulted. It was also decided that the Cortes was to remain open at least between 1 October and 31 December of every year. The principle of sharing sovereignty between monarchy and parliament was to be reformed as well. Emphasis was placed on the fact that sovereignty lay with the Cortes, the only body entitled to pass laws. The monarch would be allowed to veto a bill, but if the next Cortes was to pass that bill again it would automatically become law. Moreover, the king would no longer appoint members of the Senate. Henceforth all senators would be elected through a corporate franchise among representatives of the economic life of the nation. Finally, regional autonomy would be recognized as a natural and basic foundation of the state and not regarded as an obstacle to national unity. The parliamentarians again demanded the creation of a national government which would hold clean elections for a Constituent Cortes.[17]

The programme of the Assembly was a personal triumph for Cambó. It was essentially a recognition of the federal aspirations of the Lliga and amounted to a profound but moderate political reform. The Catalan leader continued his crusade to overthrow the government and clear the way for his initiative. On 22 October he declared in *El Heraldo de Madrid* that the Conservative administration had to go since it lacked moral authority, economic plans or valid ideas for post-war reconstruction. The next government ought to be the product of the country's will and not of a dynastic faction. The following day in a speech at the Centro Autonomista de Dependientes (Autonomist Centre for Clerks) in Barcelona, Cambó kept up the pressure. He argued that the ruling oligarchies had bankrupted the country. The Juntas had not created the crisis in June but only made it public knowledge. According to Cambó, in any democratic state such indiscipline would not have been tolerated: the fact that in Spain it had had the support and encouragement of the population revealed the crisis of authority of the political system. No remedies had been attempted to solve the evils complained of; instead the government had resorted to condemning the Assembly, which was working for a peaceful solution. The Dato cabinet had then sown discord and intrigue in order to provoke a general strike which the army had had to crush with violence and which consequently had led to the inevitable confrontation between people and army. Thus, concluded Cambó, the *Turno* was morally dead and should not continue any longer. Public interest required a complete change of the system, with new men, representing genuine sectors of public opinion, in charge of a coalition government. Then and only then the military and other problems could be solved.[18]

The *Mauristas* were no less forthright in their attacks. *La Acción* noted that Dato had hitherto managed to retain the confidence of the crown only by imposing silence on public opinion and following a campaign of deceit and misinformation. He had united workers, bourgeoisie and army in common opposition to a collapsing political order. Dato was portrayed as the most cynical and unprincipled politician of the *Turno* group. He was a man who still tried to cling to the fiction that everything was normal when it was glaringly obvious that everybody was against him and what he stood for. Claiming to speak for the only remaining healthy monarchist sector in the country, the *Maurista* organ warned the king of the dangers ahead if he granted the decree of dissolution to the government. In an editorial called 'From the people to the king', *La Acción* claimed that it was the duty of loyal monarchists to tell Alfonso that it would be a step towards national catastrophe if the old politics of *caciquismo* prevailed once more against the will of the entire nation. Thus the monarch should act while he still had time, rather than recognize too late that he had been badly advised and even deceived by those who had not informed him of the real desires of the nation.[19]

On 21 October Maura himself broke his perennial silence. In what was a bitter onslaught against the system and a display of his liberal principles, the old Conservative leader publicly stated his opposition to the government for the first time since August. He accused the Dato ministry of having put civil supremacy in the gutter by bowing to the demands of the Juntas. According to Maura, the crisis of authority was worsening daily. In a clear allusion to Dato's insistence that his government enjoyed the confidence of the monarch, Maura added:

> It is sad to see these blind politicians taking refuge in proofs of royal confidence which they were never short of, while distancing them-selves from what they really need, the support of the people. It is a foolish attempt to associate the crown with the vile interests of a faction.[20]

Two days later, *La Acción*, feeling fewer scruples than Maura in supporting the initiatives of the army, encouraged the officers to take the final step and force the government out of office.

Simultaneously, the Juntas were lambasting the government at will. On 8 October their leader, Colonel Márquez, wrote to the Minister for War, General Fernando Primo de Rivera. With no effort at subtlety, he harshly attacked the actions of the cabinet in response to the August disturbances. Márquez suggested that the carelessness shown during those days gave the impression that the government had been deliberately encouraging the con-flict to come to a head and then suppressing it with a severity that was bound to diminish the popularity of the army with the people.[21]

On 17 October, Primo de Rivera, alleging health problems, resigned and was replaced by Marina, the general most favoured by the Juntas. In fact, this was another instance of Dato attempting to placate the officers. Primo de Rivera had refused to bow to the Juntas' demands to remove the Military Governor of Valencia, General Carbó, one of those blacklisted. Under pressure from the government to comply, he had preferred to resign. Dato's move did not pay off. *El Ejército Español* and *La Correspondencia Militar*, the two main military newspapers, called his action 'a disgusting act of servility'. They concluded that the old general had given his fellow min-isters a lesson in honesty and honour, and warned that Dato was making another mistake by trying to seek shelter behind the prestige of General Marina.[22]

The ex-Minister was to prove his loyalty two days later when he declared his total support for Dato and the belief that he should continue in power. Primo pointed out that he had the backing of 22 generals who all agreed that the Juntas had made a terrible error with their intervention in politics and deviation from their original worthy objectives. Rather naively Primo de Rivera stated that Dato should be allowed to fix the new elections or otherwise the mob would be the new ruler of Spain.[23] *La Correspondencia Militar* replied that the Juntas were not political and did not support any particular party, but as patriots the officers had the duty and right to oppose the system of oligarchs and *caciques* which was embodied in the existing administration.

On 24 October, in an interview with *El Heraldo de Madrid*, Márquez made a devastating criticism of the government. The Colonel once more wrapped up his arguments in regenerationist rhetoric. He stressed that the Juntas were moved purely by patriotism and therefore had no interest in politics. Márquez claimed that any political offer made to them by either right- or left-wing groups had always been rejected. He pointed out that the hardships suffered by the population were shared by the army and so they identified with the popular clamour for radical solutions. More alarming for the government was Márquez's confirmation in the last part of his statement that although the Juntas were not willing to step into the political arena, nobody should be surprised if they looked to the crown for redress.[24]

Not even after the 'Tragic Week' of 1909 had the echoes of discontent and opposition to a monarchist administration reached such scandalous levels. All sectors of public opinion were in total agreement. From the left-wing *El Socialista*, *España* and *El Liberal* to the Catholic *El Debate*, the military *La Correspondencia Militar* and the *Maurista La Acción*, all concurred not only that the position of the government was untenable, but also that the *Turno Pacífico* had to be replaced by a new political formula.[25] The Dato cabinet was totally isolated and fighting against everyone. The profound nature of the crisis was also confirmed by the attitude of the leaders of the Liberal party. Like rats escaping from a sinking ship, they were already distancing themselves from a doomed system and talking as if they had always been part of the regenerationist movement in Spain. Santiago Alba was busy drawing up a programme of economic reconstruction and political cleansing. The former minister said that his plan sought to appeal to both Socialists and Regionalists.[26] The Marquis of Alhucemas was declaring that the *Turno* did not exist any more.[27] Even Count Romanones, probably the best living example of a *Turno* politician, was arguing that a new order based on new political practices had to be created. A bewildered *La Epoca* wondered how it could be possible that Romanones was now also a regenerationist.[28] On the front page of its edition of 26 October, *La Acción* called for a miracle and presented a cartoon of a huge broom sweeping away Dato, Sánchez Guerra and Romanones, the representatives of the old order.

The miracle did happen. There had been rumours since 23 October that the Juntas were planning to deliver a final message to the monarch. It finally arrived on the night of 26 October and, shattering Dato's last hopes that the army could be divided, was drawn up by the infantry but signed unanimously by the whole corps. It was irrefutably the ultimate proof of the strength of the army and consolidated its position as power-broker in the state. The main points were:

The Infantry has come to the conclusion that the procedure of government has not changed, nor has any new spirit been observed which might direct the country towards the progress which is required for it to achieve the state of preparedness and defence now made necessary by the approaching end of the war in Europe . . .

Furthermore, morality, justice, equity and consideration for the law are neither respected nor observed, nor can any hope be entertained that in its future acts this government may be inspired by such considerations, since the party politicians have neither expressed regret nor shown any intention of mending their ways. On the contrary, they have adopted a stance in opposition to the Juntas de Defensa whose action should have served as a regenerative force for them to employ. Instead this government regards them as a hostile force to be exterminated by any means, from violence to calumny, passing through a whole range of insidious allegations, enticements and bribery more appropriate to Byzantine politicians than to men who aspire to rule the destinies of free people . . .

The Infantry deems it advisable respectfully to bring these dangers to the notice of His Majesty.[29]

It represented a death warrant for the government. Gustavo Peyrá wrote to Maura: 'If Dato had been waiting for the bayonets to speak in order to leave office, he now had the signal he had been waiting for.'[30] The message amounted to an ultimatum. The king was very respectfully urged to act upon their document within 72 hours. The army demanded the creation of a national government which would respect the popular vote. That could be ensured by entrusting the post of Minister of the Interior to a neutral person, untainted by the business of electoral falsification. In return, the officers would guarantee to the crown that no Constituent Cortes could challenge the dynasty because, in such an event, it would automatically be dissolved by them. The king could not fail to pay heed to the army's wishes. The following day he notified his Prime Minister that he had to consult other politicians in order to solve the pending crisis. It was a diplomatic way of letting Dato know that his services were no longer needed.

According to Hardinge, Dato believed until the last moment that he could survive the political crisis. As late as 25 October he had expressed his intention to stay in office, dissolve the Cortes and hold new elections.[31] The Conservative leader seems to have taken the support of the monarch for granted. He must have realized the increasing political isolation of his government, but still Dato believed that he possessed some important assets which, if used carefully, could guarantee his survival. The dangerous situation of the summer had been successfully defused. The labour movement had suffered an important set-back and the Lliga had failed to enlist the support of the Catholic and Conservative middle classes who followed Maura. There were many hostile forces in the country but they were not co-ordinating their actions. Further-more, the monarch could not forget that his throne had probably been saved by the existing government. On several occasions the king had shown his gratitude and trust, and made very clear his refusal to have Maura back in power.[32] In early October, Alfonso had advised Dato of his readiness to grant a decree of dissolution of the Cortes which would permit him to manipulate fresh elections in his own interests. The Prime Minister had preferred to wait and see the dangers that the new gathering of parliamentarians represented. The new resolutions passed by the Assembly were not likely to have pleased the king especially since their implementation would mean a curtailment of the royal prerogatives. Then on 20 October, Alfonso sent a cable to Dato on his saint's day encouraging him to carry on with his good work.[33]

The main danger was posed by the Juntas. The government, however, had hopes that the military could be divided and the faction which followed Márquez isolated.[34] Some voices of dissent had begun to be heard within the armed services. A certain Colonel Moratinos from Barcelona had issued a statement criticizing the growing involvement of officers in politics.[35] Yet if Dato was relying on his strategy to divide the army and on the king's confi-dence, his hopes were to be dashed. The army closed ranks, court-martialled Moratinos and approved an ultimatum to be submitted to the monarch. Alfonso was not prepared to take the suicidal step of supporting a loyal poli-tician against the whole country and the army. Dato therefore had to go. The king frankly admitted to the Italian ambassador, Count Bonin, that he had no alternative but to act in the way desired by the army as the future of the dynasty depended on the maintenance of military goodwill.[36] It was not the first time that he had dismissed faithful servants for cynical motives.[37]

The fall of the Conservative government on 27 October initiated a crisis which, owing to its length and final outcome, would be crucial in the evolu-tion of the constitutional monarchy. Confusion, uncertainty and doubts about the future were the order of the day. All the main dynastic politicians, with the exception of Dato, agreed that an era had come to an end. With the Liberal party broken, and the Conservatives forced out of office, the political formula of the *Turno Pacífico*, the foundation of the established order since 1875, had to be abandoned.

In the autumn of 1917, the existing governing elites had to resolve a series of difficulties in order to retain control of the apparatus of the state. Firstly, although following separate routes, the programmes of Assembly and Juntas were remarkably similar. They echoed the desires of the country by demand-ing political renovation and a thorough change of methods. They opposed the survival of the dynastic factions at the centre of decision-making. Except for *Maurismo*, those factions were all artificially based and lacked a real ideo-logical programme with which to mobilize parts of the electorate. Natalio Rivas, a former minister and influential personality in the Liberal party, com-mented that there was no way that the *Turno* men could accept free elections as they would be wiped out of existence.[38] Additionally, it was unlikely that the different monarchist groups could shelve their internal disputes and agree to work together. Factionalism was a symptom and not a cause of the crisis. Finally, whatever political solution came out of the existing crisis, it would have to take account of the fact that the army had become politicized and would not be easily persuaded to give up its privileged position. Maura himself acknowledged the fact when he pointed out that the new government ought fully to restore civil supremacy or otherwise responsibility would have to be handed over to those who would not let others govern.[39]

As emerged during the following day, the solution pursued by the king was to find someone who could put together a monarchist coalition which would attract the backing of the Juntas and win over the moderate sectors of the Assembly represented by Catalan Regionalists and Reformists.[40] Alfonso first entrusted the Conservative Joaquín Sánchez de Toca with that task. A member of the Board of Directors of the Bank of Spain and of several sugar companies, former minister in 1902 and Speaker of the Senate in 1914, Sánchez de Toca represented the soft and paternalist side of the Conservative party, more open to dialogue with the opposition. He attempted to form a coalition to include the dynastic groups, the Reformists and the Regionalists. He was opposed to a Constituent Assembly and indeed to any constitutional reform, but declared in favour of granting an amnesty to all those imprisoned for the events of August. The only person willing to support Toca was Romanones. For the parliamentarians it was not enough, and the monarchists declined. Toca's own fellow Conservatives were infuriated. Sánchez Guerra believed that the amnesty was a manoeuvre by Romanones which he described as an infamy.[41] It was then the turn of the Marquis of Alhucemas, the leader with the largest minority in Congress. He did not fare much better. His overtures were also rejected by Cambó and Melquiades Alvarez and he had to decline.

On the fifth day of the crisis Alfonso finally resorted to the services of Antonio Maura. By 2 November he too had declined. The edition of *La Acción* for that day gave a full explanation of the unsuccessful steps taken by the veteran leader. In fact, there was very little that was original in Maura's plan. He had also rejected any possibility of constitutional change and instead had concentrated on forming a strong coalition with men drawn from all the factions. The Marquis of Lema was to continue at the Foreign Office; Juan de la Cierva, a hard-liner who had been his Minister of the Interior in 1909 and was now emerging as the man defending the interests of the Juntas, was to be Minister for War; a Germanophile Liberal, Alcalá Zamora, would be in charge of Education; and González Hontoria, an Allied sympathizer belonging to the Liberal-*Romanonista* faction, would be in Justice. An obscure officer, Admiral Ferrándiz, would take over the Navy department; three leading *Mauristas*, Goicoechea, Ossorio and the economist Flores de Lemus, would be in charge of Interior, Public Works and the Treasury respectively. Finally, Maura thought of appointing Cambó, Alhucemas and the Reformist

Azcárate as ministers without portfolio. His scheme was rejected by nearly everyone. Support came only from Romanones and Azcárate. Melquiades Alvarez made it clear that Azcárate was speaking on a personal basis and not representing his party. The proud Maura had gone begging, cap in hand, to the different dynastic groups. The enlightened politician, who for years had preached a revolution from above and had been vilifying the country's leaders since 1909, had finally turned up on their doorsteps. It was no wonder he was rebuffed.[42]

As the days went by, the atmosphere of despair and confusion in the ruling circles grew. On 30 October a crucial event took place. Cambó was summoned to the Palace. That day the Assembly had been convened at the Ateneo of Madrid to discuss the current situation. When news filtered out that the king had called for Cambó, the parliamentarians cheered. They thought that victory for their plan was within reach. The time for a peaceful and bloodless revolution from above had arrived. The Catalan leader made a triumphal speech claiming that the Assembly's principles were about to succeed.

However, amidst the reigning optimism of the moment, they had overlooked the subtle game of the Catalan industrial bourgeoisie. Indeed, they did not notice that after his meeting with the monarch, Cambó declared to the press that he had told Alfonso that the only possible solution to the crisis was to create a wide coalition to replace the discredited *Turno* and appoint a neutral person as Minister of the Interior to ensure a fair election. The Catalan leader was swiftly moving away from the positions held by the others. Constitutional reform was no longer one of his demands. He was giving the crown a valid way out.

After Maura's abortive attempt to create a coalition, Alhucemas was entrusted with the task again. Two days later he was successful. The government crisis had lasted a record eight days but was at least temporarily over. The new government was to be:

Prime Minister:	Marquis of Alhucemas (Liberal Democrat)
Foreign Office:	Marquis of Alhucemas
Interior:	Viscount Matamala (neutral)
Treasury:	Juan Ventosa (Lliga Regionalista)
Education:	Felipe Rodés (left, Catalanist)
War:	Juan de la Cierva (leader of his own right-wing Conservative faction)
Justice:	Joaquín Fernández Prida (*Maurista*)
Navy:	Amalio Gimeno (Liberal *Romanonista*)
Public Works:	Niceto Alcalá Zamora (Liberal independent)

The outcome of the October crisis was a victory for the crown, the Catalan industrial bourgeoisie and the Juntas. All of them were now at the centre of decision-making. The real losers were the forces pushing for democratization, and to a lesser extent the traditional governing elites. It was a warning of what would take place six years later when Miguel Primo de Rivera, Captain General of Catalonia, established a military dictatorship. This time the constitutional practices were conserved but the liberal political order paid a very high price: the consolidation of the alliance of an unreformed and all-powerful crown with the increasingly politically active officer corps had been sealed at the expense of the ailing dynastic parties.

The king had preserved his privileged position in the political order by taking advantage of the fact that neither the Catalan bourgeoisie nor the Juntas were antimonarchist *per se*. Alfonso had pushed for a solution in which the ambitions of both were satisfied and in exchange they forgot all their demands for constitutional reform.[43] The officers' recently acquired political role was confirmed by the presence of Juan de la Cierva in the cabinet. Cierva, *cacique* of Murcia and a man of shady reputation and authoritarian manners, had accepted what Maura had refused: to be the officers' political voice. Cierva clearly did not have the charisma nor the following which Maura possessed and the most he could aspire to, at least for the time being, was to be in charge of the War Department. Yet from the first moment he was to make clear his particular status in the cabinet as a minister appointed personally by the monarch and enjoying the support of the Juntas.[44]

The Regionalists' strength had been confirmed by the presence for the first time of two of their men in a central government. Cambó had refused to join the government but had placed his friend Juan Ventosa at the head of the Treasury. Moreover, to disguise his manoeuvre, the Lliga leader had per-suaded Felipe Rodés, a left-wing Catalanist with Republican leanings, to accept the Education portfolio. Their plan to achieve Catalanist hegemony in Madrid had been successfully completed. Politics could no longer be con-ducted without their support.

The Lliga's manoeuvre was a shock to the other parliamentarians. The Regionalists deserted them and joined forces with the hated governing oli-garchy. Melquiades Alvarez himself had been approached by Alhucemas, and when the latter refused to endorse the Assembly programme, he declined to join the government. On behalf of the other members of the Assembly, he stated that he could neither join nor support a solution which did not make its central objective the political renovation of the country by means of a Constituent Cortes. He could see that the presence of Cierva in a coalition cabinet was a guarantee that no profound transformation would happen. His surprise was total when Cambó, seated next to him when Alhucemas made his offer, swiftly accepted. Cambó's switching of allegiance was regarded as a betrayal by the left. His move had been decisive in saving the regime and dashing all hopes of political democratization.[45]

Cambó's sudden about-face in November 1917, abandoning the progres-sive forces for an alliance with the oligarchy in Madrid, was not surprising. It was simply a defence of his class interests. After the August revolt and bearing in mind the events taking place in Russia, the bourgeoisie was scared. The situation might get out of control. Forced to choose between its hostility to the established ruling oligarchies and its fear of the working class, the bourgeoisie followed the course it had consistently adopted since 1848: to use the proletariat as a travelling companion to put more pressure on the ruling class but, once the power of the latter had been broken, to seek an accommodation with the traditional governing elite in order to become part of the new ruling bloc.

In Cambó the industrial bourgeoisie found a highly competent machiavellian leader. Unlike the dynastic politicians, he knew what he wanted and how to get it. For months he threatened, manipulated and plotted with and against everybody. He created the Assembly and he also killed it as soon as his basic goals had been achieved: the hegemony of the two dynastic parties representing the landowning classes embodied in the *Turno* was destroyed; Catalan Regionalism was at the centre of decision-making with two portfolios including the Treasury; and the post of Minister of the Interior was in the hands of a neutral person.

When Dato was toppled, Cambó held out as long as he thought wise. He knew he had a good hand and played it well, but as the government crisis continued, he became worried that the stakes were too high. There was a risk that not only would the *Turno* parties be swept away but also that in consequence, either a military dictatorship or a period of anarchy would destroy his initiative. He felt that it was time to abandon the game and settle for what he considered to be an acceptable outcome.[46] Cambó even tried to justify his move by accusing his former partners in the Assembly of having been behind a far-reaching revolutionary process all the time. He professed himself as zealous as ever for political reform and declared himself happy with the creation of a coalition cabinet which put an end to the *Turno*. Cambó added that any ordinary Cortes, freely elected, was as competent as a Constituent Assembly to deal with constitutional reforms as with any other subject.[47]

Regardless of all the rhetoric, his disloyalty to the Assembly was an evident fact. The settlement of the 1917 crisis had given a breathing space to the monarchy in a moment of despair and possible deadlock, while a thorough political reform had been delayed if not finally abandoned. It was no wonder that Cambó's manoeuvre appeared to the other parties of the left as a betrayal for the sake of two seats in the Alhucemas ministry.[48] They declared that the new coalition cabinet looked like a patchwork contrivance put together to tide over the existing crisis. In fact, Cambó's main mistake was to refuse to play the role of Kerensky when there was no Spanish Lenin to render that role dangerous.

9

THE YEAR 1918

The structural crisis of the liberal monarchy

The year 1917 revealed that Spain's ruling order was plunged into a deep crisis of authority and legitimacy. This had begun at the turn of the century, gathering momentum during the war years as a near-feudal political structure was faced with the challenge of new economic and political realities. Still the old discredited governing classes were strong enough to prevent the triumph of the forces seeking thorough change. Antonio Gramsci, the leading Italian political thinker, has defined that situation as an 'organic crisis of the state'.[1]

From late 1917 onwards the social situation worsened. Both cities and countryside were seething with discontent produced by food and fuel shortages. The *crisis de subsistencias* was causing widespread desperation. An index based on a figure of 100 for overall prices in 1914 had shot up in September 1918 to 161.8 in the cities and 172.8 in the countryside. The price of a kilo of bread had increased 62.1 per cent; of meat, 78.2 per cent; potatoes, 80 per cent; rice, 50 per cent; sugar, 56.7 per cent; a litre of milk, 40 per cent and a dozen eggs, 85.3 per cent. Salaries were lagging far behind. Over the same period they had increased by a mere 25.6 per cent and 35.1 per cent for the average male and female worker respectively.[2] In December 1917 the government established a new organization called the Comisaría de Subsistencias with the task of setting quotas for the export of basic products and combating profiteers and speculators. Like similar bodies in the past, it failed utterly to accomplish anything positive.

Famine, unemployment and misery forced the distressed population to acts of violence and disorder. Throughout 1918 disturbances became a common feature all over the country. They took the form of food riots, demonstrations for cheaper goods and assaults on shops and bakeries, these often involving women and children. There were clashes and sporadic rioting in Valencia, Salamanca, Madrid, Santander, Corunna and Cadiz. In early January a general strike broke out in Malaga and Alicante and in both places several women were shot dead while demanding cheaper food. Women broke into several bakeries in Barcelona, where a state of war was subsequently declared. Three people were killed in Noblejas (Ciudad Real) during food riots. The following month there were several casualties in Palma de Majorca due to protests at the lack of charcoal, and mutinies and arrests in Barcelona and Valencia. The atmosphere of chaos and violence continued for the rest of the year, but by then the epicentre of the disturbances had shifted from the cities to the Andalusian countryside.

The Socialist movement did not profit from the widespread feeling of gloom and desperation. Disturbances were spontaneous acts of rebellion as the militant masses were left leaderless. *El Socialista* and *España* accurately reported the violent events and accused the government of doing nothing, either to alleviate the suffering of the people or to put an end to the huge profits enjoyed by wheat-growers and shipowners. However, after the experience of the previous August the Socialist leadership was not prepared to undertake more revolutionary initiatives. A proposal by the CNT on 17 January 1918 to launch a joint general strike demanding amnesty was rapidly rebuffed by the Socialists. They claimed that it would only give the government an excuse to postpone the general elections and suspend constitutional guarantees in the country.[3]

The UGT–PSOE emerged demoralized from the experiences of the summer of 1917. Recovery for the Spanish Marxists meant a return to their traditional reformist practices. Thus they swiftly confirmed their alliance with the Republicans, organized the electoral campaign and pursued the release of their comrades in prison.[4] The PSOE's Madrid branch voted in favour of selecting the members of the strike committee as candidates for the next local elections.[5] On 25 November a pro-amnesty demonstration of 30,000 people gathered in Madrid. Yet the approach adopted by the Socialists was one of extreme caution. Julián Besteiro wrote from his prison cell that Pablo Iglesias and the editor of *El Socialista*, Mariano García Cortés, were behaving disgracefully in trying to erase the memory of the August strike.[6]

The Bolshevik take-over in Russia was not altogether welcomed by the Spanish Socialists. Totally dominated by their pro-Allied views, they received the news with misgivings. *El Socialista* mentioned it for the first time on 9 November 1917. It described this crucial event merely as the triumph of the maximalist tendency in Russia. The following day the newspaper's attitude was entirely negative. It feared that the Bolshevik revolution might become an obstacle to the Allied victory:

> We regret the news we have received from Russia. We believe that for the time being the mission of that great country is to devote all its energy to the task of crushing German imperialism . . . If the events of today were to give rise to a separate peace, to a desertion of the Western Alliance which is faced with the enemy of all liberties and popular rights, what will then be left of that revolution?

The PSOE's leaders clearly sided with the Menshevik position in Russia. They were deeply upset by news of the Bolshevik victory. On 29 March 1918 Pablo Iglesias wrote that the 'Russian perturbation' would not last long. Comment on the Russian Revolution totally disappeared from the pages of *El Socialista*. Despite, or perhaps because of, the glaring reality of social distress and a political vacuum in Spain, the Bolshevik example was not analysed, simply ignored. Instead the Socialists concentrated on electoral practices (despite the notorious corruption of the Spanish political system) and in the international arena they continued to express their support for the Allied cause. This approach encouraged the creation of an antileadership tendency within the Socialist movement. It brought together the neutralist minority and the revolutionary wing of the party around a new journal, *Nuestra Palabra*, founded in the summer of 1918. They organized several pro-Bolshevik meetings from that autumn. The objective was both to combat the reformist trend within the organization and to reform the rigid orthodoxy and oligarchical structure of the party. *Nuestra Palabra* was to be the cradle of the future Spanish Communist party, created when the final split occurred in the spring of 1921.[7]

The CNT did not let the opportunity pass. Unlike the Socialists, deeply chastened by their experiment with revolutionary politics, the Anarcho-Syndicalists felt confirmed in their belief in direct action.[8] By launching a vigorous campaign against the high cost of living and the miseries of the toiling classes, Anarcho-Syndicalism became after 1918 the leading workers' organization in Spain. In its rapid growth, the CNT benefited from the growing militancy of the workers and their prevailing rebellious mood. It confirmed its supremacy both in the southern countryside and in the industrial northeast, even making inroads into traditional Socialist strongholds such as Asturias and Vizcaya. Its naturally revolutionary instincts and antiparliamentary leanings were in tune with the wishes of the distressed masses. The CNT certainly paid more attention to the Russian Revolution than did the UGT.[9] Ironically, unlike the more moderate Syndicalists who showed restraint on receipt of information from Russia, it was the more orthodox Anarchists who could not contain their enthusiasm. Since they were virtually unaware of the role played by the Communist party, the revolution appeared to them as a confirmation of their own vision of revolutionary spontaneity.[10]

The impact of the Russian Revolution was especially formidable in the Andalusian countryside, where in May 1918 the hitherto independent Andalusian Regional Confederation of landless labourers, the Federación Regional Andaluza (FRA), joined the CNT. The anarchic mood of rebellion had never been extinguished in that region. Working under staggeringly poor living conditions on large estates or *latifundios* and practically at the mercy of semi-feudal landowners, peasants in southern Spain had a tradition of sporadic uprisings and insurrections that were put down with cruelty by the authorities. The instrument of repression was usually the brutal Civil Guard, although at times of greater tension the army was used.

The outbreak of the war in 1914 had found the rural south disorganized and apathetic. The general strike in August 1917 went almost unnoticed. However, news of the Russian Revolution was to change everything. Knowledge of the Bolshevik victory and the subsequent land expropriation provided the impulse needed to trigger an upheaval in the Spanish countryside. Overnight hundreds of workers' centres sprang up and membership of the Anarcho-Syndicalist movement expanded. The first strikes began in March of 1918 with Córdoba becoming the epicentre of the movement. Buildings were set on fire, land seized, crops burned, and hundreds of enthusiastic Anarchists travelled from village to village spreading news of the Russian Revolution. On 27 October 1918 an Anarcho-Syndicalist Congress was held at Castro del Río (Córdoba) with the task of co-ordinating the revolutionary wave. A minimum programme was approved demanding higher wages, an eight-hour working day, expulsion of foreign workers unless there was full employment and the suppression of *destajo* (piecework).

The landowners were thunderstruck. Despite the apparent moderation of the demands, if implemented they would represent a real revolution in the countryside. The power of the landowners rested on their knowledge that there was an unlimited reserve of hands that they could exploit at will. Peasants worked from sunrise to sunset for miserable wages. Furthermore, outside workers acting as blackleg labour were often brought from distant areas to put extra pressure on the local workers. Thus the rising militancy and organizational activity of the peasantry in 1918 threatened the status quo in the countryside. Naturally, the rural bosses were not prepared to accept their world being turned upside down. A terrible conflict loomed ahead which would reach its climax during the years 1919 and 1920.[11]

Simultaneously, a crucial event was taking place that led to the rapid reconstruction and expansion of the CNT after 1918. The Catalan regional branch of the CNT, the Confederación Regional del Trabajo, held a congress at Sants (Barcelona) between 28 June and 1 July 1918. Several fundamental resolutions were passed. Workers could have different political leanings but the CRT stressed direct action as the only valid weapon of their struggle. Much of the appeal and strength of the CRT stemmed from its adoption of industrial unionism in the form of the so-called *sindicatos únicos*. The new *sindicatos únicos* attempted to include all the workers in a given area working in different jobs but in the same industry. Henceforth the whole labour force would be divided into thirteen industrial activities or *ramos*. The number of strikes would be reduced, but at the same time the duration of the conflict would be longer and the strength of the movement greater. The Catalan labour movement was transformed from weak, disunited unions sustained by small groups of activists into a powerful mass organization.[12]

The CRT's new strategy, later adopted by the CNT, represented the triumph of the pragmatist Syndicalists Salvador Seguí and Angel Pestaña, who now became President of the CRT and editor of *Solidaridad Obrera* respectively. By late 1918 the CNT had 114,000 members with over 70,000 in Catalonia alone. By a year later its growth had been remarkable. The national organization could boast almost 800,000 militants, over half of them in Catalonia.[13] Thus in 1918 the CNT laid the foundations which would allow it to replace the UGT as the main movement representing the interests of the working classes. The amalgamation of the proletariat into *sindicatos únicos* provided an extremely efficient weapon with which to conduct the social struggle. The bourgeoisie soon realized that the newly reorganized CNT presented a serious threat. In order to safeguard its class interests, it would seek the destruction of the *sindicatos únicos*. Years of violence and terror were forthcoming.

While social distress, economic dissatisfaction, ideological militancy and brutal class struggle were emerging into the open, the political deadlock in the state was becoming a reality. The ruling *Turno Pacífico* had been left behind by the times, but the incorporation of the Catalan bourgeoisie gave a new lease of life to the regime. In the last year of the war the monarchist factions ended up cobbling together coalitions fighting for survival and continuity but paying lip service to the idea of change. They temporarily halted the downfall of the ruling order but could not solve the crisis. Lacking clear-cut ideological principles and riddled by factionalism, they found it impossible to agree on a common agenda. Bogged down by problems of legitimacy and credibility from the outset, they failed miserably to tackle the serious economic and social problems confronting the nation. Problems multiplied on all fronts, and a population already suffering grinding deprivation became restive.

The coalition cabinet that had been led by the Marquis of Alhucemas since November 1917 never worked as a team but followed different directions while the socio-economic crisis worsened by the day. They behaved not as a real administration but as a shadow of one. Public opinion was never enthusiastic about the government of supposed renovation.[14] At best, as in the case of the *Maurista* Angel Ossorio, the monarchist coalition was regarded with uncertainty and given the benefit of the doubt since nothing could be worse than the former Dato administration. The left rejected it outright and considered it to be an obstacle to the victory of democratic principles. Romanones, whose own faction was represented in the coalition by one minister, called it an 'engendro caótico' ('chaotic freak').[15] Santiago Alba's response was even more indicative of the increasing factionalism and disintegration of the dynastic parties. He accused Alhucemas of having wasted a precious opportunity to create a modern and radical government which could include leftist representatives. Alba thus stated openly his intention to break with the faction of the Liberal party led by the Marquis. He left Julio Burrell, a former

Minister of Education and one of his closest supporters, to launch a vicious attack on the government. Burrell wrote that the cabinet was merely a coalition of men who, with the exception of the Catalanists, did not represent anyone. He was in tune with the majority of the country when he pointed out that it was difficult to see how the authoritarian Cierva could work with the antimilitarist Rodés, or the Regionalist Ventosa and Rodés with the Centralist Alcalá Zamora; but above all Burrell wondered how a government containing people like Alhucemas and Cierva could preside over any political renovation.[16] Thereafter Alba founded his own group, the Liberal Left, which by early 1918 possessed its own journal, *La Libertad*.

Indeed the government could not have offered a more chaotic image than when on its first day in power three different statements were released to the press. One came from Cierva, clarifying the distance that separated him from the other members of the cabinet and stressing that his presence was due to the personal insistence of the monarch. A second statement emanated from the Catalanists, claiming their adherence to the principles of the Assembly and their determination to reform the political system; and a final one was delivered by the other ministers, declaring that the existing coalition was not a fusion of parties but a transitory union imposed by circumstances. They, 'men of goodwill', aimed at continuing the policy of neutrality and dealing with urgent socio-economic problems, and intended to summon a new parliament without any kind of ministerial interference. With this inauguration the new government could not avoid being viewed as a pathetic experiment and as a marriage of convenience which was doomed to break up at the first serious set-back.

Initially the general impression was that the most serious threat to the survival of the cabinet was represented by the Catalanist ministers. Cambó's crucial role in the creation of the coalition government led many to believe that Alhucemas, a weak and malleable leader, was just a puppet.[17] The Catalan leader was considered to be the real power, the mastermind pulling the strings behind the scenes. This seemed apparent as the Lliga was making no secret of its plan to extend its political influence beyond the Catalan borders. In December Cambó and the other leaders of Catalan Regionalism initiated a huge propaganda tour throughout northern Spain, Valencia and even Andalusia. The idea of a peaceful political revolution which could appeal to the national bourgeoisie was still very much on the cards. The neutrality of the administration in the forthcoming elections offered Cambó a golden opportunity to sell his programme to similar groups all over Spain.

In February 1918, *El Liberal* published a controversial article describing how during a lunch at the Restaurante del Parque in Barcelona, Cambó had stated that he had advised the king to form the Alhucemas coalition. The Catalan leader claimed that he could have been in the government except that he did not want to take on that responsibility. In fact, he said that he did not need to be a minister, since it was easier to control Alhucemas, a weak little man, from outside or through Ventosa, the Lliga minister in charge of the Treasury. Cambó then boasted that after the next general election the Regionalists would have 70 or 80 deputies, so it would be impossible to rule Spain without them. The Catalan politician claimed that he would be presiding over the next government which would automatically grant Home Rule to Catalonia. Yet Cambó reminded his audience that he was not a separatist. On the contrary, he said, the duty of the Lliga was to rule not only in Catalonia but in Spain. Catalonia must become the Prussia of the Iberian kingdoms. The Lliga would naturally be at the centre of that political initiative.[18] Thus Cambó was bent on an immediate general election. The Cortes was finally dissolved in early January 1918 and the election was called for 24 February.

Yet the real danger, not only to the government but to constitutional politics, came from Cierva. The latter's immediate goal was to neutralize the Juntas' political leanings by the passing of a military reform law tailored to their demands. It raised salaries, increased employment opportunities and established promotion by strict seniority in both war and peace. The main problem affecting the army, that of excess personnel, was deliberately ignored for fear of alienating the officers.[19] The hope was that a satisfied army would not only drop all its regenerationist dreams but would be more willing than ever to serve as the praetorian guard of the monarchy. Cierva constantly visited barracks and met officers. He went out of his way to praise the Juntas and describe them as a movement born out of patriotism. All their excesses, including vetoes, were condoned by the minister.[20] In turn he sought to purge the reformist and idealist elements from their ranks, in particular Colonel Márquez, and to manipulate the officers to build his own power base. This inevitably hastened the erosion of civil supremacy.

On 26 December, *El Imparcial* published an article written by the Conservative Sánchez de Toca. Undoubtedly his words were partly motivated by the role played by the Juntas in the fall of the Dato administration. Nevertheless, his message was an accurate and precise attack on the officers' trade unions. He described the Juntas as a corrosive element in the army, the opposite of what the armed services ought to be. According to Sánchez de Toca, Syndicalism was a basic form of economic struggle which was to be expected and accepted in the working classes but never in the army. He described military syndicalism as a source of abuses and authoritarian demands, the negation of discipline and the violation of the soldier's oath to defend the flag. Sánchez de Toca begged the Minister for War to put an end to this situation.

Sánchez de Toca's appeal went unheard. Cierva had other things on his mind. On the same day as *El Imparcial* issued Sánchez de Toca's article, an isolated Márquez resigned as Chairman of the Central Junta at Barcelona. As an idealist committed to bringing about a real cleansing of politics, Colonel Márquez represented the kind of dangerous officer who had to be eliminated if Cierva wanted to succeed. Through a strategy of rewards and promises the minister had no great difficulty in winning over the officers and eroding the colonel's position. When the final showdown between the leading *juntero* and the Murcian *cacique* arrived, Márquez found himself abandoned by his former colleagues and forced to resign. He was replaced by Colonel Echevarría, who had been Chairman of the Provisional Central Junta in June 1917.

Márquez refused to be silent and on 30 January 1918 *El Mundo* published his version of the clash with the minister. The colonel regretted the readiness with which his resignation was accepted by the other members of the Central Junta and accused Cierva of having worked for his dismissal. According to Márquez, in October Cierva had contacted the officers' representatives in Madrid (Commandant Espino and Captains García Rodríguez and Villar) through Julio Amado, editor of *La Correspondencia Militar*. Those officers had exceeded their powers. Without consulting the other *junteros*, they had first supported the retention of General Marina at the War Department and had later thrown their support behind Cierva. Márquez, from the beginning, had opposed Cierva's strategy of buying off the officers through rewards and promises. Thus he objected first to sending a letter of congratulations to the new Minister for War and then to answering a questionnaire sent by Cierva to several leading officers. When the *junteros* in Madrid returned to Barcelona, they forced a vote which brought about Márquez's resignation.

In a second letter to *El Sol* (13 March 1918) Márquez bitterly attacked the Juntas, suggesting that they had nothing in common with those of June 1917. According to the colonel, the Juntas had lost touch with their original objectives and only served as a pedestal for one man, Cierva. The alliance of the minister and the Juntas constituted the greatest threat to the life of the nation. He concluded with these words for his former companions:

> You will open an abyss between the army and all classes of the nation. You must not forget that any army without the love and esteem of the nation which supports it is destined to plunge itself into the lowest depths and to weep tears of blood in company with it.

Márquez was court-martialled two days later and expelled from the army. The alliance between Cierva and the officers had been cemented in January 1918 with the dissolution of the so-called Unión de las Clases de Tropa or Juntas of NCOs. They were set up immediately after those of the officers and from the outset regarded by the latter as an embarrassment and potential threat. Their demands were moderate in the extreme, but their existence represented a parallel source of power in the barracks that the officers could not tolerate.[21] The officers found in Cierva the perfect ally to proceed against the NCOs.

After spreading various unfounded rumours that the Juntas of NCOs were preparing a revolution in collaboration with the PSOE, the government decreed their dissolution. On the morning of 4 January all troops were confined to barracks and the NCOs brought before their commanding officers. They were given the choice of dismissal or signing a declaration swearing their loyalty to the monarchy and pledging themselves to break up their Juntas. Several hundred who refused were automatically expelled from the army. Anticipating possible revolt, the minister had taken precautionary measures such as interrupting telegraphic and telephonic communications all over the country and mobilizing the Civil Guard.[22] The king and the officers were delighted with the energetic attitude of the Minister for War. The former, scared by the news arriving from Russia, was delighted to see 'revolutionaries' purged from the army.[23] Cierva, who could now even claim to be the saviour of the regime, was at the peak of his career. This authoritarian and despotic character, backed by the army and with the sympathy of the monarch, was becoming a threat to Liberalism in the country.[24]

Both the local and the general elections, in November 1917 and February 1918, respectively confirmed the growing crisis of legitimacy and decline of the dynastic parties. However, no political force could really draw solace from the results. Those groups based on public opinion made consistent advances in the large towns, but *caciquismo* reigned supreme over rural Spain where elections were actually won.

In the local elections of November 1917, *Mauristas* and the Republican–Socialist alliance triumphed in Madrid. A similar process was seen in the major cities. In Barcelona Regionalists and Republicans swept away the dynastic competition. Yet in the countryside, official candidates were returned. Almost all the newspapers claimed that the results, especially those in the capital, indicated the erosion and decline of the *Turno* parties and the consolidation of alternative forces on both the right and left of the political arena.[25] Public opinion was gradually turning against the bulwarks of the Restoration system. It was impossible to defeat them in the countryside, but it was felt that an overwhelming swing in the cities could prove enough to bring the regime down.[26]

The general election of 24 February 1918, supposedly the gateway to political renovation, proved to be disappointing. Hopes that it would be conducted without official manipulation were soon dashed. The Minister of the Interior, the apolitical Viscount Matamala, was the guarantor of a clean vote. He certainly did not intervene in the results and even issued a statement ordering the civil governors to take measures against electoral cheating and corruption. If Matamala fulfilled his task, the same could not be said of his deputies. They were busy fixing the elections in the traditional way to benefit Alhucemas's Liberals, Dato's Conservatives and Cierva's friends. Romanones, an old expert in these practices, complained to Alhucemas virtually up to the eve of the ballot, about all sorts of manoeuvres which favoured Conservative or *Ciervista* candidates to the detriment of his own followers.[27] Clearly, if Romanones's political friends were suffering from unfair treatment and even persecution, electoral manipulation was certain to be more acute in the case of Republicans or Socialists. The election of February 1918 was falsified, but nevertheless the fact that it was organized by a coalition government, with a neutral at the Ministry of the Interior, limited to a certain extent the fixing of the results and encouraged more competition than in the past. Yet the provinces remained essentially under the control of the *caciques*, who had no intention of withdrawing to allow a free vote. Their activities, together with the break-up of the dynastic parties, only helped to produce a new parliament more fragmented and ungovernable than those returned in the past.

The final results confirmed the tendency already indicated in the local elections of November 1917: the overwhelming supremacy of the dynastic groups in rural Spain and a certain advance of democracy in the large cities. Furthermore, it brought to light the final disintegration and factionalism of the monarchists. The Liberal party was the clear winner, but its representation was divided between 94 followers of Alhucemas, 40 of Romanones, 25 of Alba and ten who were friends of two other independent Liberal leaders, the Germanophile editor of *El Día* and current Minister of Public Works, Alcalá Zamora, and the former minister and editor of *El Imparcial*, Rafael Gasset. The Liberal party was damaged beyond repair. The Conservative party presented a similar picture. There were in the new Cortes 94 *Datistas*, 29 *Mauristas* and 25 *Ciervistas*. The Catalan Regionalists won a majority in their region with 20 deputies, but the strategy of creating a nationwide coalition did not succeed except in the Basque Country. There were 15 other Spanish Regionalists, seven of them members of the Basque Nationalist Party. Republicans and Reformists did not fare particularly well. They returned 15 and 8 deputies respectively, slightly fewer than in 1916. Significantly enough, those like Marcelino Domingo or Azzati who represented radical positions triumphed and those defending more moderate stances such as Lerroux or Melquiades Alvarez failed to get elected. The moral victors were the Socialists, whose representation rose from one deputy to six. The four members of the strike committee were returned: Julián Besteiro for Madrid, Largo Caballero for Barcelona, Andrés Saborit for Oviedo and Daniel Anguiano for Valencia.[28]

Any hope of sweeping renovation was dead and buried. The dynastic groups, totally opposed to any political transformation, were still in control. Most of their representatives owed their seats to the established practices of influence, intrigue and bribery. Yet an important breach with the past had taken place. In earlier elections, the government which dissolved the Cortes had always returned with a working majority from the polls. For the first time, in 1918 a parliament was produced in which no party had an absolute majority. The two traditional leading groups appeared to have been broken up by internal dissent into a constellation of small factions.[29] Political deadlock and instability were the immediate consequences.

The coalition cabinet lasted only one more month, a period marked by agony and impotence. Even before the elections a disappointed Cambó, feeling the growing threat presented by Cierva, warned that a new crisis might not have an easy solution.[30] The impression of the general election had not yet faded when the Minister for War took off his mask and began to bully his fellow ministers into accepting his decisions. Knowing that he could count on the backing of the king and the Juntas, Cierva soon began to behave as a dictator.

At the first cabinet meeting after the general election, Cierva brought about the resignation of the government. He asked why a cabinet which could not rely on a clear majority in the Cortes should be allowed to continue. His objective was to get rid of the two Catalanist ministers who represented the renovationist tendency in the government and could present the most serious objections to his military reform plan. He succeeded when the king requested Alhucemas to remain as Prime Minister and both Catalanists, Rodés and Ventosa, were replaced by Liberals, the former Major of Madrid, Luis Silvela, and a wealthy Catalan manufacturer, the Count Caralt, respectively.[31] A satisfied Cierva then declared to the press that he could not devote all his energy to satisfying the fair demands of the officers in his forthcoming bill without a strong government behind him.[32] He then proceeded with his own agenda.

In early March he presented his military reform bill. It did not reform anything. On the contrary, it represented a further swelling of the defence budget by the fantastic amount of 92 million pesetas. It deliberately avoided the sensitive subject of a reduction in the number of officers and instead increased the number of active posts by 1,714. The proposed pay scale increased salaries for all ranks, rewarding the already comfortably off senior officers more than the truly impoverished lower ranks.[33] It was a sop to the Juntas. The country was starving and the state was shifting much-needed capital to appease the officer corps. Furthermore, showing a total contempt for constitutional formalities and without warning, on 6 March Cierva introduced his bill by royal decree, alleging that he wanted to avoid any delay in its passage through the recently created parliament. The political establishment was shocked. Most dynastic politicians were prepared to appease the Juntas but Cierva's unilateral action amounted almost to armed robbery.[34]

Sánchez de Toca, a fierce critic of the Juntas in the past, wrote in *El Liberal* that they were a monster taking over the sovereignty of the state.[35] Romanones and Melquiades Alvarez declared that the political class should unite to prevent the Minister for War from sabotaging civil supremacy. Romanones told the Prime Minister that to yield to pressure at such a moment would be cowardice. He warned that if this occurred he would no longer collaborate with the government and all his friends in the administration would leave office.[36]

The authority of the state was being trampled upon. The officers, with the complicity of one minister, were showing who was the *de facto* power in the country. A delegation from the Central Junta in Barcelona had arrived in the capital. There were all sorts of wild rumours. It was said that hot-heads in the army had threatened to go and break Sánchez de Toca's head and to arrest Romanones and take him to the French border.[37] Cierva himself took on the role of defending the honour of the army. Once more without informing any of the other members of the cabinet, he delivered a statement arguing that Sánchez de Toca's declarations were just a product of 'mean political interests and sad memories of frustrated ambitions'.[38] Alhucemas, realizing that all authority had escaped from his hands, presented the resignation of his entire cabinet, and a case unique in history occurred when all complied except Cierva. He was acting as a dictator and, backed by the army, refused to leave office.[39]

In that chaotic situation all eyes turned to Maura as the man who might save the day. It was believed that he had enough authority and charisma both among officers and politicians to form a new cabinet and restore civil supremacy. Yet as in June 1917, Maura refused to climb to power by dealing with the Juntas. In a second lesson in liberal principles, he declined to be in charge of a new government and affirmed that Alhucemas should continue in power and open the Cortes as quickly as possible. Maura declared that if civil supremacy was not to be respected then those who showed such disrespect should take on the responsibility of government themselves. Asked by journalists if he would support a solution presided over by Cierva, the veteran statesman answered that to that man he would give 'neither advice, nor support, nor vote'.[40]

A formula that barely concealed the humiliation of the civil authority was finally reached. All the ministers agreed to withdraw their resignations and accept Cierva's royal decree, but in turn the military reforms would not be implemented until July, after parliament had discussed them.[41] The hand of the monarch was clearly behind this formula. He wanted to please his army above all else, constitutional guidelines were of secondary importance. Alfonso even summoned Romanones to the Palace and told him in strong terms to drop his opposition to Cierva and his bill.[42] Thus, the crisis of authority in the political system continued to grow. The demoralized dynastic politicians once again had to bow before the obstinate pressure of an authoritarian politician who could rely on the backing of both king and army. To add insult to injury, the Juntas refused to dissolve themselves although they declared that henceforth they would acquire a technical character as their only concern was the well-being of the services.[43]

Cierva's position was stronger than ever after the crisis in mid-March. Furthermore, Benito Márquez, the only officer who could have prevented him from manipulating the Juntas, was expelled from the army in March 1918. Having won the day on the military issue, Cierva was to display his authoritarianism when faced by civil disorder. Following the emergence of military Juntas de Defensa in June 1917, similar bodies had been set up throughout the public sector and the bureaucracy. The corporatist fever that had gripped the country since the summer of 1917 was clear proof of the collapse of the authority of the state. Encouraged by the success of the officers in obtaining economic gains and power, the civil Juntas sought to emulate their military counterparts. Yet here they were to run into Cierva's determination to restore authority by force. His ruthless dissolution of the Juntas of NCOs in January had already revealed that he was prepared to treat the officers differently from others. On 21 February 1918 the Juntas of Postal and Telegraph workers initiated a passive strike, demanding that a grant of three million pesetas be allocated to them without delay in order to meet the cost of increased staff and new material. They enjoyed the solidarity of all the other civil Juntas in the bureaucracy.[44]

Cierva took upon himself the task of dealing with them in his usual manner. By two royal decrees on 13 and 16 March, the management of the postal and telegraphic services was transferred from the Interior Ministry to the War Office. The militarization of those services was ordered and, as with the NCOs, the staff were presented with the choice of accepting the dissolution of their Juntas or being sacked. As the conflict threatened to spread to other sectors the government dissolved by decree the Juntas at the Treasury, Interior and Public Works. Public opinion was on the side of the civil servants. Nearly everybody agreed that the way the same cabinet yielded before the army but employed force to deal with others was shameful. There was widespread fear that the country was heading towards a one-man dictatorship.[45]

Cierva's tough stand backfired. Civil servants en masse abandoned their posts and refused to disband their organizations. The military, lacking trained personnel, were unable to run the services. Chaos was total. Mail was not delivered and communications were brought to a standstill. In the meantime, the Prime Minister behind Cierva's back began to pursue a conciliatory solution and initiated talks with the strikers. The Minister for War, who wanted to fight them to the end, presented his resignation, forcing the fall of the cabinet. On 19 March the Cortes was opened only to be closed a few minutes later when the fall of the government was announced. For some ministers it was both debut and farewell.[46]

The situation was as critical as, if not more so than, it had been in October 1917. There was widespread turmoil in cities and the countryside caused by rampant inflation and food shortages. The strike of the civil service had paralysed the country. The political vacuum seemed insuperable. The *Turno* had been destroyed and the coalition which had replaced it had been found wanting. Ironically, there was no challenge to the regime from Republicans or Socialists. The former lacked strength and the latter limited its opposition to expressing solidarity with the struggle of the civil servants. But the constitutional system was hanging by a thread. Cierva had caused three government crises in less than a month. He was now in a position to make his bid for power, backed by the resolution of the Juntas not to accept anyone else at the

War Office. He could offer a political alternative: a cabinet presided over by himself with leading *junteros* as ministers; the only way to restore law and order.[47]

The crisis appeared insoluble. Maura was asked to form a cabinet but he failed to win enough support. Politicians were demoralized. Cambó argued in *La Tribuna* that only a strong monarchist coalition could work and halt the crisis.[48] Romanones, well aware of what the army was plotting, and knowing that his sovereign was half inclined to try Cierva's experiment, came up with the final solution.[49] It consisted of the monarch summoning all the main faction leaders to the Palace at the same time. Once there the king made an earnest appeal to them to bury all their differences and work together to resolve the existing deadlock. He threatened to abdicate if they could not agree on a common agenda. The idea, launched by Cambó in his article and then put into practice by Romanones with the complicity of the monarch, paid off. By the following morning the most impressive government in the history of the Restoration monarchy had been created.[50] The new cabinet was presided over by Antonio Maura, the most charismatic and prestigious monarchist leader. It contained four former Prime Ministers, two party leaders, one ex-minister and former Speaker of the Senate, and two members of the military, one of whom had recently been Minister for War and had worked alongside the Juntas.

Prime Minister:	Antonio Maura (*Maurista*)
Foreign Office:	Eduardo Dato (Conservative)
Interior:	Marquis of Alhucemas (Liberal Democrat)
Public Works:	Francesc Cambó (Lliga Regionalista)
Justice:	Count Romanones (Liberal *Romanonista*)
Treasury:	Augusto González Besada (Conservative)
Education:	Santiago Alba (left Liberal)
War Office:	General Marina
Admiralty:	Admiral Pidal

The formation of a coalition cabinet of outstanding politicians caused general rejoicing. It was received with enthusiasm and admiration.[51] A constitutional formula had prevailed over Cierva's bid for power. Amidst a general feeling of gloom and impotence, the regime had managed to produce what appeared to be the highest model of national authority. However, not even the new national government could break the political deadlock. The dynastic politicians were unable or unwilling to meet the growing demands generated by the war. Once the enchantment of the moment vanished, the artificiality of the flamboyant new administration was revealed in full. Officers and king continued acting as an anticonstitutional party with powers of veto. The result was social conflict, political instability, and, in the end, an irretrievable structural crisis in the liberal system.[52]

It is extremely revealing that Antonio Maura, the man who was supposed to supervise the reconstruction of the political order, did not share the optimism of the others. On his very first morning in office he confided to his son Gabriel: 'They kept me away for ten years, years which could have been the most useful of my life, and now I am seized to preside over the whole lot. Let us see how long the charade lasts.'[53] Maura was right. The National Government proved a ramshackle affair. It lasted just long enough to see the end of the war in Europe, but it failed miserably to solve the urgent problems of the country. It fared slightly better than the previous administration, but only because the names of its members could impress public opinion and give a false image of strength and consistency. Also, there was no Cierva at hand ready to subvert civil supremacy. Yet the record of the so-called 'Ministerio de Primates' would be very poor. In the international field, the desperate maintenance of neutrality despite all the evidence of German aggression looked not unlike impotence and humiliation. In domestic matters, nothing constructive was ever achieved, as the government could never overcome its internal dissent and personal incompatibilities.

Since the fall of Romanones in April 1917 the domestic crisis and the subsequent collapse of authority had virtually overshadowed the question of neutrality which had been so important during the last months of the Count's administration. It re-emerged in 1918 and for a second time threatened to involve Spain in the Great War. However, unlike Romanones, eager to side with the Western Powers, the National Government went to shameful and painful extremes to avoid doing so.

By the beginning of 1918, the Central Powers seemed to be gaining the upper hand. The Italians were routed at Caporetto by the Austro-German forces in the autumn of 1917 and only held out due to the arrival of massive Anglo-French reinforcements; submarine activities were resulting in crippling losses for the Allies; and after their successful bid for power, the Bolsheviks asked for an immediate armistice on all fronts, while the US contribution to the war effort was not expected to be felt until the summer. In December 1917, peace negotiations began between Bolshevik and German delegates. All the hopes that a revolution in Russia would soon be followed by workers' insurrections in Central Europe were dashed. There were huge peace demonstrations and strikes in Germany and Austria in January 1918, but their governing classes could still control the situation by convincingly pointing at the collapse of the Russian army as proof of their impending victory.

The Bolshevik government first tried to stall the negotiations in an attempt to win time, but they were forced back to the peace conference when the German military machine resumed its advances in the East. On 3 March 1918, the Russo-German treaty was signed at Brest-Litovsk. The Bolsheviks had to accept the harsh reality of the battlefield and surrender vast provinces and areas of the former Russian Empire which now came under the control of the Central Powers.[54] On 7 May, Romania also sued for peace. For the first time, Germany and her allies were freed from the nightmare of a war on two fronts and now could concentrate their power against the Western Allies. On 9 March, they began their last offensive and the biggest gamble of the entire conflict: an all-out assault against the Anglo-French defensive lines in a desperate effort to secure victory before the huge American reserves were able to reach the war zone.

In Spain, the revolutionary events in Russia and then the general strike of August helped to consolidate the position of Germany as the best friend of the existing regime. Ironically, it was the Central Powers, clearly ignoring Spanish neutrality, who continued to pursue an aggressive campaign, sinking vessels and subverting the social order through their financing of anarchist activities, while the Allies were themselves keen on propping up the existing regime.[55] After the events in Russia the previous year, Britain and France were extremely reluctant to interfere in Spanish internal affairs. They believed that as in Russia, the fall of the monarchy in Spain would inevitably lead to a situation of chaos from which only Germany would profit. Consequently, the Western Powers were eager to distance themselves from their Republican and Socialist 'friends'. Even France, facing the prospect of an all-out German offensive after the collapse of the eastern front, severed links with her Republican and Catalan supporters. In her hour of greatest need, France was anxious to show her respect for the existing status quo. Therefore, to placate the Spanish authorities, the French government in late 1917 replaced its ambassador Leon Geoffray with the more moderate Joseph Thierry.[56]

In fact, Spanish administrations confronting the international question found their hands tied. Crown, church and armed forces identified, especially after the fall of the autocracy in Russia, with the ideological values represented by the Central Powers and despised the principles of democracy and self-determination for which the Allies stood. Thus fighting alongside the Allies was to them a terrible mistake. They believed it would strengthen the hand of the anti-regime forces in Spain and lead to the tragic fate which had befallen Tsarism. They were therefore prepared to turn a blind eye to all the excesses committed or induced by Germany. After all, the sinking of some vessels or a few anarchist actions would not bring down the ruling order. Thus, though nominally the defender of order and authority, Germany could with impunity continue subsidizing ultra-left groups in an attempt to destroy Spanish commerce intended for the Allies.[57] The fragility and weakness of the liberal monarchy in Spain made it impossible to put into practice a coherent, firm and purposeful foreign policy.

In late 1917 the Western intelligence services observed how the Germans were providing vast amounts of money to purchase votes and *caciques* in order to return a friendly Cortes. There were rumours that the Central Powers had approached the Juntas and, in exchange for the future entry of Spain into the war on their side, they had offered to place at their disposal submarines, Zeppelins, aeroplanes, and a vast territorial booty which included Portugal and her colonies, Gibraltar, Tangier, French Morocco and Algeria. A worried Clemenceau suggested that British and French propaganda should combine their efforts. Britain turned down the proposal as she believed that France was popular only among Catalan, Republican and anticlerical circles.[58] There was a conviction that Spain could not afford to quarrel with the Allies, with whom her destiny was linked by reasons of geography and economy. The Allies commanded the supplies of cotton, oil and coal which Spain needed to continue her economic life. Furthermore, until the end of the war Britain believed that the existing regime, despite all its inadequacies, was the best possible in the circumstances, the alternative being a revolution which could only end in a military dictatorship:

> The end of the present system means revolution, and it is a very long way from being certain that a revolution would place the Republicans or any Liberal element of any kind in power. The present cabinet is the only alternative to a military government . . . it originated in a crisis caused by the pretensions of the army and the dictatorial airs assumed by its chosen statesman, the then Minister for War, Cierva, towards whom the king is believed for a moment to have leaned . . . The most powerful force in the country is the army, representative with the Church of law and order. It would certainly defeat the Left if the country was thrown into a revolutionary struggle . . . The Left is practically to a man, as a matter of principle, as strongly pro-Allied as the officers of the army and the men of the official world are for the most part pro-German . . . We have to pay the penalty of our principles; and perhaps we do not sufficiently realize how such phrases as 'making the world safe for democracy', 'final destruction of the poison of militarism', and the like, inevitably alienate the aristocratic and officer class in Spain.[59]

Faced with aggressive German diplomacy, succesive Spanish governments in 1918 offered a sad image of complacency, fear and submission, constantly looking the other way and disinclined to do anything. Complaints continued to pour into the Spanish Foreign Office about Morocco. The rebel leaders, Raisuli and Abd-el Malek, were openly supplied and advised by German agents with total impunity. Spanish Morocco was regarded in Western chancelleries as a hot-bed of German intrigue: a colony characterized by incompetence, jobbery and both active and passive pro-Germanism on the part of its authorities.[60] The weakness of the Spanish cabinets was at its worst in relation to the question of German espionage in the peninsula and on the matter of protecting the merchant fleet from submarine attacks.

Violence had always been present in the class struggle, especially in Anarchist fiefs, yet it began to acquire a particularly vicious character towards the end of the Great War. In Barcelona, vessels departing from the port with

166

cargo bound for Allied ports were torpedoed with great accuracy; production was sabotaged, disturbances paralysed the activity in many factories and industrialists were assassinated. In January 1918 the killing of José Barret, one of the leading Catalan employers in the metallurgy industry, shocked public opinion. Many Syndicalists were arrested and constitutional guarantees were suspended in Barcelona for over two months. Yet the question of who benefited from the crime remained. An industrialist who was popular among his workers and in whose factory there was no reason for social conflict had been attacked. One month later the left-wing newspaper *El Parlamentario* accused a former policeman, Guillermo Belles, of being a German agent who had infiltrated Anarchist groups in order to have Barret murdered. Belles had been questioned but released after the personal intervention of Manuel Bravo Portillo, the chief of Barcelona's political police.[61]

Two months later the recently founded newspaper *El Sol*, which owing to the intellectual quality of its staff had a large influence on public opinion, published a facsimile of a letter from the First Secretary of the German Embassy, Eberhard von Stohrer, to Miguel Pascual, one of the leading Anarchists in Madrid. It was evidence that the Anarchist leader was receiving money for the printing of revolutionary leaflets. It was an operation which counted on the blessing of the German ambassador himself, Prince Ratibor. There was no doubt about the veracity of the letter produced by the French Intelligence Services. When he agreed to be interviewed by *El Sol*, Pascual's revelations were shocking. He said he had paid several visits to the German embassy, where he was received by both Secretaries, von Stohrer and Grimm. He had been given instructions to create disturbances, organize revolutionary strikes to interfere with the export trade to the Allies, and foment attacks of every kind upon Count Romanones when he was in power. Pascual believed that his acceptance of German money did not clash with his own political leanings. He and many like him were more than willing to co-operate with the Germans since both Anarchists and Germans pursued the same goals. Pascual also claimed that he had been the first Anarchist whom the Germans had approached in the capital. They had singled him out soon after the Anarcho-Syndicalist Congress at Ferrol in April 1915, where he had given a speech in favour of international neutralism. Germany did not have many agents in Madrid as the city was mainly under the control of the UGT, a pro-Allied organization which the Germans had not managed to penetrate. It was very different in Barcelona where many militants including Francisco Roldán, the ex-General Secretary of the CNT, were in their pay. In fact, he had been told many times by von Stohrer to adopt the international line followed by the CNT organ, *Solidaridad Obrera*, published in Barcelona.[62]

The response of the Alhucemas cabinet, then close to its final collapse, was not only to ignore the offence revealed by the newspaper but also, at the request of Prince Ratibor, to ban the distribution of *El Sol*. By then thousands of copies had already been sold. *El Sol* agreed to publish Ratibor's version a few days later, but it failed utterly to dispel belief in German complicity in Anarchist campaigns. Ratibor acknowledged that Pascual had received some payment for his propaganda, but only because it was believed that he was a good Spanish patriot. As soon as it was discovered he had revolutionary ideas he had been dismissed. *El Sol* commented that even if the improbable account of the German ambassador was true, he had abused his diplomatic status, since he had financed material against politicians and industrialists of his host country. The government simply chose not to pursue the matter.[63]

Continuous revelations of German infiltration and manipulation of the CNT had an impact upon that organization. In June 1918 Angel Pestaña and a new team of collaborators replaced the former staff, thoroughly discredited by its acceptance of foreign financial aid, to re-organize *Solidaridad Obrera*. The newspaper had been kept afloat by undisclosed income and in turn had been publishing neutralist editorials.[64]

On 9 June the newspaper published a crucial article which revealed the close links of German intelligence with the local authorities. It had been the constant complaint of Western diplomats that the submarines which destroyed the Spanish mercantile marine with such contemptuous disregard for her neutrality were aided in their task by well-informed confederates on shore. In early June the suspicious sinking of the French vessel, *Provence*, near the Spanish north-east coast led to the conclusion that the port commandant at the small Catalan town of Palamós had been supplying German spies with timely information on the sailing of ships and particulars of their cargoes. A few days later, *Solidaridad Obrera* published two letters written by Manuel Bravo Portillo, chief of Barcelona's political police, showing that he was guilty of the same offence. The newspaper provided documentary evidence that Bravo Portillo had informed on the movements of the steamer *Joaquín Mumbrú* which left Barcelona on 20 December and was torpedoed in January near Madeira. The captain of the German submarine told the crew of the *Mumbrú* that he was merely following orders from Barcelona.

Solidaridad Obrera stated that it was providing the information 'to whoever might be interested'. It appeared that the authorities were not. On 17 June experts found that Bravo Portillo had indeed been the author of the letters and yet he was not lodged in gaol until the night of 20 June, giving him every opportunity to destroy compromising papers. Two accomplices were also arrested: Guillermo Belles, the ex-policeman who had been linked by *El Parlamentario* with the killing of the industrialist Barret, and Royo de San Martín, a morphine addict and gambler. The sudden death of the latter on 29 June aroused suspicions that he had been poisoned.[65]

The consequent investigation produced a startling and incredible story of corruption and depravation. Bravo Portillo's activities had been known by at least two civil governors, but his good connections in the social world had placed him in an untouchable position. He was married to the daughter of a vice-admiral, had served in the past as private secretary to General Weyler, the most senior officer in the army and a well-known Germanophile, and his brother was a commandant and leading *juntero* at the local garrison. He had been working for Germany since 1915 under the immediate orders of its two leading agents in the Catalan capital, Albert Honnermann and Friedrick Ruggeberg, and received a salary of 50 pesetas a day apart from expenses incidental to his services. His task was to provide information leading to the torpedoing of vessels and also to organize disruption in the factories of industrialists producing material for the Allied war effort. To those ends he made good use of informers and several members of the police force. One of these, Guillermo Belles, had made contact with some Anarchists working at Barret's concern, which produced shells 24 hours a day for the French army. There had been several unsuccessful attempts to launch strikes or to blow up the factory. Belles finally ordered the killing of the industrialist, almost certainly with the consent of Portillo and his German masters. The murder was carried out by Anarchist gunmen under the orders of Eduardo Ferrer, the Anarchist President of the CNT's Metalworkers' Trade Union and police informer. Bravo Portillo, who publicly boasted of his energy in defending law and order, distinguished himself in the persecution of Syndicalists who had nothing to do with the killing of Barret. He was denounced and his removal was demanded in the Cortes by the Catalan deputies Francesc Macià and Marcelino Domingo for his repressive methods. Among other acts, Portillo had sent his friend José Ezcurra, a lieutenant in the Civil Guard, to the Canary Islands to collaborate with the Germans, and with Royo, he had been toying with the idea of assassinating the French ambassador although in the end that proposal was abandoned. The sinister police chief had also been involved in all kinds of illegal practices such as gambling, extortion and blackmail. In fact, gambling brought about his downfall. Portillo could not prevent police from discovering illegal gambling, or the arrest of some friends of Royo. Feeling betrayed and fearing for his life, Royo produced the evidence which put them all behind bars.[66]

The arrest of Bravo Portillo showed the penetration of German intelligence at all levels of society. The Portillo affair was deliberately covered up by the authorities. Despite the vast amount of evidence against him provided by experts and witnesses, the case was dismissed in what amounted to a scandalous subversion of justice.[67]

In early July, as the truth of German activities was beginning to come to light, the government hurriedly passed an Espionage Bill which caused public uproar. Owing to its timing and the urgency with which it was introduced, the bill drawn up by the Foreign Minister Dato appeared to be a concession to the German embassy, which had been under constant attack since Pascual's revelations in March. Its preamble declared that the government had increasing difficulty in maintaining neutrality when it was continually threatened by campaigns which, however respectable in intention, produced lamentable results. The bill, therefore, forbade under severe penalties:

1   The furnishing to the agents of a foreign power information relating to the neutrality of Spain or of a nature to injure any other foreign power. The penalty will be imprisonment or a fine of between 500 and 20,000 pesetas.

2   The publication or circulation of any news which the government has prohibited as 'contrary to the respect due to the neutrality or security of Spain'; or the spreading of news of a nature to alarm Spaniards. The penalty will be imprisonment or a fine of between 500 and 100,000 pesetas.

3   The insulting or holding up to hatred or contempt the chief of a foreign state, or a nation, army or diplomatic representative, either by word of mouth or in print or picture. The penalty will be imprisonment or a fine of between 500 and 100,000 pesetas.

The legislation against spies naturally produced a loud chorus of protest. The French ambassador, Thierry, called it a sweeping and ill-considered measure.[68] The left-wing pro-Allied press was unanimous in denouncing such a strait-jacket. *El Sol* noted that henceforth spies in Spain might be fined 20,000 pesetas, but those who exposed them or their patrons would have to pay 100,000 pesetas.[69] What was even more shocking was the haste and lack of explanations with which Dato presented his new bill in parliament almost at the same time that a German espionage network had been discovered in Barcelona. The fact that a well-known Allied supporter like Count Romanones expressed in public his backing for the bill did not change anything. It was generally regarded as a desperate attempt by the government to gag the free press in order to avoid an embarrassing situation with Germany. At a time when the maintenance of strict neutrality was becoming impossible, the government was stubbornly sticking to it. Romanones had been right when he said that there were neutralities which were fatal. Dato introduced his bill in the Cortes on 4 July and it was immediately described by Republicans as a betrayal of liberal principles and a violation of the constitution. It was put to a vote two days later and made a question of confidence by Maura. The deputies of the left withdrew from the chamber.[70]

The Spanish government was not Germanophile. In relative terms, unlike the former cabinet which had as ministers people like Alcalá Zamora and Cierva, the current composition seemed to be leaning to the Allies.[71] Yet the spectre of the Russian Revolution made a deep impression on a country like Spain where social revolts due to the *crisis de subsistencias* continued unabated, and the attitudes of army and crown were decisive. Thus the flamboyant National Government acted with a weakness that in practical terms amounted to an unconditional surrender to Germany's bullying and terrorizing methods. That position was finally confirmed in the summer of 1918, when the indiscriminate German sinking of merchant ships reached such levels that it seemed for a while that the government was prepared to stand up to it with honour.

It was no longer possible to maintain neutrality with decorum and the moment had arrived to take forceful action. Yet words were not matched by deeds and from the brink of intervention, the government retreated once more to shameful capitulation.

Throughout 1918 the submarine campaign increasingly threatened the economic life of the nation. Germany extended her submarine blockade even further, first on 21 November 1917 and then again on 11 January 1918. Between April 1917 and July 1918, 37 Spanish vessels met the same tragic end as the *San Fulgencio*. On 13 July, the steamer *Ramón de Larriñaga* bringing oil from New York was torpedoed when about to enter Spanish waters. Eight members of its crew were killed. The gravity of the incident prompted Maura to act. After days of reflection he informed his Foreign Minister that 'the limits of Spanish patience have been reached. A resolution must be adopted without further delay.'[72] On 8 August the Council of Ministers was entirely devoted to the international question. The discussions lasted for two days. Romanones was the only one backing tough action. According to the Count, Spain should take advantage of the Allied victories on the continent and seize all the German ships interned in Spanish ports. The military ministers were radically opposed to any modification of the position of strict neutrality.[73] Finally, on 10 August a compromise was reached: a new statement would be sent to Germany.

For the first time, the protest amounted to an ultimatum. The Spanish note was supposed to be a perfect exercise in both energy and moderation. The government was prepared to stand up to Germany. The statement made clear that owing to the submarine campaign, over 20 per cent of the merchant fleet had been destroyed and 100 sailors killed. The situation had gone so far that ships bringing goods exclusively destined for Spanish consumption were being torpedoed, with a disastrous effect on the material interests of the country. The cabinet therefore resolved that it had to adopt effective means for ensuring the maintenance of maritime trade and for protecting the lives of the sailors. Consequently, in the event of any fresh torpedoing, it would replace the tonnage sunk by seizing German ships lying in Spanish ports.[74]

However, at no time had the National Government believed that the statement could lead to a rupture with the Central Powers. The message, despite its strong tone, was constantly accompanied by references to their determination to maintain the most strict neutrality. It stressed that it was a measure imposed upon them by necessity and that it did not imply the indefinite appropriation of those vessels. The Germans responded by ignoring the statement and continuing brutal attacks on the Spanish fleet. This placed the Maura cabinet in the position of having to choose between putting into practice its ultimatum and risking war with Germany, or humiliation and retreat.

In the space of ten days after the delivery of the statement, two more Spanish vessels were torpedoed. The German ambassador's excuse that there had not been enough time to give new instructions to all the submarines might be sincere and yet raised the question of what the old instructions were. Yet Germany, after dictating her terms to Spain for so long, would not modify her traditionally bullying approach. She warned that seizure of any of her vessels would immediately be met by rupture of diplomatic relations and war.[75]

The government panicked, fearing the worst. The Germanophile press returned to its insidious attacks. It was suggested that Dato, in collusion with Maura and Romanones, had passed the *Ley de Espionaje* so as to be able to force the country into war.[76] There was talk of catastrophe to come if the country was dragged into the conflict. Once more appealing to slogans of *españolismo*, those newspapers described German atrocities against Spanish ships as justified acts of war and warned that many Spaniards would prefer civil war rather than to be told by 'certain powers to defend a flag that was not theirs'.[77] Yet they had it all wrong. The Western Powers were far from pushing Spain into the war. In late August, an extremely worried Dato approached the Allied representatives in Spain asking what support Spain would receive if she was forced to break off diplomatic relations with Germany.[78] The Spanish ambassadors in London and Paris initiated discussions on the question while the Germanophile Polo de Bernabé, ambassador at Berlin, kept threatening with his resignation – a threat that he never fulfilled.[79]

The response from the Western Powers was not the one expected from nations trying to impose their terms on a neutral. With victory within their reach, the entry of Spain into the war could make little difference. The Allies, unlike Germany, had maintained a policy of non-interference in Spanish internal affairs and they did not modify their behaviour now. Only the United States seemed to encourage a forceful act on the part of Spain. Unlike the French and the British, the Americans were keen on forcing the Spanish hand by strong and merciless commercial pressure, refusing her a single bale of cotton or gallon of oil. That proposal was rapidly opposed by the French and British, who regarded their industrial and mining concerns in Spain as of paramount importance and therefore advocated a conciliatory approach.[80] On 31 August Joseph Willard, the US ambassador at Madrid, published an article in *El Liberal* affirming that if Spain wanted to save her honour she would have to break off diplomatic relations with Germany. He argued that German threats, espionage and control of the press had already been tried in his country and had failed. Willard repeated the same promise that he had made a few days before to Dato. The United States would give all its support and do all in its power to meet the industrial and material needs of Spain.[81]

In fact, the French and British did not want to see a Spanish move at the last minute which could give her grounds for territorial claims or excessive economic demands. Both agreed that they would be glad to see Spain on their side and were willing to support her financially, industrially and militarily, but they also insisted that they were not prepared to push her into the war. It was for Spain, and Spain alone, to decide what course she ought to pursue to safeguard her honour and protect her interests.[82]

Yet there was never a serious risk of Spanish intervention. Neither king nor army were prepared to let it happen. The former, after the experiences of the previous August in Spain and the revolutionary events in Russia, would stick to neutrality to the end, never mind the honour of the nation. Moreover, Alfonso believed that the Central Powers would not be defeated and still hoped he could be the arbiter of the peace. The army, aware of the nation's military weakness, was also determined to avoid intervention at any cost. The government of notables would have to swallow its pride and negotiate on the terms dictated by Germany.

On 30 August, at a turbulent cabinet meeting, most ministers were prepared to enforce the ultimatum and seize one German vessel. But they were stopped by the Minister for the Navy, who hinted that he was speaking on behalf of the king and army.[83] A few days later, Dato wrote to Maura confirming that idea: the monarch had told him that under no circumstances was he prepared to permit a departure from strict neutrality.[84] The energy shown by the Spanish government on 10 August vanished into thin air. The Maura cabinet was left in a ridiculous and humiliating position at precisely the moment that the Allies were about to win the war. It would have been better if they had never voted for a strong measure which was not in their power to enforce. The real victory was for German diplomacy, which was able to dictate the conditions.[85]

Maura and his ministers could only hope to find a solution which might permit them to save face. First, they decided to postpone any drastic action until further reports had confirmed Germany's guilt in the sinking of the Spanish ships. Then, they expressed their willingness to give her more time to warn her submarines. When by 12 October three more vessels had been sunk, the government finally announced that seven ships of the German fleet in Spanish ports would soon be seized. Spanish public opinion of the government was tinged with sadness, if not ridicule, when it emerged that far from being a show of strength, this amounted almost to an act of charity on the German part. In fact, the seven ships would not be seized but borrowed – as soon as the German embassy decided which ones to lend.[86] To add insult to injury, in the end the numerous Austrian and German vessels in Spanish ports were never used to restore the battered Spanish merchant fleet. Before any concrete agreement had been reached, the armistice was signed. One of its clauses was the surrender of the Central Powers' fleet in neutral ports to the Allies. It was a just reward for a shameful and bankrupt foreign policy. Six of the ships lent by Germany remained in Spanish hands. They were all given the name *España* and numbered from one to six.[87]

In the domestic sphere, the National Government also performed very poorly. The cabinet never worked as an harmonious body. Its members had been compelled to join forces temporarily by the attitude of the army. As soon as they believed that the situation had been normalized, all the personal jealousies and rivalries emerged again so that the initial consensus disappeared and any hope of propping up the constitutional system was dashed.

In general, the principles which divided them were hollow or imaginary, but the personal interests were very real. The Conservatives were not at ease in the coalition. They were presided over by Maura who had vilified them for years. Moreover, the Conservatives could not be pleased to work alongside people like Alba or Romanones, and particularly Cambó, who appeared to them to have benefited from the peculiar circumstances which they themselves had helped to create in the summer of 1917 and which had resulted in the downfall of the Dato administration. The Conservatives could not help regarding them as unscrupulous politicians always ready to run with the hare and hunt with the hounds. There were also other internal problems, such as the personal hostility between Alba and Cambó, the rivalries between the different Liberal leaders and the question of Catalan Regionalism, which had not been overcome.[88]

Bearing in mind all the possible sources of conflict, Maura did not promise to embark upon a far-reaching programme. Instead, after solving the dispute with the civil service and re-establishing constitutional guarantees in Barcelona, he declared that his government would deal mainly with four issues: amnesty for political offences, army reforms, the reform of procedure in parliament and the budget.[89] The first three were rapidly dealt with, but the budget proved to be beyond the grasp of the government.

The debate on the bill for the reform of the internal regulations of the Spanish parliament began on 26 April and was approved by the deputies on 8 May. The introduction of the guillotine which limited the amount of time to discuss an issue met with protests from the left. They argued that there were more important problems of national interest and that this bill would curtail the liberty of the deputies and be used to hurry through the passage of the bill for military reforms.[90] On the same day the bill of amnesty became law and the four Socialist deputies were released from gaol at Cartagena and allowed to take their seats in the Cortes. One month later, and despite the total opposition of the left, the bill for military reform was finally passed.

The first cracks in the coalition government appeared in early June when discussing the role of the Conservative government during the revolutionary events of 1917. On 4 June several left-wing deputies presented a motion approving the conduct of the former Speaker, Villanueva, with regard to his efforts to obtain the release of the arrested deputy Marcelino Domingo. In reality, although the motion was intended to be a vote of censure against the Dato cabinet, it also represented a question of confidence in the current administration in which, as Minister for Foreign Affairs, Dato was a leading member. It left the ministers with the choice of either voting against a motion defending the rights of a deputy, and thereby saving the coalition, or voting for it and bringing the government down. Although the government survived, when the motion was rejected by 129 votes to 18 its credibility as a united body was undermined. Cambó, Alhucemas and Romanones instructed their followers to vote against the motion, but they all brought out qualified explanations which implied a tacit disapproval of the course followed by the Dato administration in 1917 and insisted that Villanueva, the former Speaker of the Chamber, had acted correctly by insisting on the rights of the deputy Marcelino Domingo. Alba did not even make the effort and his friends abstained.[91]

During the summer, the March coalition disintegrated. The Conservatives began to consider that the circumstances which had compelled them to join the government no longer existed and expected to return to the pre-June 1917 situation. At the same time, the two up-and-coming personalities in the monarchist camp, Alba and Cambó, had ambitious plans of their own which were bound to clash with the concepts of the 'old guard'.

The budget brought all those differences of opinion to the surface. The Conservative Finance Minister, González Besada, backed by his leader Dato, planned to pass an unexceptional budget. His main concern was to balance the numbers and curb inflation. He was opposed by Cambó and Alba, who wanted to take advantage of the immense wealth which the war had poured into Spain to develop her resources on a larger scale. Unlike Besada with his traditional views, Cambó and Alba were keen for the state to take an interventionist and active role in developing the economy and therefore wanted a budget of thousands of millions of pesetas for the reconstruction of the country. They initially joined forces to fight Besada, but soon quarrelled with each other.

Alba wanted to be the leader of a new populist formation on the left of a re-constructed power bloc which hopefully would attract support from antidynastic groups. Cambó would play a similar role on the right. Alba seems to have resented the fact that as Minister for Public Works, Cambó had been given the chance to shine that he had not had at Education.

In the summer of 1918 the Catalan leader was commonly perceived as the soul of the government. Unlike the other ministers, Cambó was willing to prove his ability as an economist in his department. He therefore embarked on a far-reaching programme for the modernization of the nation's economic infrastructure. His proposals touched on road building, a mining code, irrigation and afforestation. He also set out in a detailed six-volume survey a railway plan which called upon the state to nationalize, and thereafter maintain and develop, the Spanish network as well as to assume responsibility for subsidizing passenger fares and freight rates. In early September Cambó travelled on a tour with the king and queen, and in a famous speech at Covadonga he played down his regionalism and instead put forward his vast financial and economic schemes to build up a greater Spain. The Catalan leader had to keep something for his own nationalist constituency and so planned to persuade the other ministers to delegate some of their responsibilities to the regional Mancomunidad, the administrative body granted by Dato to placate the Regionalists in 1913.[92] Alba feared that for a second time his rising star could be eclipsed by the success of the Lliga's leader. He hesitated between forming a common front with Cambó and fighting him. Finally he opted for the latter.

Thus in August and September, Maura saw himself increasingly isolated as a leader of a government which was collapsing due to its internal quarrels. First, the 'modernizers' Cambó and Alba with the backing of Alhucemas were opposing the plans of Besada; and secondly, Alba was leading an offensive against Cambó's nationalization plans and intentions of delegating powers to the Mancomunidad. Maura had to go out of his way to ensure the survival of the cabinet. The Conservatives and Cambó, joined by Ventosa who had been appointed Minister of Supply, were threatening to quit. Alhucemas with the backing of Alba was declaring in the press that he would be prepared to form a government which would include the Socialist Besteiro (in charge of Employment). The Prime Minister only managed to keep the government alive by persuading Cambó to postpone his Regionalist demands and Besada to add 400 million to his original budget.[93]

Alba himself inflicted a mortal blow on the government in late September. He was aware that the cabinet was disintegrating and hoped to take advantage of the situation and emerge as the leader of a new Liberal coalition by being the first to leave. Thus he demanded 20 million pesetas for increases in schoolmasters' wages. In fact, he was simply seeking an excuse to resign and found it when the others only gave him 11 million.[94] He left office on 2 October. Up until that moment, Maura had managed to maintain the coalition. Alba's departure inevitably produced a domino effect and in one month the National Government had collapsed.

Alba's real intention could not be hidden for long. He rejected any compromise and refused to withdraw his resignation. Yet he agreed not to make public his departure from the administration until the king returned from his summer holiday in San Sebastián a few days later. Nevertheless, on 3 October *El Liberal* published Alba's version of the causes of his resignation. The former minister asked if the country wanted to have a worthy education system and accused Maura and Cambó of torpedoing his initiatives and forcing him to quit.

For a month, the spectacle presented by all the monarchist leaders was pitiful. Alba had opened the door and now all the rivalries and squabbles which had hitherto been kept hidden came to view. Cambó did not waste time in providing a response and on 5 October in *La Veu* he alleged that Alba was an ambitious and unscrupulous politician who had fabricated an artificial crisis so as to leave office and then had broken his promise not to reveal his resignation. Romanones replaced Alba at Education and Maura himself took over Justice.

The solution did not last. There was the widespread feeling that the government was about to collapse.[95] A few days later, the Cortes was re-opened and there appeared the sad spectacle of one minister attacking another and all of them claiming to be the successor of the still-existing National Government.[96] Alba spoke against Cambó, Romanones and Maura. According to the ex-Minister of Education, the Count had wanted his portfolio and so had conspired against him. Cambó had tried to introduce his Regionalist plans by threats and had always had the support of a declining Maura. Alba asked Cambó whether he really believed that his region was oppressed in Spain, and if the answer was no, why he made veiled hints that Catalonia would find in France what was denied her in Spain. In turn, Alba was attacked mercilessly by the others. They accused him of cheating, lying, breaking his promises and working for himself rather than the country. According to them, they could have never opposed any of his initiatives since he had not presented any in all his time at Education. He had only come up with demands for money for the schoolmasters knowing all the time that what he asked for was impossible. Civil servants and other workers had recently obtained increases of up to 30 per cent, and he was demanding rises of 80 per cent for the schoolmasters.[97]

Alba's move did not pay off. He was ridiculed and rebuffed by the left and did not manage to emerge from the crisis as the leader of a new leftist and populist force.[98] Nevertheless he had left the government mortally wounded. Well aware of this, Maura declared that his cabinet would continue in power just to pass the budget. Spain had been without a budget since 1914. Three days later Dato initiated his particular campaign to claim the empty throne and resigned. In early November, Alhucemas made a speech in the chamber which sounded like his plans for a future government. He quarrelled with Cambó by denying the need for Catalan autonomy. Even in Restoration Spain it was unusual for two members of the same cabinet to reveal their differences in public. The final blow came the following morning when Besada read out his budget and was opposed by none other than Sánchez Guerra, the second in command of his own Conservative party. It was an illusion to pretend that a government still existed. Maura resigned.[99]

The fall of the National Government virtually coincided with the armistice in Europe. By the summer of 1918 the tide had begun to turn dramatically in favour of the Allies. In fact, it was becoming evident to everybody, except the Spanish monarch and the most steadfast among the Germanophiles, that victory was imminent for the Allied forces. The German offensive planned by General Ludendorff in the spring had turned by the summer into disaster. It had been all the time a desperate gamble and a race against the clock to knock out the Anglo-French armies before the vast American resources could be used in earnest. In early June, the German armies were 40 miles from Paris but the troops were exhausted, the supply lines overstretched and the reserves almost depleted. Once again, as in 1914, the Western Powers launched a counter-offensive that this time proved to be crucial. Soon their immense superiority in terms of material resources and manpower

began to be felt. The German front lines gave way and by August the hitherto mighty German army was in open retreat. At the same time, her allies
were being routed everywhere else. Amidst revolution and mutinies, the Central Powers collapsed. On 28 September Bulgaria accepted defeat. One month
later, the Austrian and Ottoman Empires sued for peace, and on 11 November, German negotiators signed at the Forest of Compiègne the armistice
terms imposed by the Allies. By then, the formerly all-powerful ruling
dynasties had been overthrown and revolution was spreading throughout
Central and Eastern Europe.

Spain's dynastic parties had spared the country from the ordeals of the war
but had not managed to save themselves from political decline. With the
demise of the Maura cabinet of 1918, the last great hope of the constitutional
Monarchy vanished. The old Conservative leader declared: '¡A ver quien es
ahora el guapo que se encarga del poder!' ('let us see who is now the smart
guy who can take power').[100]

10

EPILOGUE

The First World War proved to be a watershed in European history. The outbreak of a conflict of such magnitude produced economic dislocation, social distress and ideological militancy which eroded the foundations of European Liberalism. Already before 1914, the supremacy of the Liberal governing elites was under threat: economic modernization, industrialization, secularization and other related contemporary phenomena were breaking down and challenging the existing hierarchical, elitist and clientelist politics. Now the formerly dominant groups were confronted with the uncertainties of popular politics, the often unwelcome prospect of more genuine democracy, and the fast-advancing threat of Socialism.[1] Four years of appalling human and material losses intensified the movements of protest which had existed before 1914. Furthermore, to the existing problems of food and fuel shortages, economic dislocation and social distress were added the pleas of displaced national minorities and the revisionist feelings of the losers of the Great War.

The armistice of 1918 did not put an end to the struggle on the continent, it only changed its appearance. The armed conflict was over but a new kind of ideological warfare had only just begun. After its success in Russia in November 1917, Bolshevism found a ready audience among the war-weary populations and began to spread westwards, initiating the richest period of revolutionary activity in Europe since 1848. Traditional rulers soon discovered that it was impossible to put back the clock. Years of misery had brought about political militancy which in turn led to the breakdown of existing forms of elitist politics. The political and social upheaval would be felt throughout the continent, from London to Moscow, heralding an era of utopian ferment and class struggle. Nevertheless, the main battlefield had two centres. First there were the newly born regimes of Central Europe, created out of the disintegration of the Hohenzollern and Habsburg Empires, which had to cope with the bitter taste of defeat and the political vacuum left by the enforced departure of their rulers. Secondly, southern Europe, where the governing class, whose hegemony had hitherto been based upon electoral falsification and patronage, proved unable to face up to the arrival of mass politics.

The year 1919 constituted the peak of the revolutionary offensive. This was a moment when bourgeois Europe seemed about to collapse. In Russia, the Bolshevik forces gained the upper hand in the civil war against the various White armies led by former Tsarist officers. In Germany, as the old regime collapsed in November 1918, councils of soldiers and workers were formed in the main cities. The spring of 1919 saw a soviet state established in Bavaria and during that year there were Communist uprisings against the Socialist-led government of the newly created republic in Berlin and in other capitals. In Hungary, the revolutionary forces also seized power in March 1919. Italian peasants occupied the land, not only in the south, but also in places in the north and centre where such action was new. During 1919, internal committees which had been created in industrial centres in Italy during the war were turned into 'factory councils' whose objective was to take over the means of production, fulfilling simultaneously the economic role of direct workers' management of the plant and the political function of self-government. The strength of the factory councils was fully displayed in the summer of 1920 when more than half a million workers occupied their factories.

In the meantime, the ruling social and economic classes were biding their time and waiting for the tide to turn. By 1920 the revolutionary thrust was exhausted. The Red Army had been defeated at the gates of Warsaw and the European labour movement was hopelessly divided between Communists and Socialists. The challenge of the working classes had either been brutally crushed, as in Hungary and Germany, or channelled towards reformist goals, as was the case in Italy. The traditional governing elites were pushed aside, and with them Liberalism and Constitutionalism were discarded as valid political forms. Instead, authoritarian solutions were advocated, not so much to suppress revolutionary socialism, which had already run out of steam, as to wipe out the gains in social and industrial legislation which the labour movement had achieved since 1914. The establishment of a dictatorship in Hungary in the summer of 1919 represented the beginning of a period of virtually uninterrupted working class defeat and a concomitant advance of the new radical right across the continent: the left was destroyed in Italy after Mussolini's seizure of power in 1922; military dictatorships were established in most southern and eastern European countries in the 1920s and 1930s; in 1933 democracy was annihilated by Hitler in Germany and within one year Austria had met a similar fate.[2]

The Spanish case cannot be separated from the wider European conflict. The First World War brought about the crisis of hegemony of the liberal monarchy in Spain. Neutrality did not spare the country from political upheaval and radical social and economic transformation. In the summer of 1917, the industrial bourgeoisie, the armed forces and the labour movement mobilized their forces and attempted to overthrow the ruling liberal oligarchy. The irony of the events of this year was that a large range of groups

sharing comparable levels of hostility and contempt for the ruling oligarchy
never managed to co-operate in a common initiative. Catalans and Republicans tried to win over the Juntas, but the latter were looking to Maura who,
in turn, refused to become involved in the conflict. The strict legalism of
Maura prevented his movement from playing a crucial role at that historic
moment. Cambó emerged as the only significant figure trying to establish a
political alternative based upon a coalition of forces with a common programme of economic and political modernization. The left, outmanoeuvred
by the cunning of the Catalan politician, was not up to the job. The Socialists, in particular, found themselves in the odd situation of being moderate
but forced by circumstances to become revolutionary, and they paid dearly
for their own ideological contradictions. The result was a situation of chaos
and turmoil, violence and revolution in which the government scored an
important victory in the short term simply by exploiting the internal disputes of the various opposing forces.

The liberal monarchy survived the revolutionary challenge of 1917, but
the constitutional regime had to pay a high price for that victory: the alliance
of throne and army was consolidated at the expense of the discredited political elites. Henceforth the officers were to act as an anticonstitutional party
with powers of veto, able to make and topple cabinets. The carefully con-
structed edifice built during the last decades of the nineteenth century collapsed and the *Turno* between dynastic parties was abandoned.

After the failure of the coalition government of 1918, the best solution
offered by the existing ruling order, the Canovite system, never regained the
initative. The organic crisis of the state was long and painful, for although
the political system was mortally wounded it was still strong enough to prevent the creation of a political alternative, and lasted until 1923.

In Morocco, Spain paid the penalty for her neutrality. Under the harassment of a proud France, which remembered the Germanophilia of key Spanish institutions, an isolated Spain found herself struggling alone against the
well-armed and well-trained Moorish guerrillas. The lack of efficient planning and the unpopularity of the campaign, which was grossly underfunded,
finally led to the disaster at Annual in the summer of 1921, when over 12,000
Spanish troops were killed and nearly the whole eastern part of the Protectorate was overrun by the Moors. The impact of the defeat resembled that of
1898. It led to a national uproar demanding the heads of those responsible
for such disaster. It was one more nail in the coffin of the dynastic politicians,
accused again of inefficiency and incapability, and of leading Spain to international humiliation.[3]

The domestic situation presented a chaotic image. Rural *caciquismo* was
still omnipotent and delivered the awaited results, but the dynastic parties
were fragmented into a variety of rival factions. The political deadlock could
not be solved. There were 30 partial crises and 13 total crises of government
between 1917 and 1923.

The Allied victory, the Bolshevik triumph in Russia and the post-war economic recession intensified the class struggle in Spain. It was evident by the autumn of 1918 that Spain was sliding into a revolutionary situation which now, unlike in 1917, possessed both an urban and a rural dimension. Yet the swift suppression of the revolutionary strike in August 1917 had halted the revolutionary impetus of the Socialist leaders and broken the coalition created against the regime. The Spanish Socialists were inflexibly opposed to any further revolutionary adventures and thereby lost the opportunity to become, at a time of growing popular discontent, supreme among the forces fighting for radical change in Spain. Their power base was rapidly taken by the CNT, which became the leading force of the organized working class, even making inroads into traditional Socialist strongholds. In 1920, the membership of the Socialist trade union, the UGT, lagged (with 211,342 members) far behind that of the CNT (which boasted a membership of 790,948). The Anarcho-Syndicalist movement, however, lacked the discipline, organization and ideological coherence of the Socialists. Rather than being an homogeneous group, the CNT constituted an amalgamation of opposite factions which ranged from moderate Syndicalists to uncompromising Anarchists.

The militancy of the masses and the revolutionary atmosphere could not be eradicated. Throughout 1918 food riots and workers' protests against the rising cost of living rocked the normal life of most cities. Workers had to cope with worsening living conditions produced by an increasing scarcity of basic commodities and mounting inflation. The situation was even worse for the peasants, who had to survive on miserable wages and unhealthy diets and who had, in most cases, only temporary jobs. News of the Bolshevik takeover and the subsequent land distribution in Russia was the ideological push needed to trigger an all-out revolutionary upheaval in the southern countryside. The traditionally rebellious mood of the Andalusian anarchist peasants had never really been extinguished and it was the Russian Revolution which now provided the necessary myth which, historically, had been needed to spark uprisings in the countryside. Between 1918 and 1920, the starving and long-suffering masses, showing an unprecedented degree of co-ordination and organization, rose throughout southern Spain demanding 'land and bread'. Authorities and the rural bourgeoisie were caught by surprise. They lost control of events and many fled in panic to the safety of the cities. Power lay in the many workers' trade unions, normally controlled by the Anarcho-Syndicalists, which had sprung up amidst the revolutionary euphoria. Thus in 1919 a kind of dictatorship of the proletariat reigned over large swathes of the Andalusian countryside.[4]

Simultaneously, the CNT experienced astonishing success and rapid advance in the industrial centres, particularly in Catalonia. In the summer of 1918, the Catalan CRT abandoned the old craft trade unions and instead adopted the model of the *sindicato único*. It was a new strategy which soon proved a formidable weapon in the hands of the resolute Syndicalist leaders. The first major test of strength for the new *sindicato único* took place in February 1919, when a strike broke out at the Anglo-Canadian hydroelectric concern known as 'La Canadiense'. The conflict began as a normal wage dispute between the management and workers who had recently joined the CRT and been sacked, but soon became the most successful strike in Spanish labour history. The co-ordination, organization and careful planning of the Syndicalists as well as the solidarity of the Catalan proletariat were stunning. The mobilization of the workers was remarkable and lasted 44 days, leaving the city of Barcelona totally paralysed. To add insult to injury, the trade union of graphic artists even put into practice the so-called 'red censorship', that is the prevention of any publication hostile to the workers' position. The victory of the labour movement was total: the current Liberal administration, led by Count Romanones, promised the introduction of the eight-hour working day and the company agreed both to re-hire its employees without penalties of any kind and to raise wages.[5] When the CNT held a Congress at the Teatro de la Comedia in Madrid in December, the organization was at the peak of its power. The structure of the *sindicato único* was adopted nationally and amidst revolutionary optimism the CNT voted for affiliating provisionally with the Comintern.[6]

The Spanish ruling classes shared with their European counterparts the fear of an imminent revolution. The revolutionary offensive in Spain, however, never really represented a challenge capable of bringing down the regime, nor did it offer a viable political alternative. There was no leading group that attempted to link the rural revolt with the urban unrest. The Socialists were not prepared to lead a violent insurrection and although the CNT stepped in and attracted massive support at a time of intensified class struggle, their own apolitical and libertarian principles prevented the Anarcho-Syndicalists from even considering a seizure of state power. Nevertheless, the expansion of the labour movement and the offensive of the CNT contributed decisively to the final disintegration of an already bruised and discredited political system. They persuaded the ruling classes to discard the existing governing class, which could guarantee neither social order nor political stability. The Spanish bourgeoisie in general, and the Catalan in particular, frightened by the growing power of the Syndicalists, finally dropped any reformist intentions that they might have harboured in the past, and sought to protect their economic interests by relying on sheer force. With the end of the war in Europe, the golden era of huge profits had ended. Industrialists could foresee an imminent economic recession in which they planned to resort to massive lay-offs of workers and cuts in production. Yet this could not be carried out with a powerful and combative CNT. Hence the Anarcho-Syndicalist movement had to be crushed. Employers would settle for nothing less than the union's total destruction. A miniature civil war was in the offing.[7]

The first loud calls for a military dictatorship appeared in 1919.[8] The bourgeoisie was clearly not prepared to surrender its social and economic privileges without a battle and hence it turned to the army for protection. The alliance between the bourgeoisie and the army acted independently of the central government in Madrid and often in open defiance of its orders. In 1919 alone two cabinets confronted with the intransigent opposition of officers and industrialists had to resign.[9] The result would be the final collapse of civil supremacy and the final crisis of authority of the dynastic parties.

In the spring of 1919 an army of 20,000 troops was sent to Andalusia. Towns were occupied after pitched battles, workers' unions were closed down and hundreds of militants imprisoned. Even more brutal and violent was the reaction in Catalonia. There constitutional guarantees had been suspended in January 1919 and would remain so for more than three years. Real power thus lay with the Captain General of that region. Under his command, an old bourgeois militia dating from medieval times, El Somatén, was resurrected and its members granted permission to carry weapons, patrol the streets and arrest strikers. Not satisfied with this, the industrialists hired gangs of thugs, one of which was led by the infamous former chief of police Manuel Bravo Portillo, whose task was to beat up and shoot leading Syndicalists. The streets of Barcelona soon became a battlefield. In November 1919, the Catalan employers launched a massive lock-out which lasted two months and left 200,000 workers jobless. One month later, the so-called Sindicatos Libres were established in Barcelona. They were a new trade union controlled by Catholic and Carlist workers. They presented the employers with a great opportunity to split the labour movement.[10] The climax of violence and repression was reached with the appointment of General Severiano Martínez Anido as civil governor of Barcelona in October 1920. For two years, this blood-thirsty and vicious officer was to run Barcelona as his private fiefdom. He disregarded civil rights and regarded the CNT militants as enemies of war. Thousands of Syndicalists and left-wing sympathizers were imprisoned or deported to distant provinces (making the journey on foot and in chains). Counter-terrorism received official protection. Gunmen of the Libres were trained and armed in military barracks and the notorious *Ley de Fugas*, allowing the shooting of captured Syndicalists 'while trying to escape', was introduced. Between 1919 and 1923 hundreds of the best militants of the CNT, including three General Secretaries, were killed.[11]

The intransigent attitude of the propertied classes and the brutal repression carried out against the CNT played into the hands of the extremists who began to dominate the organization after 1919. Just when the CNT seemed to have reached its apex of efficiency and strength, its energies were to be channelled into a crazy wave of assassinations and terror. This was not only to end the collective discipline which had yielded its best fruits in the past, but was also ironically to play into the hands of those who only needed an excuse to smash the labour movement.[12] Moreover, the irony of indiscriminate repression was that the moderate Syndicalist leaders, and not the lesser-known Anarchists, became the targets of employers' gunmen. It was the extremists in the CNT who were best equipped and prepared to operate clandestinely and who were most disposed to meet violence with violence. From 1919, Anarchist 'action groups' responded in kind and industrialists, overseers and strikebreakers were gunned down. The most outstanding victims of Anarchist violence were the Conservative Prime Minister Eduardo Dato and the Archbishop of Saragossa, shot dead in March 1921 and June 1923 respectively. The endless spiral of violence spread from Catalonia to other regions. Spain resembled a country in civil war: seldom did a day pass without the newspapers reporting fresh assassinations or new acts of vandalism.

Following the disaster of Annual in the summer of 1921, the services of Antonio Maura were once more required to save the political system from collapse. He again formed a national government, which included among others Juan de la Cierva and Francesc Cambó. As in 1918, the attempt failed miserably. Once the temporary cement provided by the Moroccan disaster disappeared, the coalition government was torn apart by irreconcilable internal political and personal rivalries. The last experience of a national coalition collapsed in March 1922. Henceforth calls for a military take-over became deafening, while the dynastic politicians saw their role reduced to that of verbally abusing one another in the Cortes which, now more than ever, functioned as a mere talking-shop. It was amidst this climate of colonial disaster, social warfare and political vacuum that the same groups which had played a crucial role in the crisis of October 1917 – king, army and industrial bourgeoisie – decided to throw their support behind an authoritarian solution in September 1923. In fact, in that year Primo de Rivera did not overthrow the last constitutional government, he merely limited himself to filling a vacuum which had existed ever since 1917.

CHRONOLOGY OF MAIN EVENTS

1914

June

Assassination of Archduke Franz Ferdinand, heir to the Austrian throne, in Sarajevo.

July

Austria invades Serbia.
Leading pro-peace French Socialist Jean Jaurès is assassinated by a fanatical nationalist.

August

War breaks out in Europe.
The Spanish Conservative government led by Eduardo Dato declares its strict neutrality.
Count Romanones, leader of the Liberal Party, indicates his pro-Allied feelings in a controversial article called 'Fatal Neutralities'.

September

German offensive halted on the River Marne. War of attrition begins on the Western Front.
Russian armies crushed in East Prussia.
Spanish political groups begin to split according to their ideological positions; Republicans and Socialists are Francophiles, Carlists and *Mauristas* Germanophiles.

November

The Ottoman Empire enters the war on the side of the Central Powers.

1915

January

Germany follows a strategy of territorial offers and purchase of Spanish newspapers to ensure Spain's continued neutrality.

April

Germany invades Poland.

Heavy casualties in the first battle of Ypres where Germany uses gas for the first time in modern warfare.

Disastrous Allied landing in Gallipoli (Turkey). The expeditionary force has to be evacuated after six months.

May

Italy joins the Allies after promises of territories belonging to the Austrian Empire.

September

Zimmerwald Conference of anti-war Socialists.

October

Bulgaria joins the Central Powers.

The PSOE's tenth congress votes in favour of the pro-Allied and Republican position adopted by the leadership.

December

The Dato administration collapses due to its inability to deal with increasing food shortages and mounting inflation. It is replaced by the Liberals led by Count Romanones.

1916

February

Battle of Verdun begins. It becomes the symbol of French resistance and determination: France loses hundreds of thousands of soldiers but resists the continuous German onslaught.

April

Kiental Conference of anti-war Socialists.

Easter rising in Dublin by Irish Republicans to secure independence is crushed by the British army.

Despite promises of a clean ballot, the general elections in Spain are rigged as usual, giving the government an overall majority.

May

Initially successful Russian offensive, led by General Brusilov, peters out in a few months due to lack of supplies and breakdown of the transport system. Demoralization among Russian troops.

Portugal joins the Allies.

In the twelfth UGT Congress, the Socialists under pressure from the rank and file decide to approach the CNT and embark together on a campaign to solve the urgent economic problems.

June

Question of Catalan self-determination raised in parliament. At the same time the Finance Minister, Santiago Alba, begins to expose his plans for radical economic reforms paid for by an extra tax on the war profits of industry and commerce.

July

Bloody slaughter in the battle of the Somme, launched by the Allies to relieve pressure on Verdun. It lasts until November causing hundreds of thousands of casualties to both sides. Tanks are used for the first time but fail to break German lines.

Historic labour pact signed between UGT and CNT.

Spanish railway workers obtain stunning victory in transport strike.

August

Romania joins the Allies.

September

Massive purchase of Spanish journals by both sides. German submarine activity begins to cause havoc among the neutral Spanish merchant fleet. First revelations that Germany has been financing and arming Moorish insurgents in Morocco.

December

Death of Austrian Emperor Franz Josef. He is replaced by his great-nephew Charles.

In Britain the Liberal-dominated cabinet of Henry Herbert Asquith is overthrown and replaced by a new war coalition cabinet led by David Lloyd George. Its objective is to pursue the war with greater effort, introducing measures such as conscription.

Unsuccessful peace initiatives launched by US President Woodrow Wilson and the Central Powers.

Romanones becomes the target of the Germanophiles when he opposes the peace initiatives and bans Alfonso from attending Franz Josef's funeral and attempting mediation between the two sides. An interview with the Austrian ambassador initiates the Germanophile press campaign to overthrow Romanones. German ambassador is caught asking for more funding to support that operation.

After voting down CNT's more radical proposals, the UGT–PSOE launches a successful one-day stoppage in protest at the government's failure to solve the economic crisis.

Alba's economic projects finally destroyed in the chamber.

188

1917

January

Germany announces the beginning of an all-out submarine offensive.
Quick expansion of movement of military unions or Juntas de Defensa.

February

Sudden closure of Spanish Cortes.
US breaks off diplomatic relations with Germany.
Romanones embarks on negotiations with Western Powers in an attempt to negotiate satisfactory conditions and then follow the American example.

March

The Tsar Nicholas II is overthrown in Russia after days of riots in Petrograd. Establishment of a Provisional Government which is promptly recognized by the Allies when it confirms its willingness to continue the war.
Manifesto signed by UGT and CNT threatens to launch a general strike to bring down the government. The Socialists clearly state their purpose: to overthrow the ruling oligarchy and support a bourgeois liberal democracy.

April

Lenin returns to Russia. He announces his opposition to the Provisional Government, claims power for the Soviets of Workers' and Soldiers' Deputies and demands an end to the imperialist war.
The United States and some Latin American Republics declare war on Germany.
Widespread mutinies in the French army after the failure of the spring offensive. France is on the brink of collapse as industrial action and popular discontent mount. Pétain becomes new Commander in Chief and quells the mutinies after promises of better conditions and no further offensives.
Romanones is forced to resign by the king, totally opposed to breaking off diplomatic relations with the Central Powers. The Count is replaced by another Liberal cabinet led by his rival the Marquis of Alhucemas.

May

Mensheviks and Socialist Revolutionaries join the Russian Provisional Government.
Pro-Allied gathering in Madrid warns Alfonso that his Germanophile position will lead to his downfall.

June

Pro-German king Constantine of Greece is overthrown. Under Prime Minister Venizelos Greece joins the Allies.
Rebellion of officers organized into Juntas de Defensa cause the fall of Alhucemas, who is replaced by Dato.

July

Last Russian offensive ends in total disaster.

After demonstrations in Petrograd, some leading Bolsheviks are arrested while others (including Lenin) are forced into hiding. Socialist Revolutionary Kerensky appointed Prime Minister.

German Chancellor Theobald Bethmann-Hollwegg is compelled to resign. Henceforth Germany is virtually a military dictatorship under the control of Generals Hindenburg and Lundendorff.

Liberals divide into several factions. The two most important are led by Alhucemas and Romanones respectively.

Assembly of parliamentarians takes place in Barcelona and commits itself to constitutional reform and to put an end to the rule of the centralist oligarchy. At the same time, a transport strike breaks out in Valencia.

August

The Dato administration uses the transport strike to provoke the labour movement into launching an ill-timed general strike. It is crushed with violence by the army after a week of fighting. The miners in Asturias hold out for several weeks but have to surrender. The government accuses the Allies of being behind the insurrection so that Spain would join their camp.

Food riots in Italian cities. Revolutionary rising in Turin is crushed after eight days of fighting. About 50 people are killed before order is restored.

September

Abortive military coup led by General Kornilov, Commander in Chief of the Russian army.

The German Socialist party officially splits with the creation of the Independent Socialist party opposed to the continuation of the war.

October

Bolsheviks win control of Soviets in many cities.

Juntas force the resignation of the Dato administration.

November

Provisional Government is overthrown by the Bolsheviks. The new administration calls for an end to the war.

Italian army is routed at Caporetto and barely manages to survive as a fighting force after hundreds of thousands of troops are either taken prisoner or desert. The front is only stabilized after the arrival of French and British reinforcements.

Government of resistance in France led by veteran Georges Clemenceau. Amidst feeling of gloom and war weariness, the new cabinet is determined to annihilate defeatism and fight to the end until victory.

190

After a record eight days without a government in Spain, the crisis is solved by the creation of a monarchist coalition led by Alhucemas in which, for the first time, there are two Catalanist ministers. The Juntas are represented by the ultra-conservative Juan de la Cierva.

December

Beginning of armistice negotiations between Russia and the Central Powers.

1918

January

President Wilson announces his fourteen points, stressing freedom of the seas and self-determination of nations as statement of war objectives.
Growth of industrial militancy and war weariness in Austria and Germany.
Killing of Catalan industrialist Barret, one of the main suppliers to France. Collusion of Anarchists and German spies in that event.

February

Spain's general elections show political deadlock with a chamber full of small factions.

March

Civil war in Russia. After German ultimatum Bolsheviks sign the Treaty of Brest-Litovsk, accepting an armistice and surrendering vast tracts of land. As a consequence, Allied contingents begin landing in Russia, supporting the emerging White Armies led by former Tsarist officers.
Germany launches massive offensive on the Western Front.
Danger of a dictatorship under Cierva, supported by the Juntas, is averted by the creation of a National Government formed by monarchist leaders presided over by Antonio Maura.
Evidence of links between Anarchist activities and German espionage revealed in Spanish press.
Insurrection in the Spanish countryside.

May

Romania sues for peace. Germany no longer has to fight on the eastern front but due to its huge territorial gains and the instability in Russia, one million German soldiers have to remain there.

June

Russian civil war escalates after the rebellion of the Czech Legion. A new front is opened with their occupation of the main railroads throughout Siberia.

191

New *Solidaridad Obrera* editorship under Angel Pestaña which offers proofs that Barcelona's chief of police, Manuel Bravo Portillo, is a leading figure in an extensive German spy network.

July

As White Armies continue their advance, Tsar Nicholas II and his family are executed in Ekaterinburg.
Law of espionage passed by the Spanish Cortes.
The CRT adopts the strategy of *sindicatos únicos*.
Lenin is shot by a Socialist Revolutionary but survives. The Bolsheviks crush opposition in the capital.

August

Beginning of a successful Allied counter-offensive.
After continuous sinking of Spanish merchant vessels, the government sends ultimatum to Germany, but further action has to be abandoned after royal veto.

September

German Army High Command admits defeat and advises the establishment of a parliamentary regime to negotiate an armistice based on Wilson's proposals.
Bulgaria sues for peace.

October

Mutinies and rebellions rock the Central Powers.
The departure of the Minister of Education, Santiago Alba, initiates the disintegration of the National Government.

November

As the war ends on the continent, revolution spreads in central Europe where former rulers have to abdicate and flee. Power is in the hands of workers' and soldiers' councils.
Maura's National Government collapses.

NOTES

1 INTRODUCTION

1 M. Tuñón de Lara, *Poder y sociedad en España, 1900–1931*, Madrid, 1992, pp. 108–19, 202–11.

2 On *caciquismo* and liberal politics see J. Varela Ortega, 'Los amigos políticos: funcionamiento del sistema caciquista', J. Romero Maura, 'El *caciquismo*: tentativa de conceptualización' and J. Tusell, 'La descomposición del sistema caciquista español', all in *Revista de Occidente*, October 1973, no. 127, pp. 17–117; R. W. Kern, *Liberals, Reformers and Caciques in Restoration Spain*, Alburquerque, 1974; J. Costa, *Oligarquía y caciquismo*, Madrid, 1975; J. Tusell, *Oligarquía y caciquismo en Andalucía*, Madrid, 1976; J. Varela Ortega, *Los amigos políticos. Partidos, elecciones y caciquismo en la Restauración, 1875–1900*, Madrid, 1977; M. Tuñón de Lara, 'De la Restauración al desastre colonial', *Historia 16,* June 1982, *Extra XXII: La España de los caciques*, pp. 53–94; L. Arranz and M. Cabrera, 'El Parlamento de la Restauración', *Hispania*, January–April 1995, vol. LV, no. 189, pp. 67–98.

3 On the impact of 1898 see H. Ramsden, *The 1898 Movement in Spain*, London, 1974; R. Pérez Delgado, *1898. El año del desastre*, Madrid, 1976; J. Harrison, 'The Regenerationist Movement in Spain after the Disaster of 1898', *European Studies Review*, 1979, vol. 9, no. 1, pp. 1–27; J. Varela Ortega, 'Aftermath of Splendid Disaster: Spanish Politics before and after the Spanish American War of 1898', *Journal of Contemporary History*, 1980, vol. 15, pp. 317–44; C. Serrano, *Final del Imperio, España, 1895–1898*, Madrid, 1984; M. Tuñón de Lara, *España: la quiebra de 1898*, Madrid, 1986; J. Smith, *The Spanish-American War. Conflict in the Caribbean and the Pacific*, London, 1994; S. Balfour, *The End of the Spanish Empire, 1898–1923*, Oxford, 1997; J. Pan-Montojo (ed.), *Más se perdió en Cuba. España, 1898 y la crisis de fin de siglo*, Madrid, 1998.

4 B. de Riquer, *Regionalistes i Nacionalistes, 1898–1931*, Barcelona, 1979, pp. 42–9; J. Harrison, 'The Catalan Industrial Elite, 1898–1923', in P. Preston and F. Lannon (eds), *Elites and Power in Twentieth-Century Spain: Essays in Honour of Sir Raymond Carr*, Oxford, 1990, pp. 53–5.

5 The best analysis of the Tragic Week is J. Connelly Ullman, *The Tragic Week: Anticlericalism in Spain, 1875–1912*, Harvard, 1968; see also J. Romero Maura, *'La rosa de fuego'. El obrerismo barcelonés de 1899 a 1909*, Barcelona, 1974; P. Voltes, *La Semana Trágica*, Madrid, 1995.

6 Quoted in G. Maura and M. Fernández Almagro, *Por qué cayó Alfonso XIII*, Madrid, 1948, pp. 240–1:

('The Conservative party cannot work any longer within the system as His Majesty's Opposition, nor rotate in government nor share responsibilities . . . the present administration or others to be formed with similar elements will have to last until another party, different from the present Conservative party, has been formed, *Idóneo* [compatible] to alternate in power with the Liberal party.')

7 Ibid., pp. 248–62; see also R. Pérez Delgado, *Antonio Maura*, Madrid, 1974, pp. 594–7; M. J. González Hernández, *Ciudadanía y Acción: el conservadurismo maurista, 1907–1923*, Madrid, 1990, pp. 30–43.

2 THE OUTBREAK OF WAR

1 Tuñón, *Poder*, p. 187.
2 Quoted in Maura and Fernández Almagro, *Por qué*, pp. 472–3.
3 On the Socialists' support for neutrality see Fundación Pablo Iglesias, Amaro del Rosal Díaz's Papers: History of the UGT (hereafter AARD-330-2), August 1914, and *El Socialista*, 2 and 4 August 1914. For the Lliga Regionalista see *La Veu de Catalunya*, 19 August 1914. Maura's backing for neutrality can be found in Biblioteca de la Real Academia de la Historia, Eduardo Dato's Papers (hereafter AD), letters from Maura to Dato, 2 and 28 August 1914. Many believed that the main cause of Spanish neutrality was military incapacity and the economic weakness of the country which made it impossible to wage a modern war. See, for instance, M. Azaña, *Los motivos de la Germanofilía, Discurso en el Ateneo de Madrid el 15 de Mayo de 1917*, Madrid, 1917, pp. 6, 18; M. Cordero, *Los socialistas y la revolución*, Madrid, 1932, p. 26; M. Espadas Burgos, 'España y la guerra', *Historia 16*, 1983, no. 51, pp. 89–90.
4 See Public Record Office, *Foreign Office Records* (hereafter FO) 371-2105/49,262, dispatch from Ambassador Hardinge to Grey, Minister for Foreign Affairs, about the Spanish army's hostility to Lerroux's pro-Allied stance, 14 September 1914; FO 371-2106/69,755, Hardinge to Grey concerning his embarrassment at being approached by Lerroux's Radical party, 11 November 1914.
5 Romanones, *Notas de una vida, 1912–1931*, Madrid, 1947, pp. 94–5; *Las responsabilidades del antiguo régimen, 1875–1923*, Madrid, n.d., p. 77.
6 FO 371-2104/72,570, Hardinge to Grey, 18 November 1914.
7 L. Araquistáin, *Entre la guerra y la revolución. España en 1917*, Madrid, 1917, pp. 6–7.
8 G. Meaker, 'A Civil War of Words' in H. A. Schmitt (ed.), *Neutral Europe between War and Revolution, 1917–1923*, Charlottesville, 1988, pp. 1–2, 6–7; also see A. Posada, *Actitud ética ante la guerra y la paz*, Madrid, 1923, pp. 13–14.
9 Archivo General de la Administración (hereafter AGA), *Foreign Office Section*, Washington, Idd. 26; boxes 8134, 8136, 8140, 8141, 8142 and 8152.
10 FO 371-2195/37,227, visit of Spanish ambassador, Merry del Val, to British Foreign Office, 11 August 1914; FO 371-2169/39,448 and FO 371-2169/40,133, Spanish officers in the British army and Navy, 17 and 18 August 1914. FO 371-2104/72,750, Hardinge to Grey on the divisions within the two dynastic parties, 18 November 1914; FO 371-2468/7611, Hardinge to Grey about his satisfaction with the current government, 20 January 1915; FO 371-2468/85,652, Hardinge to Grey about the hostility of the German ambassador, Prince Ratibor, towards the Spanish Minister for Foreign Affairs, Marquis de Lema, 23 June 1915.
11 See, among others, H. Cenamor Val, *Los españoles y la guerra: neutralidad o intervención*, Madrid, 1916; J. Román, *Voces de guerra*, Barcelona, 1916; L. Araquistáin, *Dos ideales políticos y otros trabajos*, Madrid, 1916, *Entre la guerra y la revolución*, and *Polémica de la guerra, 1914–1916*, Madrid, n.d.; L. Ballesteros, *La*

guerra europea y la neutralidad española, Madrid, 1917; Posada, *Actitud ética*, F. de la Reguera, *España neutral*, Madrid, 1967; F. Díaz Plaja, *Francófilos y Germanófilos. Los españoles y la guerra europea*, Barcelona, 1973; Meaker, 'Civil War of Words'; see also FO 371-2471/73,963 and FO 371-2760/20,756, secret reports, 29 July 1915 and 17 April 1916.

12 Díaz Plaja, *Francóphilos,* pp. 150–2, 162; Cenamor Val, *Los españoles y la guerra,* pp. 228–30; see also FO 371-2471/103,219, memo from British Consular agent Butler on the attitude of Spanish bishops towards the war (29 July 1915); FO 371-2472/44,697, Germanophilia of Spanish clergy confirmed during the tour of the Bishop of Southwark, 5 October 1915.

13 FO 371-2471/103,219, memo from British Consular agent Butler on the position of the army, 29 July 1915; FO 371-2105/49,962, Hardinge to Grey on the Germanophilia of the army, 14 September 1914; FO 371-2468/115,649, Hardinge to Grey on plans of certain officers to annex Portugal, 19 August 1915.

14 FO 371-2471/103,219, memo from Butler on *Maurista*s and Carlists as the two most Germanophile political groups in Spain, 29 July 1915.

15 FO 371-2412/51,655, Hardinge to Grey commenting on Maura's speech, 29 April 1915. Maura's speech at the Royal Theatre is in A. Maura, *Tres discursos*, Madrid, 1918, pp. 9–35.

16 FO 371-2762/185,472, Hardinge to Grey commenting on Maura's second speech, 12 September 1916; Maura's speech at Berlanga is in Maura, *Tres discursos*, pp. 39–53.

17 On the role of Alfonso XIII during the war see V. Espinos Moltó, *Alfonso XIII, espejo de neutrales*, Madrid, 1977; see also Princesa Pilar de Baviera and C. Chapman-Huston, *Alfonso XIII*, Barcelona, 1945, pp. 165–89; J. Cortés Cavanillas, *Alfonso XIII*, Barcelona, 1966, pp. 148–61; M. Fernández Almagro, *Historia del reinado de Alfonso XIII*, Barcelona, 1977, pp. 205–61.

18 The Spanish king was believed until 1916 to favour the Allied cause. See, for instance, FO 371-2105/49,204, Hardinge to Grey, 14 September 1914; FO 371-2760/20,576, secret report, 2 February 1916. But Alfonso moved towards the Germanophile camp in 1917. See Romanones, *Notas*, p. 100; FO 371-3033/96,587, memo by British Military Attaché Jocelyn Grant, 5 May 1917; FO 371-3033/92,539, opinion of the French ambassador, 7 May 1917.

19 Meaker, 'War of Words', pp. 24–31; Díaz Plaja, *Francófilos*, pp. 24–5, 190–1, 339–43.

20 The best collection of documents and information about the Volunteers can be found in Arxiu Nacional de Catalunya, Dr Joan Solé i Pla's Papers. The thorough work by D. Martínez Fiol, *Els Voluntaris Catalans a la Gran Guerra, 1914–1918*, Barcelona, 1991, pp. 105–28, destroys the myth of the existence of 15,000 Spanish Volunteers, 12,000 of them Catalans. This author proves that there were 2,118 Volunteers, 935 of them Catalans. See also A. Balcélls, 'Los Voluntarios Catalanes en la Gran Guerra (1914–1918)' in *Historia 16*, May 1986, no. 121, pp. 51–62; FO 371-2471/73,963, memo from Butler on Catalans, 29 July 1915. On Cambó's ambiguous position see J. Pabón, *Cambó*, Barcelona, 1952, vol. 1, pp. 448–9; F. Cambó, *Memorias*, Madrid, 1987, p. 219.

21 For Lerroux's interventionism see D. Martínez Fiol, 'Lerrouxistas en pie de guerra' in *Historia 16*, October 1990, no. 174, pp. 22–30.

22 Most Socialists, Syndicalists and Regionalists describe Lerroux as a demagogue and unprincipled adventurer. See, for instance, Cordero, *Los socialistas y la revolución*, pp. 27–8; A. Saborit, *La huelga de agosto de 1917*, Mexico, 1967, pp. 27, 35; P. Foix, *Los archivos del terrorismo blanco: el fichero Lasarte 1910–1930*, Madrid, 1978, p. 101; Cambó, *Memorias*, p. 187. Modern historiography has to a certain extent

restored Lerroux's tarnished reputation by trying to find a balance between his opportunism and collaboration with Liberal governments in Madrid and his ability to create a modern political party by mobilizing elements of the proletariat and petty bourgeoisie, formerly unrepresented within the Spanish political system. See Romero-Maura, *'La rosa de fuego'*, Madrid, 1989; J. Alvarez Junco, *El Emperador del Paralelo. Lerroux y la demagogia populista*, Madrid, 1990; J. R. Mosher, *The Birth of Mass Politics in Spain. Lerrouxismo in Barcelona, 1901 1909*, New York, 1991. On Francophile feelings among the Republicans see FO 371-2471/73,963, memo from Butler, 29 July 1915; FO 371-2105/49,204 and FO 371-2106/69,755, Hardinge to Grey, 24 September 1914 and 11 November 1914; FO 371-2471/69,000, Hardinge to Grey on rumours of Radicals planning to attack German ships in Barcelona, 12 June 1915. On Lerroux's position at the outbreak of the war see A. Lerroux, *La verdad a mi país. España y la guerra*, Madrid, 1915, p. 51; O. Ruiz Manjón, *El partido republicano radical, 1908–1936*, Madrid, 1976, pp. 110–11.

23 M. García Venero, *Melquiades Alvarez: historia de un liberal*, Madrid, 1974, pp. 316–18; M. Suárez Cortina, *El reformismo en España*, Madrid, 1986, pp. 148–55.
24 M. Buenacasa, *El movimiento obrero español, 1886–1926*, Paris, 1966, pp. 55–7; C. Forcadell, *Parlamentarismo y bolchevización*, Barcelona, 1978, pp. 215–29; A. Bar, *La CNT en los años rojos: del sindicalismo revolucionario al anarcosindicalismo, 1910–1926*, Madrid, 1981, pp. 359–431.
25 A. Fabra Ribas, *El socialismo y el conflicto europeo. ¡El Kaiserismo: He ahí el peligro!*, Valencia, 1915; see also M. Tuñón de Lara, *El movimiento obrero en la historia de España*, Madrid, 1972, pp. 574–81; J. L. Gómez Llorente, *Aproximación a la historia del socialismo español*, Madrid, 1976, pp. 105–6; Forcadell, *Parlamentarismo*, pp. 84–92. For a fuller consideration of the 1915 debate see AARD-330-2 (1915).
26 FO 371-2106/64,601, Hardinge to Grey, 29 October 1914.
27 FO 371-2106/60,039, Director of the Intelligence service to Hardinge, 13 October 1914.
28 E. Montero, 'Luis Araquistáin y la propaganda aliada durante la primera guerra mundial', in *Estudios de Historia Social*, 1983, nos. 24–5, pp. 245–8.
29 FO 371-2105/58,868, 2105/64,599 and 2105/69,076, Hardinge to Grey, 13 and 23 October, 9 November 1914.
30 FO 371-2468/103,725, Hardinge to Grey, 29 July 1915. The Ambassador was against the entry of Portugal into the war. He wrote: 'The present benevolent neutrality of Portugal is more useful to us than her active military help, especially if we have to buy it by the sacrifice of sympathy and goodwill in the peninsula.' See also FO 371-2472/100,366, Foreign Office to British Ambassador at Lisbon, Lancelot D. Carnegie, 24 July 1915. The Foreign Office pointed out the following advantages of Portugal's entry into the war:

(1) Take possession of 44 enemy ships now in Portuguese ports.
(2) Increase efficiency of our patrol of the western coast of the peninsula by using Portuguese ports.
(3) Complete the blockade of German East Africa.

And the following disadvantages:

(1) Lose Portugal as intermediary for buying Brazilian, Danish and other neutral-owned munitions.
(2) Lose our freedom in the settlement of Africa after the war. We might be faced with the alternative of ingratitude or surrender to Portugal of some part of Northern German South-West Africa and Southern German East Africa.
(3) We might be faced with trouble from Spain or internal revolution at Lisbon.

The ambiguous conclusion was that Portugal should not become a belligerent as she was more useful rendering services in her condition of neutrality. It was impossible, however, not to see the strength of the argument that Portugal had earned the lasting enmity of Germany without establishing any binding claim on the benevolence of Britain.

31 FO 371-2470/3456, Hardinge to Grey, 9 January 1915.

32 FO 371-2470/14,004, Hardinge to Grey, 5 February 1915.

33 According to Romanones, Dato claimed that the German ambassador had offered Tangier, Gibraltar and Portugal in exchange for Spanish support in the war. See Romanones, *Notas*, p. 103. In FO 371-2470/29,115, the king confirmed to Monsieur Cooreman the German offer of Gibraltar, Morocco and free hand in Portugal, 13 March 1915; FO 371-2472/144,697: the Spanish monarch said exactly the same thing to the Bishop of Southwark (5 October 1915); FO 371-2472/159,874: information confirmed by Leopoldo Romeo, the pro-Allied editor of *La Correspondencia de España*, 28 October 1915.

34 FO 371-2105/40,112, secret report by War Admiralty Staff, 17 August 1914.

35 FO 371-2050/38,811, Foreign Office memorandum, 13 August 1914.

36 Fernández Almagro, *Historia*, p. 212.

37 FO 371-2412/46,393, Grey to Hardinge, 20 April 1915.

38 Maura, *Tres discursos*, p. 23.

39 See *ABC* (11 April 1915) and *El Mundo* (12 April 1915).

40 Both mentioned above, in note 32.

41 FO 371-2412/65,976, 25 May 1916.

42 FO 371-2470/29,500, 15 March 1915.

43 FO 371-2412/65,976, Hardinge to Grey following Russian support for the Spanish claim on Tangier, 25 May 1915; FO 371-2472/100,366: War Office and Admiralty consider Spanish claim, 24 July 1915; FO 371-2412/160,862 and 2412/166,839, conversations of Grey with Cambon, 28 October and 11 November 1915.

44 R. Carr, *Spain, 1808–1975*, Oxford, 1982, pp. 481–2.

45 On the impact of the war on the economy see Instituto de Reformas Sociales, *Informes de los inspectores de trabajo sobre la influencia de la guerra europea en las industrias españolas*, Madrid, 1918, and *Movimientos de precios al por menor durante la guerra*, Madrid, 1923; I. Bernís, *Consecuencias económicas de la guerra*, Madrid, 1923; J. L. García Delgado, S. Roldán and J. Muñoz, *La formación de la sociedad capitalista en España (1914–1920)*, Madrid, 1973; J. Vicéns Vives, *Historia de España y América*, vol. V, Barcelona, 1972.

46 J. de la Cierva, *Notas de mi vida*, Madrid, 1955, p. 180; Romanones, *Responsabilidades*, p. 82.

3 THE DOMESTIC CHALLENGE

1 Many sources describe Romanones as the perfect example of a professional politician associated with the corrupt practices of the *Turno* era. See, for instance, Saborit, *La huelga*, pp. 27, 95–6, 262; Cierva, *Notas*, p. 58; Cambó, *Memorias*, pp. 239–40; T. G. Trice, *Spanish Liberalism in Crisis*, New York, 1991, pp. 45–7; J. Moreno Luzón, 'Romanones: Conquistador de clientelas. Gran Señor', *Historia Contemporánea*, 1996, nos. 13–14, pp. 281–8. For views on the Count by famous essayists and novelists of that period see J. Tusell, *La política y los políticos en tiempos de Alfonso XIII*, Madrid, 1976, p. 61; S. Forner Muñoz, *Canalejas y el partido liberal demoncrático*, Madrid, 1993, p. 38.

2 Romanones (*Notas*, p. 13) claims that there was no united and strong Liberal party after the death of the historical leader, Práxedes Sagasta, in 1903. In his

own defence, Romanones notes that he managed to seize the leadership of the party after the assassination of the then Prime Minister and leader Canalejas as a result of the role played by the monarch. His main rival for the post, the Marquis of Alhucemas, seemed to be the best candidate but Alfonso, always willing to put into practice the principle of *divide et impera*, threw his support behind Romanones.

3 Most authors absolve Dato of any part in the internal coup which ended Maura's leadership of the Conservative party. In fact, Dato seems to have tried to persuade Maura until almost the last moment to form a Conservative government. It was Maura's own obstinacy as well as Romanones (with the connivance of the monarch) who brought about his fall. There is abundant evidence of this in the private archives of both Maura and Dato. See Fundación Antonio Maura, Antonio Maura's Papers (hereafter AM), Leg. 19, letters from Cierva to Maura, 25 June and 26 October 1913; Leg. 34, letters from Dato to Maura, 12 July and 19 October 1913. See also AD, letter from Maura to Dato, 23 October 1913. Dato's position is strongly defended in C. Seco Serrano, *Perfil político y humano de un político de la restauración. Eduardo Dato a través de su archivo*, Madrid, 1978, pp. 61–73, and V. Martín Nogales, *Eduardo Dato*, Alava, 1993, pp. 56–9. More critical are the views of Maura and Fernández Almagro, *Por qué*, pp. 257–60; J. Gutiérrez Ravé, *Yo fui un joven maurista*, Madrid, 1944, pp. 129–30, 183; González Hernández, *Ciudadanía*, pp. 39–40. Dato's premiership is heavily attacked in Fernández Almagro, *Historia*, pp. 191–3. He argues that the Dato cabinet was created to remove a man, Maura, rather than to follow a programme: 'Andando de puntillas Dato había aprendido a llegar lejos. Maura pisando fuerte iba camino del destierro' ('Walking on tiptoes Dato had learned to go far. Maura treading firmly was on his way to exile').

4 Parliamentary Records, 1914–1918 (hereafter DSC), 10 May 1916.

5 Araquistáin, *Entre la guerra*, p. 101.

6 For the origins and evolution of Spain's labour movement prior to the First World War see, among others, Buenacasa, *El movimiento obrero español*, pp. 19–40; D. Abad de Santillán, *Contribución a la historia del movimiento obrero español*, 3 vols., Puebla, 1965, vol. 1, pp. 30–117; F. Romeu Alfaro, *Las clases trabajadoras en España (1898–1930)*, Madrid, 1970, pp. 44–89; Tuñón de Lara, *El movimiento obrero*, pp. 62–445; Gómez Llorente, *Aproximación a la historia del socialismo español*, pp. 104–59; Bar, *La CNT en los años rojos*, pp. 13–316; P. Heywood, *Marxism and the Failure of Organized Socialism in Spain, 1879–1936*, Cambridge, 1990, pp. 1–28; B. Martin, *The Agony of Modernization. Labour and Industrialization in Spain*, Ithaca, 1990, pp. 41–145; F. Olaya Morales, *Historia del movimiento obrero español (siglo XIX)*, Madrid, 1994, pp. 321–853; S. Juliá, *Los Socialistas en la política española, 1879–1982*, Madrid, 1997, pp. 15–85.

7 Tuñón de Lara, *El movimiento obrero*, pp. 30–9.

8 Heywood, *Marxism*, p. 36.

9 Instituto de Reformas Sociales, *Movimientos de precios*, pp. 16–17.

10 J. A. Lacomba, *La crisis española de 1917*, Málaga, 1970, p. 31.

11 Labour conflicts are well presented in *El Socialista*, *El Liberal*, *El País* and *El Heraldo de Madrid* (January–May 1916). See also J. M. Farré Morego, *Los atentados sociales en España*, Madrid, 1922, pp. 214–17.

12 J. Andrade, *La burocracia reformista en el movimiento obrero*, Madrid, 1935, pp. 8–9, 29–30.

13 *El Socialista* (20, 22 January and 24–27 February 1916, 1, 8, 13, 18–20 March 1916); *España* no. 51 (13 January 1916), no. 52 (20 January 1916) and no. 58 (2 March 1916).

14 Fundación Pablo Iglesias, Amaro del Rosal Diaz's Papers. UGT's Papers. National Committee Resolutions, 1916–1918 (hereafter AARD-IX).

15 See DSC (28 June, 4 and 7 November 1916). Newspapers supporting opposite political tendencies had welcomed and backed Urzaiz. See, for instance, *España*, nos. 51–54 (20 January–3 February 1916), in which the work of Urzaiz is praised, and no. 58 (2 March 1916). Araquistáin, in an editorial called 'La crisis', argued that the sacking of Urzaiz was a victory for Romanones and the plutocracy. In another article called 'El mastín y el zorro' ('Fox and hound'), another journalist, Luis de Olarriaga, claimed that the plutocracy must have been delighted with the departure of Urzaiz and the rise of two Castilian caciques, Villanueva and Alba. In *España* no. 94 (9 November 1916), Araquistáin, echoing Urzaiz's words in the Cortes, entitled his editorial: 'Todo el régimen es una prevaricación' ('The whole regime is prevarication'). Similar editorials favourable to Urzaiz can be found in *El Socialista* (20 January, 25–26 February and 5–6 November 1916). See also the Maurista journal *La Acción* (28 February, 29 June, 7 August, 7 and 29 November 1916). On 6 November 1916 *La Acción* called the system 'a fetid pond' and its representatives 'a tribe of gipsies prepared to trade with everything regardless of the fact that they are leading the country to total ruin'.

16 Archivo Histórico Nacional, Serie A, Home Office Papers (hereafter AHN). Leg. 27 A, Exp. no. 6, instructions from Alba to governors for the elections of 9 April 1916.

17 F. Soldevilla, *El año político de 1916*, Madrid, 1917, pp. 92–5. All the leading politicians of the Restoration – Dato, Romanones, Maura, Gasset, Alhucemas, Montero Ríos, Sagasta, etc – had one or more relatives in the Cortes. Over twenty national newspapers had their editors or members of their staff returned as Deputies. Examples were *La Tribuna*, *La Acción*, *El Socialista*, *El Liberal*, *El Imparcial*, *El Diario Universal*, *El Heraldo de Madrid*, *El País*, *La Mañana*, *El ABC* and *El Correo Español*.

18 *El Socialista*, 3, 5, 22 and 25 April 1916; *España*, nos. 63–5 (6, 13 and 20 April 1916).

19 AARD-IX, 1916.

20 *El Socialista*, 24 May 1916.

21 AARD-330-2, 1916.

22 A. Saborit, *Julián Besteiro*, Mexico City, 1961, pp. 87–8. See also Saborit, *La huelga*, p. 44. According to Saborit, Acevedo did not believe in his own proposal and was actually expecting a negative response from the UGT which he knew to be reluctant to collaborate with the CNT.

23 Heywood (*Marxism*, pp. 40–1) stresses that the rapprochement between the CNT and the UGT was partly due to the Socialist leaders' realization that they should be able to subsume the still smaller CNT within a united trade union federation in which they would retain the upper hand. Nevertheless, it seems that pressure from below in both organizations was the main cause of their pact of alliance.

24 AARD-330-2, 1916.

25 Details of the UGT Congress can be found in *El Socialista*, 19–25 May 1916.

26 The most important objective of the railway workers was the recognition of their trade union. See A. Saborit, *Asturias y sus hombres*, Toulouse, 1963, p. 164; García Venero, *Melquiades*, p. 357; for Romanones's despair see Real Academia de la Historia, Romanones's Papers (hereafter AR), Leg. 8 Exp. no. 1, letter to Fermín Calbetón, Spain's ambassador to the Vatican, 18 July 1916. The Count wrote: 'You cannot imagine what I have been going through with this strike . . . It has been the most difficult situation that Spain has faced for many years . . . It has

lasted eight days that have seemed to me like eight years.' For the events during
the railway strike and its aftermath see *El Socialista*, 8–20 July 1916; *España*
no. 77 (13 July 1916); Soldevilla, *El año político*, pp. 286–307.

27 The campaign was carried out in *El Socialista*, 22–26 August 1916. Romanones
was accused of being behind economic and mining interests in Morocco. He was
one of the main shareholders of the mining company La Colonizadora.

28 AARD-IX, 1916.

29 Fundación Pablo Iglesias, Papers of the Madrid Branch of the Socialist Party
(hereafter AASM-LXX-2).

30 Some leading pro-Entente editorials in *El Socialista*: 2 February 1916 ('Lucha de
clases', 'Class struggle'); 10 February 1916 ('La Internacional y la guerra', 'The
International and the war'); 2 May 1916 ('Los socialistas y la guerra', 'The socialists and the war'); 20 July 1916 ('Interview de Fabra y Ribas a Iglesias', 'Fabra
and Ribas visit Iglesias'); 26 August 1916 ('Nuestra actitud', 'Our attitude'); 22
September 1916 ('Impresiones de la guerra por Julián Besteiro', 'Julián Besteiro's
impressions of the war'); 30 December 1916 ('Enseñanzas de la realidad', 'Lessons
of reality'); 12 January 1917 ('La causa aliada', 'The allied cause'); 5 February
1917 ('A qué llamamos neutralidad', 'What we call neutrality'); In *España* no.
107, 8 February 1917 ('La nota de Alemania', 'Germany's note'); no. 108, 15
February 1917 ('Ante el furor germánico', 'Before the wrath of Germany'); no.
112, 15 March 1917 ('Los socialistas demandan urgentes medidas del gobierno',
'Socialists demand urgent action from government'); no. 113, 22 March 1917
('Sobre la revolución en Rusia', 'On the Russian Revolution').

31 Neutralist editorials in *Solidaridad Obrera*, 17 August and 16 November 1916; 3
and 5 February 1917.

32 AARD-IX, 1916.

33 Soldevilla, *El año 1916*, pp. 428–31.

34 AARD-IX, 1916.

35 See *ABC*, 18 December 1916; *La Acción*, 18–19 December 1916; *La Epoca*, 19
December 1916.

36 AHN, Leg. 16 A, Exp. no. 6 (labour conflicts).

37 Saborit, *La huelga*, p. 52; see also *El Socialista*, 20 December 1916; 7 and 12
January 1917.

38 Article by Iglesias in *El Socialista*, 8 January 1917. Attack on the bankruptcy of
the Junta de Subsistencias in *El Socialista*, 23 February 1917. See also AARD-IX,
1917.

39 *El Socialista*, 2 March 1917.

40 Ibid., 7 March 1917.

41 Ibid., 15 and 27 March 1917.

42 Ibid., 28 March 1917.

43 FO 185-1343/168, Hardinge to Balfour, 2 April 1917.

44 Saborit, *Besteiro*, p. 95.

45 The government was attacked by nearly all the main newspapers. See, for instance,
El Socialista, 29 March and 2 April 1917; *El Liberal*, 29 March 1917; *El Heraldo
de Madrid*, 29 March and 1 April 1917; *El País*, 29 March 1917; *El Imparcial*, 29
March 1917; *La Epoca*, 28–29 March 1917; *La Acción*, 27–29 March 1917.

46 A. Mayer, *The Persistence of the Old Regime*, New York, 1974. Although Spain is
not considered in this work, all the conditions underlined by Mayer to prove the
persistence of old regimes in Europe in 1914 were present there.

47 On the early period of the Lliga Regionalista see J. Pla, *Cambó. Materials per a una
historia d'aquesta ultims anys*, 3 vols., Barcelona, 1930; M. García Venero, *Historia
del nacionalismo catalán, 1793–1936*, Madrid, 1944; Pabón, *Cambó*; B. de Riquer,

La Lliga Regionalista: la burguesía catalana i el nacionalisme, Barcelona, 1977; J. A. González Casanova, *Federalismo y autonomía. Cataluña y el estado español, 1868– 1938*, Barcelona, 1979; A. Balcells, *Historia contemporánea de Cataluña*, Barcelona, 1981; A. Jutglar, *Historia crítica de la burguesía en Cataluña*, Barcelona, 1984; F. Cambó, *Memorias*, Madrid, 1987; A. Balcells, *Historia del nacionalisme catala. Dels origins al nostre temps*, Barcelona, 1992.

48 Vicens Vives, *Historia*, p. 350.

49 J. Harrison, *The Spanish Economy in the XXth Century*, London, 1985, pp. 39–40. García Delgado, Roldán and Muñoz, *La formación de la sociedad capitalista en España*, vol. 1, pp. 76–7.

50 The anger felt by the Lliga is well illustrated in the documents and articles in Arxiu Nacional de Catalunya, Enric Prat de la Riba's Papers, April 1916.

51 De Riquer, *Regionalistes i Nacionalistes*, pp. 90–2. Santiago Alba's links with Valladolid's wheat lobby can be seen in Varela Ortega, *Los amigos políticos*, pp. 347–8. For the results of the general election of April 1916 see Soldevilla, *El año 1916*, pp. 82–90.

52 Harrison, *The Spanish Economy*, p. 41.

53 E. Aunós, *Itinerario histórico de la España contemporánea, 1808–1936*, Barcelona, 1940, pp. 329–30.

54 *ABC*, 22 March 1916.

55 The Catalan question was covered in the editorials of several national newspapers: *El País, El Liberal, El Heraldo de Madrid, El Imparcial, La Acción, El ABC*, etc. (May–June 1916). Several leading politicians participated in the subsequent debate in the Cortes: Cambó (Lliga Regionalista); Romanones, Ortega y Gasset, Alcalá Zamora and Ríus (Liberal party); Marcelino Domingo (Catalan Republican); Nougués (Federal Republican); Rodés (Republican Nationalist).

56 On *Maurismo* see Maura and Fernández Almagro, *Por qué*; González Hernández, *Ciudadanía*; J. Gutiérrez Ravé, *Yo fui*; R. Punset, 'Maura y maurismo. Perspectiva histórica de la revolución desde arriba', *Sistema*, November 1979, no. 33, pp. 129–41; J. Tusell and J. Avilés, *La derecha española contemporánea. Sus origenes: el Maurismo*, Madrid, 1986; González Hernández, 'Sobre Antonio Maura', pp. 107– 24; J. Tusell, *Antonio Maura. Una biografía política*, Madrid, 1994.

57 AM, Leg. 82. Letters from Gustavo Peyrá to Maura, 12 and 28 June 1916.

58 DSC, 7 June 1916.

59 Cambó, *Memorias*, pp. 223–4.

60 The best study of Santiago Alba's economic projects is M. Cabrera, F. Comín and J. L. García Delgado, *Santiago Alba. Un programa de reforma económica en la España del primer tercio del Siglo XX*, Madrid, 1989.

61 Pabón, *Cambó*, vol. 1, pp. 448–9.

62 Cambó, *Memorias*, p. 246.

63 Cabrera *et al.*, *Santiago Alba*, pp. 143–6.

64 *La Veu de Catalunya*, 3–6 June 1916; *ABC*, 24 May 1916; see also García Delgado *et al.*, *La formación*, pp. 255–322; Cabrera *et al.*, *Santiago Alba*, pp. 369–410.

65 DSC, 17 June–12 July 1916. According to Cabrera *et al.* (ibid., pp. 410–18), Alba was ready to seek a compromise with those opposed to his projects. Nevertheless, Cambó (*Memorias*, p. 235) claims that the Lliga's obstructionist strategy was provoked by Alba's intransigence. Many newspapers' editorials agree that the Liberal cabinet was looking for an excuse to close the Cortes. See, for instance, *La Acción*, 8 and 14 July 1916; *La Epoca*, 23 July 1916; *El Socialista*, 24 July and 6 August 1916. This view seems to be confirmed by Romanones expressing in a letter to Calbetón on 12 July 1916 his intention to close the Cortes as soon as possible (AR, Leg. 8, Exp. no. 1).

66 *El Socialista*, 5, 7 and 27 June, 6 August and 1 October 1916; *España* nos. 72–5, 79 and 89 (8, 15, 22, 29 June, 27 July and 5 October 1916). Cambó (*Memorias*, 229) claims that he agreed to give a speech at the Socialist Casa del Pueblo at Madrid in order to prevent Alba from doing so.

67 Cambó, *Memorias*, pp. 239–40.

68 DSC, 31 October 1916.

69 DSC, 20–1 November 1916. See also *ABC*, 21 November 1916.

70 Real Academia de la Historia, Natalio Rivas's Papers. 'Memorias del reinado de Alfonso XIII, 1902–1931' (hereafter ANR), Leg. 8903 (December 1916).

71 Tusell and Avilés, *La derecha española*, pp. 107–8; Cambó, *Memorias*, pp. 242–3; Pabón, *Cambó*, vol. 1, pp. 469–70.

72 Ibid., p. 469; Cambó, *Memorias*, pp. 236–7; Lacomba, *La Crisis española*, p. 109.

73 On the role of the army in Spanish politics during the nineteenth century see S. Payne, *Politics and the Military in Modern Spain*, Stanford, 1967; E. Christiansen, *The Origins of Military Power in Spain, 1808–1854*, London, 1967; M. Alonso Baguer, *El ejército en la sociedad española*, Madrid, 1971; J. R. Alonso, *Historia política del ejército español*, Madrid, 1974; G. Cardona, *El poder militar en la España contemporánea hasta la guerra civil*, Madrid, 1983; C. Seco Serrano, *Militarismo y civilismo en la España contemporánea*, Madrid, 1984; M. Ballbé, *Orden público y militarismo en la España constitucional, 1812–1983*, Madrid, 1985; J. Lleixá, *Cien años de militarismo en España*, Barcelona, 1986.

74 Ballbé, *Orden público*, pp. 226–7.

75 Ibid., pp. 247–8; Lleixá, *Cien años*, p. 60.

76 C. P. Boyd, *Praetorian Politics in Liberal Spain*, Chapel Hill, 1979, pp. 27–9; Ballbé, *Orden Público*, pp. 249–50; Cardona, *El poder militar*, pp. 7–9.

77 Boyd, *Praetorian Politics*, p. 10.

78 Payne, *Politics and the Military*, pp. 76–81.

79 Ibid., p. 59.

80 Ballbé, *Orden político*, pp. 273–8.

81 Connelly Ullman, *The Tragic Week*, pp. 285–8.

82 Boyd, *Praetorian Politics*, p. 41.

83 Ibid., pp. 51–2.

84 Ibid., pp. 52–5.

85 B. Márquez and J. Capó, *Las juntas militares de defensa*, Havana, 1923, p. 24.

86 J. Buxadé, *España en crisis. La bullanga misteriosa de 1917*, Barcelona, 1917, pp. 33–43; see also Seco, *Militarismo*, pp. 257–63.

87 Márquez and Capó, *Las juntas*, p. 27.

88 Romanones, *Notas*, pp. 135–8, 141–4.

4 THE INTERNATIONAL CHALLENGE

1 Soldevilla, *El año 1916*, pp. 73–4.

2 In all his speeches in parliament throughout 1916, Romanones stressed his commitment to official neutrality and asked for the patriotic support of the chamber. See DSC, 10 May, 6 June, 13 October and 4 November 1916.

3 AR, II I A (correspondence with ambassadors), letter from León y Castillo, 22 April 1916.

4 AR, II I A, letter from Polo de Bernabé, 16 March 1916.

5 AR, II I A, letters from Romanones to León y Castillo, 25 January, 23 February, 23 and 30 March 1916.

6 AR, II I A, letters from León y Castillo to Romanones, 5 and 14 February, 27 March 1916.

7　FO 371-2711/29,361, Grey informs Hardinge of the meeting of the Spanish ambassador in Paris with the French Prime Minister, 10 February 1916.

8　AR, II I A, letters from León y Castillo to Romanones, 27 March, 10, 17 and 22 April, 8 and 22 May 1916.

9　AR, II I A, letters from Romanones to Merry del Val, 22 and 24 June 1916. See also AGA, London, idd. 77. Box 7046, 1916.

10　FO 371-2711/188,140, Hardinge to Grey, 10 December 1915.

11　FO 371-2711/19,049, Grey to Hardinge, 31 January 1916.

12　FO 371-2711/58,754, Grey to Hardinge, 31 March 1916.

13　FO 371-2711/72,158, Hardinge to Grey, 15 April 1916.

14　AM, Leg. 259, 4 September 1916.

15　Maura, *Tres discursos*, pp. 37–75. FO 371-2762/182,808: Hardinge wrote to Grey that Romanones had been successful in inducing Maura to support him in his pro-Entente foreign policy (15 September 1916).

16　On 13 September 1916 *La Tribuna*, a Germanophile newspaper, noted: 'Maura has betrayed his old friends at the request of important persons.' The pro-Allied press welcomed Maura's speech and *España* no. 86 (14 September 1916) suggested that if Maura kept delivering such pro-Western speeches he would soon be abandoned by the *Mauristas*.

17　FO 371-2762/182,208, Foreign Office to Hardinge, 13 September 1916.

18　FO 371-2762/189,921, Hardinge to Grey, 16 September 1916.

19　Romanones, *Notas*, p. 117; Romanones, *Responsabilidades*, p. 84.

20　FO 371-2760/20,756, secret report, 2 February 1916.

21　FO 395-117, secret report, October 1917, underlining the superiority of German propaganda in comparison to that of the Allies. It stressed that Germany was lavishing large sums of money in Spain to gain control of the press.

22　AHN, Leg. 48 A, Exp. 18, 2 February 1929. See also AR, Leg. 96, Exp. 33: on German espionage in Spain, written on 19 April 1919.

23　*La Acción*, 23–6 June 1916.

24　FO 371-2760/20,756, secret report, 2 February 1916.

25　FO 371-2761/87,617, Vaughan to Grey 8 May 1916.

26　*El Imparcial*, 24 June 1916.

27　For French protests about German submarine activities and the subsequent Spanish impotence see AGA, Paris, box 5946 (1916).

28　AR, Leg. 63, Exp. 46 (September 1916); see also FO 371-2762/189,923, Hardinge to Grey, 23 September 1916.

29　AGA, London, box 7039 and Paris, box 5955 (1916).

30　AR, Leg. 63, Exp. 31, April 1917.

31　AGA, Paris, box 5947 (1916).

32　FO 371-2762/229,037, Hardinge to Grey, 11 November 1916.

33　On the pro-German activities of the Governor of Fernando Poo see FO 371-2762/229,041, Grey to Hardinge, 14 November 1916 and FO 371-2762/260,662, Grey to Hardinge, 23 December 1916.

34　FO 371-2762/46,070, Grey to Hardinge, 14 February 1917.

35　AGA, Paris, box 5947. See also AR, Leg. 63, Exp. 46.

36　AR, Leg. 63, Exp. 46.

37　AGA, Paris, box 5957.

38　AR, Leg. 63, Exp. 46; Romanones, *Notas*, pp. 108–10; FO 371-2762/261,551. secret report, 26 December 1916.

39　For the pro-Allied press see *El Liberal*, *El Socialista*, *El Imparcial* and *España*; and for the pro-German press see *La Acción*, *El Día*, *La Tribuna*, *España Nueva* and *El Debate*. All in December 1916.

40 Espinos Moltó, *Alfonso XIII*, pp. 191–3, 201–3; see also AGA, Paris, box 5948.
41 FO 371-2762/256,871, Hardinge to Balfour, 14 December 1916.
42 ANR, Leg. 8903, 5 December 1916.
43 FO 371-2762/256,871, Hardinge to Balfour, 14 December 1916.
44 For the note see *El Liberal*, 28 December 1916. For Romanones's opposition to the king's intention to attend the funeral at Vienna see AR, II I A: letters from Romanones to Fermín Calbetón, 26 and 28 December 1916. See also ANR, Leg. 8903, 5–10 December 1916.
45 For the Austrian ambassador's attack on the Count see AHN, Leg. 48A. Exp. 18; see also FO 371-3033/11,492, January 1917. The telegram sent by the German ambassador was published by *El Imparcial* and *El País* (4 and 9 January 1917 respectively).
46 The most outstanding newspapers in the anti-Romanones campaign were *El Día*, *La Tribuna*, *La Nación*, *La Acción*, *El Debate* and *España Nueva*. See also ANR, Leg. 8903. According to Rivas, Alcalá Zamora, Liberal deputy and editor of *El Día*, supported a new Liberal cabinet headed by the pro-German General Weyler (18 December 1916).
47 FO 371-3033/11,492, Hardinge to Balfour, 17 January 1917.
48 *La Acción*, 9–10 January 1917.
49 *España* no. 107 (8 February 1917).
50 AR, II I A, letters from Romanones to León y Castillo, 3 and 6 February 1917, and to Merry del Val, 10 February 1917.
51 DSC, 1 February 1917.
52 *El Imparcial*, 8 February 1917.
53 DSC, 17 February 1917.
54 AR, II I A, León y Castillo to Romanones, 10 February 1917; see also FO 371-3035/39,928, Balfour to Hardinge, 20 February 1917.
55 AR, II I A, León y Castillo to Romanones, 6 February 1917, and Calbetón to Romanones, 17 February 1917.
56 AR, Leg. 63, Exp. 28, February 1917.
57 AR, Leg. 63, Exp. 28, April 1917; AR, II I A, Romanones to León y Castillo, 28 March 1917.
58 Germanophile newspapers such as the Republican *España Nueva* and the Anarcho-Syndicalist *Solidaridad Obrera* (18 and 20 March 1917 respectively) claimed that the revolution against the Tsar had been produced by the war weariness of both people and troops. By contrast, *El Socialista* in a series of editorials under the title *Contra el espíritu alemán* ('Against the German spirit', 17–24 March 1917) argued that the revolution had not been against the war but against reactionary circles in Russia seeking a separate peace with Germany. On 6 April 1917 Pablo Iglesias demanded the severence of diplomatic relations with Germany.
59 AR, II I A, Romanones to León y Castillo, 14 April 1917. The same day the latter had written: 'We must act now otherwise it will be too late.'
60 Public Record Office, Cabinet papers (CAB) 23/2. War Cabinet, no. 91, 8 March 1917.
61 CAB. 24/7. GT.132, March 1917; see also FO 371-3035/75,548, Vaughan to Balfour, 12 April 1917.
62 FO 371-3035/75,927, Vaughan writes to Balfour concerning the attitude of the US ambassador, 13 April 1917.
63 FO 371-3030/11,488, Jocelyn Grant to Balfour, 9 January 1917.
64 CAB 24/7. GT.161, 14 March 1917.
65 FO 371-3035/75,549, Conclusions of the Foreign Office after considering the advantages and disadvantages of Spain's entry into the war, 12 April 1917. CAB

23/2. no. 115: appointment of an interdepartmental committee to report on the issue of exchanging Gibraltar for Ceuta. The committee was chaired by Lord Curzon and was formed by two representatives from the Foreign Office, Sir Eyre Crowe and Lord Drogueda, one from the Admiralty, Rear Admiral Hope, and one from the War Office, Major General Maurice (6 April 1917). CAB 27/51. C.115: almost unanimously the committee came out against the proposed exchange of Gibraltar for Ceuta, 10 January 1919.

66 FO 371-3033/77,074, War Cabinet to Vaughan, 13 April 1917.
67 FO 371-3033/76,696 and 3033/77,736, Vaughan to War Cabinet, 13 and 14 April 1917.
68 *El Socialista*, 6 April 1917.
69 *El Debate*, 13 April 1917.
70 *El Debate, La Acción, España Nueva, ABC, Solidaridad Obrera*, April 1917.
71 The king's declarations in F. Soldevilla, *El año político de 1917*, Madrid, 1918, p. 115; Villanueva's in *El Debate* and *El Día*, 13 April 1917; Dato's in *La Epoca*, 14 April 1917; Alhucemas's in *La Mañana*, 14 April 1917; the army's in *La Correspondencia Militar*, 13 and 14 April 1917.
72 AR, II I A, Romanones to Calbetón, 18 April 1917.
73 AR, Leg. 63, Exp. 46, April 1917.
74 *La Acción*, 21 April 1917.

5 THE GATHERING STORM

1 *El Imparcial*, 21 April 1917.
2 AGA, Paris, box 5960.
3 CAB 24/15. GT.394: Impression of the Alhucemas cabinet in Britain, 1 June 1917. The note sent by the new Liberal government can be found in *La Epoca*, 27 April 1917.
4 AD, Mail from diplomats. Quiñones, a Spanish diplomat at Paris, wrote to Dato on 9 May 1917: 'A los ojos de los franceses, los españoles hemos perdido nuestra hidalguía' ('In the eyes of the French, we Spaniards have lost our dignity'). For French reaction to German submarine attacks in Spanish waters see AGA, Paris, box 5962, 9–15 May 1917.
5 *La Epoca*, 19 April 1917.
6 *España* no. 118 (26 April 1917). Romanones (*Notas*, p. 103) suggests that the king went over to the pro-German camp in 1917. FO 371-3033/96,587, Jocelyn Grant to Balfour, 5 May 1917.
7 *España* no. 118, 'Una crisis Germanófila' ('A Germanophile crisis', 26 April 1917); *El Socialista*, 'Saldo de Coronas' ('Balance of crowns', 29 April 1917).
8 *El Liberal*, 26 April 1917.
9 *La Acción*, 26 April 1917; *ABC*, 28 April 1917.
10 *El Socialista*: García Cortés's pro-neutrality editorial (1 May 1917) was followed one week later by Araquistáin's pro-interventionist answer (7 May 1917).
11 *Solidaridad Obrera*, 5, 9 and 10 May 1917.
12 AARD-IX, May 1917.
13 Fundación Pablo Iglesias, Papers of the Madrid Branch of the Socialist Party (AASM-LII-2, 21 May 1917). The CNT's note was published in *Solidaridad Obrera*, 25 May 1917. For the internal debate in the UGT see AARD-IX, May 1917.
14 Saborit, *La huelga*, p. 55.
15 Maura, *Tres Discursos*, pp. 57–73.
16 FO 185-1338/90,790: editorials from French newspapers – *Le Figaro, Le Matin, La Victoire* – on Maura's speech, 1 May 1917.

17 *El Liberal*, 1 May 1917; *España* no. 119 (3 May 1917).
18 *El País*, 28 May 1917.
19 The Allies' support for the Provisional Government in Russia was not missed by the Germanophile journals. They hinted that the Allies were behind that revolution and that they were also backing an insurrection which would establish an interventionist Republic in Spain. See *El Día*, 28 May 1917, and *La Acción*, 30 May 1917.
20 FO 185-1344, no. 299, Hardinge to Balfour, 6 June 1917.
21 *La Epoca*, 4 June 1917.
22 FO 185-1344, no. 268, Hardinge to Balfour, 19 May 1917.
23 Romanones, *Notas*, pp. 135–7.
24 On the events leading to the officers' rebellion of June 1917 see F. Soldevilla, *Tres Revoluciones (Apuntes y notas). La junta de reforma. La asamblea parlamentaria. La huelga general*, Madrid, 1917, pp. 1–30; Lacomba, *La crisis*, pp. 112–35; Buxadé, *La bullanga*, pp. 41–63; Márquez and Capó, *Las juntas*, pp. 23–40; Seco, *Militarismo*, pp. 257–67.
25 Márquez and Capó, *Las juntas*, p. 36.
26 *La Correspondencia Militar*, 6 June 1917.
27 Márquez and Capó, *Las juntas*, p. 36.
28 Ibid., appendix 2, pp. 178–9.
29 Soldevilla, *Tres revoluciones*, pp. 63–5.
30 *La Epoca*, 2 June 1917; *ABC*, 3 June 1917.
31 *La Correspondencia Militar*, 2, 6, 8 and 10 June 1917.
32 Márquez and Capó, *Las juntas*, pp. 41–2.
33 Romanones, *Notas*, p. 137.
34 AR, Leg. 1, letter from Romanones to Alhucemas, 10 June 1917.
35 AR, Leg. 1, Romanones to Dato, 12 June 1917; see also *La Correspondencia Militar*, 12 June 1917.
36 AR, Leg. 1, Romanones to Groizard and Villanueva, 23 June 1917.
37 AR, Leg. 1, Romanones to Groizard and Villanueva, 27 June 1917.
38 The internal quarrel in the Liberal party can be followed in Soldevilla, *El año 1917*, pp. 268–79. The former ambassador to the Vatican, Fermín Calbetón, became one of the Liberal notables mustering support for the Count and leading the campaign against the other camp. For his role see AR, Leg. 1, 29 June 1917.
39 Expression used by the Republican writer Alvaro de Albornoz in *El Parlamentario*, 27 June 1917.

6 TWO PARLIAMENTS IN ONE COUNTRY

1 Lacomba, *La crisis*, pp. 15–16.
2 Romanones, *Notas*, p. 141.
3 Soldevilla, *El año 1917*, pp. 255–7.
4 *El Heraldo de Madrid*, 6 June 1917.
5 AM, Leg. 389, Carp. 10, June 1917.
6 Suárez Cortina, *El reformismo*, pp. 170–1.
7 *El Socialista*, 8 June 1917.
8 Ibid., 12 June 1917.
9 García Venero, *Melquiades Alvarez*, p. 339.
10 AM, Leg. 259, 12 June 1917.
11 *La Acción*, 11 and 13 June 1917. AM, Leg. 399, Carp. 18: letter from Francisco Salcedo Bermejillo to Goicoechea, leader of the *Maurista* youth, apologizing for the incident in which he struck the monarch's portrait. He offered his resignation

which was not accepted. Goicoechea wrote to the king's secretary, the Marquis of Torrecilla, confirming that monarchism was one of the pillars of *Maurismo*. The following day the Marquis replied that the king had been notified and was grateful for the *Mauristas*' loyalty (11–12 June 1917).

12 M. Burgos y Mazo, *Vida política española. Páginas históricas de 1917*, Madrid, 1918, pp. 59, 64–73.
13 *La Veu de Catalunya*, 14 June 1917.
14 Lacomba, *La crisis*, pp. 174–8; Pabón, *Cambó*, vol. 1, pp. 501–7.
15 Cambó, *Memorias*, p. 255.
16 Soldevilla, *Tres revoluciones*, p. 16.
17 M. Domingo, *¿Qué espera el Rey?*, Madrid, 1930, pp. 25–31.
18 Maura and Fernández Almagro, *Por qué*, p. 298; AM, Leg. 399, Carp. 18: letter from Dr Zúñiga Garrido to Maura. The former stressed that he was a monarchist but he was prepared to follow blindly Maura even against the monarchy (11 June 1917). AM, Leg. 401, Carp. 3: Letters from various *Mauristas* criticizing the monarch for endorsing the *Turno* instead of calling Maura, June 1917.
19 AM, Leg. 29. Maura's abstentionist stand was applauded by Cierva. He confided to his former chief that if Dato was overthrown political anarchy would follow (12 July 1917).
20 F. J. Romero Salvadó, 'Maura, Maurismo and the Crisis of 1917', *Journal for the Association for Contemporary Iberian Studies (ACIS)*, Spring 1994, vol. 7, no. 1, p. 22.
21 AM, Leg. 402, Carp. 22. Two officers from the regiment Cazadores de Estella to Maura, 6 June 1917.
22 AM, Leg. 389, Carp. 10: Gustavo Peyrá to Maura, 20 June 1917. AM, Leg. 402, Carp. 22, Gabriel Maura to Antonio Maura, 22 June 1917.
23 AM, Leg. 389, Carp. 10, Maura to Peyrá, 23 June 1917.
24 AM, Leg. 389, Carp. 10, Peyrá to Maura, 25 and 28 June 1917.
25 Maura and Fernández Almagro, *Por qué*, p. 487. Two letters from Antonio to Gabriel Maura, 23 and 30 June 1917.
26 AM, Leg. 362, Carp. 2, Miguel Maura to Antonio Maura, 24 June 1917, and Gabriel to Antonio Maura, 26 June, 3 and 8 July 1917.
27 AM, Leg. 390, Carp. 7: *Maurista* Centre at Chamberí to Maura, 4 July 1917; Leg. 185, Alfonso Nadal to Maura, 6 and 11 July 1917; Leg. 80, Ossorio to Maura, 9 July 1917; Leg. 19, Cambó to Gabriel Maura, 10 and 11 July 1917.
28 Maura and Fernández Almagro, *Por qué*, pp. 487–8. Antonio to Gabriel Maura, 6 July 1917.
29 Romero Salvadó, 'Maura, Maurismo', p. 23.
30 AM, Leg. 390, Carp. 7, Maura to *Maurista* Centre at Chamberí, 7 July 1917; Leg. 397, Carp. 7, Maura to Ossorio, 12 July 1917; Leg. 185, Catalan *Mauristas* to Maura and reply, 15 July 1917. Fundación Antonio Maura, *Gabriel Maura's Papers* (AGM), Leg. 113, Carp. 4, Gabriel Maura to Abadal, 17 July 1917.
31 AM, Leg. 402, Carp. 22, Peyrá to Maura, 10 July 1917.
32 Dato's role in the summer of 1917 is strongly defended by Seco Serrano both in *Perfil político y humano*, pp. 80–4 and *Militarismo y civilismo*, p. 270.
33 L. Simarro, *Los sucesos de agosto en el parlamento*, Madrid, 1918, pp. 331–6.
34 Soldevilla, *El año 1917*, p. 288.
35 AD, letters from former ministers, Fernando Primo de Rivera to Dato, 28 July 1917; see also ANR, Leg. 8911, July 1917.
36 *La Epoca*, 26 June 1917.
37 AHN, Leg. 42 A, Exp. 1, instructions from Sánchez Guerra to civil governors, 25–26 June 1917.
38 *La Epoca*, 8 July 1917.

39 *La Epoca*, 13 July 1917.
40 *El Heraldo de Madrid*, 6 July 1917. See also M. Bajatierra, *Desde las barricadas. Una semana de revolución en España. Las jornadas de Madrid en agosto de 1917*, Tortosa, 1918, pp. 20–3; Cordero, *Los Socialistas*, pp. 30–4.
41 Pla, *Cambó*, vol. 3, p. 136.
42 Márquez and Capó, *Las Juntas*, pp. 48–50.
43 Ibid., p. 46.
44 J. J. Morato, *Pablo Iglesias Posse. Educador de muchedumbres*, Barcelona, 1931, p. 160.
45 *Solidaridad Obrera*, 17 July 1917.
46 For the publication of illegal leaflets see Burgos y Mazo, *Vida política*, pp. 74–83; Bajatierra, *Desde las barricadas*, p. 20. Cambó's pamphlet was published in *España* no. 130 (19 July 1917).
47 AHN, Leg. 42 A, instructions from Sánchez Guerra to civil governors, July 1917; see also Lacomba, *La crisis*, pp. 187–93. According to Burgos y Mazo (*Vida política*, p. 84) Lerroux and Cambó agreed to set up a Federal Republic. Lerroux could have his Republic and Cambó virtual independence for Catalonia.
48 AM, Leg. 362, Carp. 2, Ossorio to Maura, 13 July 1917; Gabriel to Antonio Maura, 14 July 17; Miguel to Antonio Maura, 14 July 1917.
49 Márquez and Capó, *Las juntas*, p. 40.
50 Soldevilla, *El año 1917*, p. 238.
51 FO 371-3036/127,522, Hardinge to Balfour, 19 June 1917.
52 CAB 24. Vol. 21. GT.1511, information Bureau, weekly report on Spain, Department of Intelligence, 25 July 1917.
53 AM, Leg. 362, Carp. 2, Ossorio to Maura, 13 July 1917. Ossorio noted: 'El Rey aún confía en su habilidad para engañar a todo el mundo' ('The king still believes in his ability to deceive everyone').
54 That meeting is denied by Cambó in his memoirs (p. 256), but is confirmed by Márquez and Capó, *Las juntas*, pp. 48–50 and mentioned by Saborit (*La huelga*, p. 256).
55 AR, Leg. 14, Exp. 19, the Assembly of parliamentarians.
56 Arxiu Nacional de Catalunya, Lluis Durán i Ventosa's Papers (hereafter ADV), notes from Cambó to Ventosa. The first sent from the restaurant in the Casino del Parque, and the second from the Palacio del Gobernador del Parque de la Ciudadela.
57 See Simarro, *Los sucesos*, pp. 365–79; Soldevilla, *El año 1917*, pp. 325–39.
58 *La Epoca* (20 July 1917). Headline: 'El triunfo del espírítu público' ('The triumph of public spirit'). Sánchez Guerra declared that there had been neither Assembly nor arrests.
59 FO 185-1346/390 and 371-3033/143,746, Hardinge to Balfour, 20 July 1917.
60 AM, Leg. 402, Carp. 22, Peyrá to Maura, 21 July 1917.
61 *La Acción*, 20 and 21 July 1917.
62 Lacomba, *La crisis*, p. 201.
63 J. A. Lacomba, 'España en 1917. Ensayo de morfología de una crisis histórica', *Revista Saitabi* (Valencia 1971), p. 152; see also S. de Madariaga, *Spain*, London, 1942, p. 237. For Madariaga, the Assembly was the great missed opportunity of modern Spanish history. It could have been the true salvation of Spain and of the monarchical system had the crown been more supportive of a parliamentary form of government.
64 See *La Acción*, 21, 25 and 26 July 1917; *El País*, 21, 23 and 27 July 1917; *El Liberal*, 21 and 26 July 1917; *El Heraldo de Madrid*, 21 and 22 July 1917; *El Mundo*, 21 and 22 July 1917; *El Socialista*, 20, 21, 27 July and 1 August 1917; *La Tribuna*, 21, 22 and 25 July 1917; *España* no. 131 (2 August 1917).

65 AHN, Leg. 48 A, Exp. 17 (29–30 July 1917). Sánchez Guerra warned the civil governors that the lifting of censorship did not mean a return to constitutional normality. Hence they should take note of any anti-government articles and act with force.
66 Lacomba, *La crisis*, pp. 206–7.
67 Maura and Fernández Almagro, *Por qué*, pp. 492–3. Cesar Silió to Maura, 21 July 1917.
68 AM, Leg. 61, Gabriel to Antonio Maura, 25 July 1917.
69 AM, Leg. 462, Carp. 2, Miguel to Antonio Maura, 30 July 1917.
70 AM, Leg. 80, Ossorio to Maura, 7 August 1917.
71 Maura and Fernández Almagro, *Por qué*, pp. 496–7. Antonio to Gabriel Maura, 30 July 1917.
72 AM, Leg. 80, Maura to Ossorio, 7 August 1917.
73 Maura and Fernández Almagro, *Por qué*, p. 495. Peyrá to Maura, 26 July 1917.
74 Márquez and Capó, *Las juntas*, appendix 13, pp. 204–8.

7 THE HOT AUGUST OF 1917

1 F. J. Romero Salvadó, 'Spain and the First World War: The Structural Crisis of the Liberal Monarchy', *European History Quarterly*, October 1995, vol. 25, no. 4, p. 543.
2 *El Socialista*, 2 April, 8 and 10 May 1917.
3 These events can be followed in national journals like *El Heraldo de Madrid*, *El Liberal*, *La Epoca*, *El Imparcial*, etc. (20 July–21 August 1917). For the Socialist view of these events see Simarro, *Los sucesos de agosto*.
4 García Venero, *Melquiades Alvarez*, p. 350.
5 AHN, Leg. 42 A, Exp. 1, June–July 1917.
6 Saborit, *Besteiro*, p. 98. Francisco Núñez Tomás and Eduardo Torralba Beci were replaced by Daniel Anguiano and Andrés Saborit respectively.
7 García Venero (*Melquiades Alvarez*, p. 350) is the only author to claim that *agents provocateurs* initiated the transport strike in July 1917. Two socialists, Saborit (*Besteiro*, p. 98) and Cordero (*Los Socialistas*, pp. 30–3), argued that the imprudence of Republicans like Marcelino Domingo and Félix Azzati was the cause of that strike. Saborit (*La huelga*, pp. 12–13) also points out that the lack of leadership of Daniel Anguiano, President of the Railway Union, determined the course of events.
8 Practically all authors agree that the government provoked the General Strike in August. See Balcélls, *El sindicalismo en Barcelona, 1916–1923*, Barcelona, 1965, p. 31; G. Meaker, *The Revolutionary Left in Spain, 1914–1923*, Palo Alto, 1974, pp. 83–4; Saborit, *Besteiro*, p. 99; Tuñón de Lara, *El movimiento obrero*, p. 589; Gómez Llorente, *Aproximación*, p. 299; Buxadé, *La bullanga*, pp. 218–19; García Venero, *Melquiades*, pp. 344–5; Fernández Almagro, *Historia*, p. 245; Cordero, *Los Socialistas*, p. 34. The exception is, not surprisingly, Manuel Burgos y Mazo (*Vida política*, pp. 107, 202), Minister of Justice in the Dato Cabinet of August 1917. Burgos y Mazo claims that the strike had been on the cards since March 1917. In fact, the government attempted to avoid clashes but could do nothing when faced by the intransigence of both the railway workers and the company.
9 Simarro, *Los sucesos*, pp. 44–5.
10 Ibid., p. 9.
11 Tuñón de Lara, *Poder*, p. 262.
12 AHN, Leg. 42 A, Exp. 1. As early as 8 August, Sánchez Guerra was ordering the civil governors to draw up lists of the leading revolutionary elements so as to

make their arrest easier as soon as the strike began. See also Leg. 48 A, Exp. 17: on 12 August Sánchez Guerra instructed the civil governors to form groups of vigilantes and policemen from among reliable people in their regions.

13 On the decision to declare the general strike see F. Largo Caballero, *Mis recuerdos. Cartas a un amigo*, Mexico, 1954, pp. 50–3; Saborit, *Asturias y sus hombres*, pp. 165–8; Morato, *Pablo Iglesias*, pp. 160–3; Cordero, *Los Socialistas*, pp. 33–4; Gómez Llorente, *Aproximación*, pp. 299–305; Saborit, *La huelga*, pp. 69–74.

14 Many lies were spread by the government during those days. In fact, the Socialist leaders had been arrested when having supper. The police allowed them to finish their meal. See S. Vidarte, *No queríamos al rey. Testimonio de un socialista español*, Madrid, 1977, p. 78.

15 Meaker, *The Revolutionary Left*, p. 82.

16 *El Socialista* (2 August 1917), editorial by Iglesias, '*¡Abajo el régimen!*' Saborit (*La huelga*, p. 25), also says that the strike was in favour of the liberal bourgeoisie.

17 Meaker, *The Revolutionary Left*, p. 51; see also Gómez Llorente, *Approximación*, pp. 293–4.

18 A. Pestaña, *Lo que aprendí en la vida*, Murcia, 1971, vol. 1, pp. 59–63. Largo Caballero, *Correspondencia secreta*, Madrid, 1961, pp. 73–4 and Saborit, *La huelga*, pp. 12, 64, disagree with Pestaña. They argue that the CNT was led by reformist leaders who were happy to collaborate with the UGT.

19 Gómez Llorente, *Aproximación*, p. 221.

20 Saborit, *Besteiro*, pp. 100–2.

21 Saborit, *La huelga*, p. 9.

22 The idea that extremists were in charge of the revolutionary movement is put forward by Burgos y Mazo, *Vida política*, pp. 64–73. He bases his argument to a large extent on the revolutionary pamphlets printed at the time. See, for example, 'Ésta es la Revolución' by Domingo, in Domingo, *¿Qué espera?*, pp. 57–79. This view is seriously weakened when contrasted with the disappointment of Anarchists: see for example Bajatierra, *Desde las barricadas*, pp. 12–13.

23 Largo's speech in Simarro, *Los sucesos*, pp. 13–20

24 Saborit's speech, ibid., pp. 50–1.

25 Prieto's speech, ibid., pp. 108–9.

26 Gómez Llorente, *Aproximación*, pp. 260, 270–2; Saborit, *La huelga*, p. 23; Meaker, *The Revolutionary Left*, p. 80; Vidarte, *No queríamos al rey*, p. 76.

27 Bajatierra (*Desde las barricades*, pp. 57–61, 69) describes the violence in the clashes between strikers and the tram drivers protected by the army. He concludes that the workers were no match for the well-armed soldiers. Tuñón de Lara (*El movimiento obrero*, pp. 586–8) says that neither the UGT nor the CNT had ruled out a resort to violence. Yet the Socialists were not prepared to go beyond mere political objectives. Buenacasa (*El movimiento obrero*, p. 63) writes that the events of the August strike helped open the eyes of many Anarcho-Syndicalists. They could no longer follow the lead of people such as Indalecio Prieto, who had openly declared that he had refused to hand over weapons and ammunition to the workers.

28 Besteiro's speech in Simarro, *Los sucesos*, pp. 167, 176.

29 Cordero (*Los socialistas*, p. 34) writes: 'We did not believe the old man [Pablo Iglesias]. We had such enthusiasm and confidence in those moments that we all unanimously voted for the general strike.'

30 Romero Salvadó, 'Spain and the First World War', p. 544.

31 Maura and Fernández Almagro, *Por qué*, pp. 498–500. Miguel to Gabriel Maura, 19 August 1917.

32 Soldevilla, *El año 1917*, p. 385; also in Márquez and Capó, *Las Juntas*, pp. 60–1.

33 Prieto's speech in Simarro, *Los sucesos*, pp. 112–38; see also Soldevilla, *El año 1917*, pp. 170–1.
34 Márquez and Capó, *Por qué*, appendix 11, pp. 195–7; Saborit's speech in Simarro, *Los sucesos*, pp. 112–38 and Saborit, *Asturias*, pp. 168–71.
35 *La Acción*, 9, 10, 15, 17 and 20 August 1917.
36 Saborit, *La huelga*, p. 13.
37 See Buenacasa, *El movimento obrero*, p. 62 and Pestaña, *Lo que aprendí*, p. 63. Lerroux bribed Francisco Martorell, a chief of police at Barcelona. Martorell was accused later by Bravo Portillo who took his job.
38 This opinion was shared by Saborit, *La huelga*, p. 8; Burgos y Mazo, *Vida política*, pp. 106–8, 161, 163; Maura and Fernández Almagro, *Por qué*, pp. 501–2. Peyrá to Maura, 28 August 1917. Besteiro claims (in Simarro, *Los sucesos*, p. 195) that Cambó was well informed of the steps being taken to launch the general strike.
39 Soldevilla, *El año 1917*, pp. 386–7; Buxadé, *España en crisis*, pp. 269–71.
40 FO 371-3033/135,629, Hardinge to Balfour, 9 July 1917.
41 FO 371-3034/144,713, Balfour to Hardinge, 19 July 1917.
42 FO 371-3034/146,627, Unthorff to Hardinge, 16 July 1917.
43 AGA, Paris, idd. 95, box 5960.
44 AM, Leg. 362, Carp. 2, Gabriel to Antonio Maura, 7 July 1917.
45 FO 371-3034/142,714, Hardinge to Balfour, 19 July 1917.
46 FO 371-3034/181,841, Hardinge to Balfour about the Marquis of Lema, 14 August 1917. FO 371-3033/132,944, Grant to Balfour about the king, 5 July 1917.
47 *La Epoca*, 19 August 1917. The headline was 'Embaucadores y embaucados', 'The swindlers and the swindled'. The Conservative newspaper said that the Socialist leaders were caught with 14 million pesetas. In Simarro (*Los sucesos*, pp. 63, 223) both Saborit and Besteiro accused Sánchez Guerra of having spread the news that the Socialists had sold out to the Allies.
48 For Burguete's statement see Márquez and Capó, *Las juntas*, appendix 11, pp. 115–17. See FO 185-136/343 and 371-3034/175,803, Hardinge complains to Balfour that the Spanish authorities are claiming that the disturbances are the work of foreign gold (24 and 31 August 1917).
49 *La Acción*, 12 September 1917.
50 AGA, Paris, idd. 95, box 5960: Instructions to Spanish consuls at Bordeaux, Toulouse, Perpignan and Pau to follow the movements of all those involved in the August events. See also AD, Correspondence from politicians. In late August Lerroux wrote to Dato denying having received any money from the French government. Lerroux demanded the release of his driver and asked why there was an order of arrest against him. He added: 'Todos sabemos el papel que hemos jugado en esta tragicomedia' ('We all know the role that we have played in this tragicomedy').
51 FO 185-1346/469, Hardinge to Balfour, 24 September 1917.

8 THE END OF AN ERA

1 For the campaign against Cambó see *La Epoca* (4, 5, 9 and 12 September 1917). See also FO 185-1347/506 and 1347/519. Dato and the Marquis of Lema confided to Hardinge that Cambó was the main threat to the government; Burgos y Mazo (*Vida política*, pp. 1–3, 111–15) singled out Cambó as the mastermind behind all the revolutionary events of 1917.
2 Pabón, *Cambó*, pp. 547–53. *El Día*, 7 September 1917.
3 AM, Leg. 19, Cambó to Maura, 27 September 1917.

4 Romero Salvadó, 'Maura, Maurismo', p. 24.
5 AD, Marquis of Lema to Dato, 3 October 1917.
6 AM, Leg. 362, Carp. 2, Gabriel to Antonio Maura, 7 September 1917, Miguel to Antonio Maura, 8 and 10 September 1917.
7 AD, Marquis of Lema to Dato, 3 October 1917.
8 AM, Leg. 362, Carp. 2, Miguel to Antonio Maura, 17 August 1917.
9 AM, Leg. 362, Carp. 2, Gabriel to Antonio Maura, 11 and 20 August 1917; Miguel to Antonio Maura, 12, 16, 17 and 19 August 1917. See also Besteiro's speech in Simarro, *Los sucesos*, pp. 239–43 and Domingo's speech, pp. 286–8, 291–4. Soldevilla, *El año 1917*, pp. 412–22; Márquez and Capó, *Las Juntas*, p. 61; Vidarte, *No queríamos*, pp. 100–2.
10 Soldevilla, *El año 1917*, pp. 437–40.
11 Soldevilla, *Tres revoluciones*, pp. 59–63.
12 Soldevilla, *El año 1917*, pp. 443–7.
13 Márquez and Capó, *Las Juntas*, p. 68.
14 AM, Leg. 402, Carp. 22, Peyrá to Maura, 4 October 1917. Peyrá informed Maura of the visit of some officers of the artillery corps of Santiago: 'uno de ellos . . . me decía que la última nota oficiosa del gobierno inspiraba asco por su servilismo. Todos expusieron su deseo vehementísimo de ver a usted al frente del gobierno . . . El clamoreo es, pues, general, y sólo falta que quien debe tener oídos oiga . . .' ('one of them . . . told me that the latest government statement had inspired nausea by its servility. They all expressed their desire to see you at the head of the government . . . The clamour is thus unanimous, and the only thing needed is that he who ought to have ears should hear . . .').
15 *La condena del comité de huelga*, Madrid, 1918. Saborit, *Besteiro*, pp. 103–4.
16 *El Socialista*, 9 and 25 October 1917.
17 Conclusions of the Assembly in *El Heraldo de Madrid*, 17 October 1917. See also AR, Leg. 14, Exp. 19, Assembly of parliamentarians. The desperation of Sánchez Guerra, unable to prevent the new gathering of parliamentarians, can be seen in ANR, Leg. 8904, 9–15 October 1917.
18 *El Liberal*, 22, 24 and 25 October 1917.
19 *La Acción*, editorial encouraging the king to act, 10 October 1917; other attacks on government, 8, 15, 17, 19, 21 and 22 October 1917.
20 AM, Leg. 389, Carp. 10, 21 October 1917.
21 Soldevilla, *Tres revoluciones*, pp. 69–71.
22 *El Ejército Español*, 19 October 1917; *La Correspondencia Militar*, 22 October 1917.
23 *El Heraldo de Madrid*, 19 October 1917. Five days later *El Socialista* commented that Spain was the only country in which an electoral farce had been publicly exposed but nothing had happened.
24 *El Heraldo de Madrid* (24 October 1917). The following day the same newspaper interviewed some of the leading *junteros* at Barcelona, who agreed with the opinion expressed by Márquez.
25 *España* no. 133 (25 October 1917): 'Todos desde Socialistas hasta Juntas quieren la caída del gobierno Dato' ('All, from the Socialists to the Juntas, want the Dato government to fall'); *La Correspondencia Militar*, 24 October 1917: 'El Imperio de la verdad' ('The reign of truth'); *El Debate*, 23 October 1917: 'La hora de dimitir' ('Time to resign'); *El Liberal*, 24 October 1917: 'La quiebra del *Turno*' ('Collapse of the *Turno*'); *La Acción*, 19 October 1917: 'Todos contra el gobierno y el gobierno contra todos' ('All against the government and the government against all').
26 ANR, Leg. 8912, programme drawn up by Alba on 29 September 1917.
27 ANR, Leg. 8904, 15 October 1917.

28 *La Epoca*, 27 October 1917. See also ANR, Leg. 8904, 26 October 1917. Rivas commented that Romanones's sudden regenerationist ideals were surely due to the fact that he had scented the crisis.

29 Márquez and Capó, *Las juntas*, appendix 16, pp. 216–22.

30 Maura and Fernández Almagro, *Por qué*, pp. 505–6. Peyrá to Maura, 26 October 1917.

31 FO 185-347/522, Hardinge to Balfour, 28 October 1917.

32 AD, Marquis of Lema to Dato, 3 and 5 October 1917.

33 Soldevilla, *El año 1917*, p. 524.

34 AD, Marquis of Lema to Dato, 5 October 1917.

35 Soldevilla, *El año 1917*, pp. 497–503.

36 CAB 24. Vol. 31. GT.2540: weekly report from the Department of Information, 7 November 1917.

37 ANR, Leg. 8904, 28 October 1917. Rivas commented that Prime Ministers had frequently been sacked during the reign of Alfonso XIII.

38 ANR, Leg. 8904, 29 October 1917.

39 *La Acción*, 28 October 1917.

40 For the course of events see *El Liberal*, *El País*, *La Acción*, *El Heraldo de Madrid* and *El Imparcial*, 28 October–3 November 1917.

41 ANR, Leg. 8904, 29 October 1917.

42 Romero Salvadó, 'Maura y Mauristas', p. 24.

43 Romero Salvadó, 'Spain and the First World War', pp. 546–7.

44 Cierva, *Notas*, pp. 188–9, contends that he was visited by several officers who told him that he was the only civilian who could restore discipline in the army and carry through an effective package of military reforms. He then met the king, who told him that he was considering abdicating. Alfonso begged Cierva to accept the post of Minister for War in a coalition led by the Marquis of Alhucemas. Cierva accepted, on condition he was allowed to publish a statement explaining that he was a member of that government only because of his sincere monarchism. On the other hand, Márquez and Capó (*Las juntas*, pp. 75–82) suggest that Cierva himself had approached the officers offering his services. According to Márquez, the representatives of the Central *Junta* in Madrid, Commandant Espino and Captains Villar and García Rodríguez, without consulting their colleagues at Barcelona, decided to back Cierva's bid for the post of Minister for War.

45 Gómez Llorente, *Aproximación*, pp. 456–7; Lacomba, *La crisis*, p. 316.

46 Cambó's intention to join a monarchist coalition with the backing of his party can be seen in ADV, letters exchanged between Cambó and Ventosa, 27 and 30 October 1917.

47 Cambó's declaration in *El Heraldo de Madrid* (4 November 1917), *La Tribuna* and *La Veu de Catalunya* (6 November 1917).

48 Cambó's role and that of the Lliga during the crisis of October 1917 remain highly controversial. His biographers (Pla, *Cambó*, vol. III, pp. 200–9 and Pabón, *Cambó*, pp. 570–2) defend Cambó by arguing that he achieved the destruction of the *Turno* and ensured, by appointing an independent to the Ministry of the Interior, that there would be a free vote. An intermediate position is adopted by González Casanova (*Federalismo*, pp. 205–6), who agrees that the Lliga betrayed the Assembly but also notes that the failure of the August revolution forced the bourgeoisie to align with the oligarchy or risk the establishment of a military dictatorship. The majority of authors are critical of Cambó's move. Cordero (*Los Socialistas*, p. 30) says that had Cambó not betrayed the Assembly the monarchy would have collapsed. Saborit (*La huelga*, p. 83) points out that in the *gitaneo*

which followed the fall of the Dato cabinet, Cambó managed to impose his views and gain two portfolios. Fernández Almagro (*Historia,* pp. 252–3) says that Cambó abandoned the spirit of the Assembly and preferred instead to take advantage of the situation in order to get two seats in the cabinet. Boyd (*Praetorian Politics,* p. 59) argues that Cambó brought down the Conservative government, yet he was prepared to sacrifice the bourgeois revolution in order to save the Monarchy and the social order. Burgos y Mazo (*Vida política,* p. 59) regards Cambó as the 'machiavellian' leader of the offensive against the regime, dominating all the others and discarding them when no longer useful. A superb analysis can be found in the editorials by Luis Bello in *España,* nos. 137 and 140 (22 November and 13 December 1917). The Republican journalist writes that the strategy pursued by the Catalan bourgeoisie always involved a commitment to *Realpolitik* and opportunism. Thus they used the Assembly for their own benefit. Once their basic goals had been reached – destruction of the *Turno,* two portfolios in the new cabinet and an independent in charge of the Interior – they destroyed the Assembly which they themselves had created.

9 THE YEAR 1918

1 A. Gramsci, *Selections from Prison Notebooks,* London, 1971, p. 276.
2 Instituto de Reformas Sociales, *Movimiento de precios,* pp. 10–11.
3 AARD-IX, January 1918.
4 Editorial by Pablo Iglesias in *El Socialista,* 4 January 1918.
5 AASM-LXX-2, 22 October 1917. The objective was to release the members of the strike committee from prison. Therefore they decided by 116 votes to choose them as candidates for Madrid at the local elections in the following month.
6 Fundación Pablo Iglesias, Julián Besteiro's Papers, family correspondence (LXV-1), letters to his daughter Lolita, 17 and 18 November 1917. In early November he described Lerroux as an adventurer of the same kind as Romanones.
7 Meaker, *The Revolutionary Left,* pp. 111–16; Forcadell, *Parlamentarismo,* pp. 245–57; Heywood, *Marxism,* pp. 54–7.
8 Martin, *The Agony of Modernization,* p. 195.
9 *Solidaridad Obrera,* 11, 14 and 19 November 1917.
10 Meaker, *The Revolutionary Left,* pp. 108–10.
11 On the 'red' years in Andalusia see J. Díaz del Moral, *Historia de las agitaciones campesinas andaluzas,* Madrid, 1973; first published in 1929; C. Bernaldo de Quirós, *El espartaquismo agrario andaluz,* Madrid, 1974; J. Maurice, *El anarquismo andaluz. Campesinos y sindicalistas, 1868–1936,* Barcelona, 1990; A. Barragán, *Conflictividad social y desarticulación política en la provincia de Córdoba, 1918–1920,* Córdoba, 1990.
12 Martin, *Agony,* p. 196.
13 Bar, *La CNT,* pp. 359–431; Martin, *Agony,* pp. 149–54; A. Balcélls, *El sindicalisme,* pp. 51–65.
14 *La Correspondencia de España* and *La Veu de Catalunya* were the only newspapers enthusiastic about the political solution. *El Heraldo de Madrid* and *La Acción* declared a partial truce. The coalition government was criticized by *El Liberal, El Socialista, El ABC, La Tribuna, El País* and *España.*
15 Romanones, *Notas,* p. 145.
16 *El Liberal,* 4 November 1917.
17 View expressed in *La Epoca* (9 November 1917), *El Heraldo de Madrid* (12 November 1917) and *El Día* (16 December 1917).

18 The article appeared in *El Liberal*, 2 February 1918. See also ADV: Cambó wrote to Durán i Ventosa claiming that the Liberal party was totally broken and that he preferred to have Alhucemas as Prime Minister rather than take that role himself, 3 November 1917.

19 Boyd, *Praetorian Politics*, pp. 94–6.

20 Soldevilla, *El año 1917*, pp. 574–5.

21 Those demands were indeed moderate. They wanted the creation of a corps of honorary officers with promotion up to the rank of major; warrant officers to have a chance of promotion to second lieutenant; and the uniforms of the sergeants and barrack conditions to be improved.

22 *El Liberal*, 3 and 4 January 1918. Cierva (*Notas*, pp. 194–6) claims that they were conspiring with the Socialists to launch a revolution. His proof is that several intercepted cables mention the word *abuelo*. There was, in fact, no evidence that the PSOE had organized any revolutionary plot within the army. After the August debacle, nothing could be further from their plans. The word *abuelo* ('grandfather') was a common reference among Socialists to their leader, Pablo Iglesias. Yet the veteran general and ex-minister Fernando Primo de Rivera was also known as *el abuelo* among soldiers. Primo de Rivera, as War Minister, had shown interest in improving the conditions of the NCOs.

23 Cierva, *Notas*, p. 196.

24 M. Burgos y Mazo, *El verano de 1919 en Gobernación*, Cuenca, 1921, p. 29.

25 The results in Madrid were as follows: 9 *Mauristas*; 6 Republicans; 4 Socialists; 1 Reformist; 4 *Romanonistas*; 1 Liberal Democrat; 1 Conservative; 2 Independents. See J. A. Martínez Martín, 'Las elecciones municipales en la crisis de la restauración: Madrid, 1917' in J. L. García Delgado (ed.), *La crisis de la restauración: España entre la primera guerra mundial y la II República*, Madrid, 1986, pp. 121–47. The editorial of *La Acción* was entitled '¡Maurismo o Republicanismo!' *El ABC*, *El Liberal*, *El Imparcial* and *El País* agreed that two ideological currents, *Maurismo* and the Republican–Socialist coalition, had triumphed over the traditional fiction of the monarchist parties. *El Socialista* regarded the election of the four members of the strike committee as a vindication of the August revolutionary movement. In contrast, *La Epoca* pointed out that in the country the monarchists had obtained an important victory and the same would have happened in Madrid if they had formed an electoral coalition.

26 The best example of that situation would be the local elections of April 1931. The monarchists once more obtained an overwhelming majority in the countryside but were defeated in the cities. The king had to flee and the Second Republic was established.

27 AR, Leg. 5, Exp. 40, letters from Romanones to Alhucemas, January–February, 1918. See also AHN, Leg. 28 A, Exp. 2 where there is abundant documentary evidence of abuses, briberies and persecutions in the weeks before the general election of February 1918.

28 All newspapers agreed that the elections had failed to give a clear mandate to any political formation. *El Socialista* considered the election of the four members of the strike committee and the success of the leftist coalition in Madrid to be a victory. *El Heraldo de Madrid* noted that nothing had changed: the old practices of electoral falsification had been used as in the past and the old governing elites were still in charge. *El Debate* also pointed out that despite all the promises of the government, the purchase of votes and other illegal methods had been employed. The Catholic newspaper warned of the steady advance of Socialism. *La Epoca* regarded the elections as a great victory for the monarchy. Yet it also said that the advance of some radicals was a reason for

worry. *El Liberal*, *El País* and *España Nueva* stressed that the fact that the members of the strike committee had become deputies was a victory for public opinion. For *La Acción* the results of the general election of February 1918 simply confirmed the trend towards truth initiated in the local election of November 1917. *España* emphasized that the results had brought about the end of the *Turno* for ever. Finally, *El Sol* argued that the new parliament was far from ideal. Some new forces had made some progress, but the old parties were still in control.

29 Lacomba, *La crisis*, p. 337.
30 See ADV, Cambó to Durán i Ventosa, 1 February 1918.
31 Pabón, *Cambó*, p. 590.
32 *El Liberal*, 28 February 1918.
33 A complete report on the military reforms can be found in *El Sol*, 10 March 1918. See also Boyd, *Praetorian Politics*, p. 100; Seco, *Militarismo*, p. 276.
34 See *El Socialista*, 8 March 1918.
35 *El Liberal*, 2 and 6 March 1918.
36 AR, Leg. 5, Exp. 40, letters from Romanones to Alhucemas, 1 and 9 March 1918.
37 FO 371-3070/48,811, memorandum on the internal situation in Spain, 11 March 1918.
38 F. Soldevilla, *El año político de 1918*, Madrid, 1919, pp. 57–8; Cierva (*Notas*, p. 204) argues that his action prevented the officers from taking the law into their own hands.
39 *El Socialista*, 8 March 1918: '¡Bajo el imperio del sable!' ('Under the rule of the sabre!'); Sánchez de Toca called Cierva 'Dictador al dictado' ('Dictator by dictate') in *El Heraldo de Madrid*, 8 March 1918.
40 Tusell and Avilés, *La derecha*, p. 141. *El Sol* (10 March 1918) argued that Maura and Cierva were often grouped together in the same political camp. Yet Maura had proved that there was a huge gap between them.
41 *El Socialista*, 10 March 1918: '¡Locura e indignidad!' ('Madness and indignity!'). Cierva (*Notas*, p. 204) claims that there was no clash in the cabinet. On the contrary, he convinced the other ministers after a friendly dialogue.
42 Alhucemas declared in *El Sol* (10 March 1918) that he was back in power because of a personal request by the king.
43 Fernández Almagro, *Historia*, p. 258.
44 Pabón, *Cambó*, p. 600.
45 *El Socialista*, *El Liberal*, *El País* and *El Sol* agreed that the country was under the threat of dictatorship by Cierva. The conservative *La Epoca* applauded the minister's show of authority. Cierva (*Notas*, p. 205) suggests that he led the battle against the civil service because the other ministers did not know what to do and begged him to take the initiative. Cierva also claims that if he had not put down the strike, Socialism would have triumphed in Spain.
46 Fernández Almagro, *Historia*, p. 259. Soldevilla, *El año 1918*, pp. 74–89.
47 Márquez and Capó (*Las juntas*, pp. 104–5) argue that there was a military plot to create a government presided over by Cierva with eight colonels. This opinion is shared by Fernández Almagro (*Historia*, pp. 259–60) and Seco (*Militarismo*, p. 277). Rumours of a military take-over headed by Cierva were also reported by the British ambassador: FO 371-3372/60,969, Hardinge to Balfour, 6 April 1918. Cierva (*Notas*, pp. 202–3) denies that he was behind a military coup and even claims that he was asked twice by Alhucemas in March 1918 to head a government, but refused as he did not want to be a dictator.
48 *La Tribuna*, 20 March 1918.

49 Romanones, *Notas*, pp. 145–7. See also FO 371-3372/60,969: Hardinge tells Balfour that the king hesitated and was only prevented at the last moment from accepting a Cierva cabinet by the wise advice of the Queen Mother 6 April 1918.

50 J. Gil Pecharromán, *Conservadores subversivos. La derecha autoritaria alfonsina (1913–1936)*, Madrid, 1994, p. 21; Fernández Almagro, *Historia*, pp. 260–1; Soldevilla, *El año 1918,* pp. 94–107.

51 Nearly all the press rejoiced at the idea of a coalition government headed by Maura to put an end to the danger of a military cabinet presided over by Cierva. See, for instance, *El Sol*: 'España recibe jubilosa al nuevo gobierno' ('A rejoicing Spain receives the new government'); *ABC*: '¡Gratitud al monarca!' ('Gratitude to the monarch!'); *El País*: '¡Triunfo del liberalismo!' ('Triumph of Liberalism!'); *La Acción*: '¡La voluntad del país!' ('The will of the country!'); even Luis Araquistáin in *España* wrote an editorial, 'Las dos caras de Maura' ('The two faces of Maura'), in which the role of the veteran Conservative leader in the crisis of March 1918 was praised.

52 See T. Carnero Arbat, 'Política sin democracia en España, 1874–1923', *Revista de Occidente*, April 1988, no. 83, pp. 53–4; and Carnero, 'Modernització, desenvolupament politic i canvi social: Espanya (1874–1931)', *Recerques*, 23 (1990), p. 79.

53 Maura and Fernández Almagro, *Por qué*, p. 311.

54 The terms of the peace treaty were extremely onerous. Russia was required to recognize the independence of Finland, the Ukraine and Georgia, and to renounce sovereignty over Poland, Lithuania, Livonia, Kurland, Estonia and the Moon Sound Islands. They either became sovereign states under a German protectorate or were annexed by Germany. Batum, Kars and Ardahan were to be ceded to Turkey. In addition, the Bolsheviks were forced to agree to considerable monetary reparations. The Treaty of Brest-Litovsk stripped the former Russian Empire of almost a third of its population; these territories accounted for almost 40 per cent of its agricultural harvest; 26 per cent of its railway tracks; and almost 80 per cent of its iron and 90 per cent of its coal production.

55 This apparently contradictory situation was discussed in *España* no. 148 (7 February 1918).

56 Martínez Fiol, *Voluntaris*, pp. 98–101.

57 FO 371-3372/fsw.017 weekly report by the Intelligence Bureau, Department of Information, 31 January 1918. See also CAB 24/35-GT.2973, weekly report by the Department of Information, 13 December 1917; FO 185-1348/586, Hardinge to Balfour, 10 December 1917.

58 FO 371-3372/3464 and 3372/5669, Balfour to Hardinge and Hardinge's reply, 7 and 10 January 1918.

59 FO 371-3372/118.836, report by Political Intelligence Department, 6 July 1918.

60 AGA, Paris, idd.95, box 5976, year 1918.

61 In January and February 1918 *El Parlamentario* carried out a campaign accusing the Germans of being behind anarchist activities. On 24 January, it named Albert Honnerman as the mastermind behind the German–Anarchist collaboration. On 25 February it demanded a thorough investigation to arrest the killers of the industrialist Barret. See also Pestaña, *Lo que aprendí*, pp. 174–5; Pere Foix, *Los archivos*, pp. 59–60.

62 *El Sol*, 4–7 March 1918. See also *España* no. 152 (7 March 1918): 'El terrorismo alemán en España', 'German terrorism in Spain'. Cordero (*Los Socialistas*, p. 41) noted that the Anarchists were easy prey for the German agents. They were

financed to strike against those industries producing for the Allies. FO 371-3373/44,846: Hardinge informs Balfour of the connections between Anarchists and Germans, 9 March 1918. On 26 January, 1918 *El Parlamentario* accused the former CNT Secretary, Francisco Roldán, of being on Honnerman's payroll.

63 *El Sol*, 10 March 1918.

64 Pestaña, *Lo que aprendí*, pp. 115–19; Bar, *La CNT*, pp. 360–70.

65 *Solidaridad Obrera*, 9 June 1918; *El Parlamentario*, 12, 26, 28 and 29 June 1918; *El Sol*, 12 and 14 June 1918; *El Socialista*, 12 June 1918.

66 It seems that Royo provided Francisco Carbonell, a former chief of police at Barcelona and rival of Portillo, with the evidence to convict Portillo. Despite the overwhelming evidence against Portillo, and the numerous witnesses testifying against him (workers, policemen, experts, etc.), the case was dismissed and the chief of police released in December 1918. See AR, Leg. 16, Exp. 25, 'The Portillo affair'; FO 371-3375/118,036, report by the British Consul at Barcelona, 29 June 1918; Pestaña, *Lo que aprendí*, pp. 123–4, 173–9; Foix, *Archivos*, pp. 59–60; Márquez and Capó, *Las juntas*, appendix 22, pp. 123–8.

67 *España* no. 192 (12 December 1918); *El Sol*, 7–8 December 1918; Márquez and Capó, *Las juntas*, appendix 22, pp. 123–8.

68 FO 371-3375/119,647, Hardinge to Balfour, 5 July 1918.

69 *El Sol*, 4 July 1918. See also *El Parlamentario*, 5 July 1918; *El País*, 4–5 July 1918; *El Socialista*, 4–6 July 1918; *El Heraldo de Madrid*, 5 July 1918; *La Correspondencia de España*, 5 July 1918; *España* no. 170 (11 July 1918). Once more *La Epoca* (5 July 1918) disagreed, claiming that Spain was still 'the most liberal country in the world'.

70 DSC, 4–6 July 1918.

71 Alcalá Zamora was the editor of *El Día*, a newspaper financed by the Germans. Cierva was an ultra Conservative who did not disguise his sympathy for Germany. He was involved with German commercial interests in southern Spain and had defended before the Supreme Court the German appeal against the sentence passed by the Tetuán *audiencia* on the murder of the vice-consul Atkinson's servant.

72 AD, Maura to Dato (28 July 1918). In AM, Leg. 252, Maura wrote to his son Gabriel that Spanish dignity could no longer accept German atrocities (29 July 1918). For Maura's anger against the Spanish Germanophiles prepared to accept all kinds of German punitive action see AM, Leg. 252, Maura to Dato (18 July 1918).

73 ANR, Leg. 8893, 8–10 August 1918.

74 Soldevilla, *El año 1918*, pp. 226–8.

75 AD, Correspondence from former Prime Ministers, Maura to Dato, 18 August 1918.

76 The strong support given by Maura to his foreign minister Dato is stressed in Tusell, *Antonio Maura*, pp. 183–6.

77 *El Día*, 11 August 1918; *ABC*, 18 August 1918. See also Burgos y Mazo, *El verano*, p. 48; Fernández Almagro, *Historia*, pp. 264–5.

78 FO 371-3374/145,426 and 3374/150,374, Hardinge to Balfour, 23 August and 2 September 1918.

79 FO 371-3371/158,724, British ambassador at Paris to Balfour, 17 September 1918. FO 371-3374/157,329, Balfour to Vaughan, 19 September 1918. AD, letters from diplomats, Polo de Bernabé to Dato, 31 August 1918.

80 FO 371-3372/118,836, Hardinge to Balfour, 6 July 1918; 3371/134,741. Hardinge to Balfour, 28 July 1918.

81 FO 371-3374/145,526, Hardinge to Balfour, 23 August 1918.

82 FO 371-3374/157,329, Balfour to Vaughan, 19 September 1918; 3374/158,384, Balfour to Vaughan, 18 September 1918; 3374/158,724, British ambassador at Paris to Balfour, 19 September 1918; 3374/161,003, British ambassador at Paris to Balfour, 23 September 1918; 3374/161,163, Balfour to Vaughan, 24 September 1918.

83 ANR, Leg. 8906, 31 August 1918. Rivas commented that in order to maintain neutrality the king was prepared to sack all his ministers.

84 AM, Leg. 272, Dato to Maura, 3 September 1918.

85 News of the king's opposition to any move against Germany filtered out, and the Socialist deputy Indalecio Prieto declared in the Cortes on 28 October that no government could undertake a coherent foreign policy with a royal veto. The French Foreign Minister, Cambon, also blamed Alfonso XIII for the weakening of the government's response to Germany. FO 371-3374/153,920, English ambassador at Paris to Balfour, 9 September 1918.

86 Burgos, *El verano*, pp. 48–52.

87 AR, Leg. 19, Exp. 8, no. 3, telegram from Minister Baldomero Argente to Romanones, January 1919.

88 Burgos y Mazo, *El verano*, pp. 37–41, 44–6; Romanones, *Notas*, p. 148; Pabón, *Cambó*, pp. 606–8. Also see ADV, letter from Cambó to Durán in which the Catalan leader claims that the coalition government could do great things and he expected to be its engine. Otherwise the monarchy will fall and the Regionalists will have to work only on behalf of Catalonia (23 March 1918).

89 Fernández Almagro, *Historia*, p. 262.

90 DSC, 27 April 1918.

91 Pabón, *Cambó*, pp. 612–29; Romanones, *Notas*, p. 149.

92 ANR, Leg. 8905, 13 July 1918. According to Rivas, Alba was already considering resignation but feared that people would accuse him of ambition and impatience, ANR, Leg. 8893, 9–10 August 1918. Alba and Cambó were forming a common front against the budget presented by Besada, but Alba reacted against Cambó's Regionalist plans.

93 ANR, Leg. 8906, 18 September 1918. All the ministers except Romanones and Maura, who abstained, opposed the projects presented by Cambó and Besada. On 13 September *El Sol* described the general opposition to Besada's budget and the offer by Alhucemas to Besteiro to join a new cabinet. Two days later *El Socialista* explained how Besteiro had turned down Alhucemas's approach.

94 Fernández Almagro, *Historia*, p. 267; Pabón, *Cambó*, pp. 649–66.

95 ADV: Cambó wrote to Durán i Ventosa on 17 October that he knew that soon he would no longer be a minister as the government could not last.

96 Pabón, *Cambó*, pp. 651–66; Burgos y Mazo, *El verano*, pp. 50–2.

97 DSC, 24–5 October 1918.

98 *España* no. 186 (30 October 1918).

99 Fernández Almagro, *Historia*, pp. 267–8.

100 Ibid., p. 267.

10 EPILOGUE

1 M. Blinkhorn (ed.), *Fascists and Conservatives. The Radical Right and the Establishment in Twentieth-Century Europe,* London, 1990, p. 4.

2 P. Preston and H. Graham, 'The Popular Front and the Struggle against Fascism' in Preston and Graham, *The Popular Front in Europe*, London, 1987, p. 1.

3 A good analysis of the impact of the Annual disaster can be found in A. Comalada, *El ocaso de un parlamento*, Barcelona, 1985.

4 Díaz del Moral, *Agitaciones*, pp. 267–73; see also Meaker, *The Revolutionary Left*, pp. 137–43.

5 Balcélls, *El sindicalisme*, pp. 73–82.

6 For more details of the CNT Congress in December 1919 see Bar, *La CNT,* pp. 489–555.

7 Martin, *Agony*, p. 218.

8 *La Acción* (8 March 1919). The editorial was entitled: 'A dictator is needed'.

9 The conciliatory policy of the Liberal cabinet led by Count Romanones in April 1919 clashed with the position of officers and industrialists prepared to fight to the death with the CNT. As a consequence, the Civil Governor of Barcelona and its chief of police were ejected from the city by local officers. Romanones took the hint and resigned. The Conservative cabinet led by Sánchez de Toca met a similar fate in December 1919 when his conciliatory initiatives were opposed by the combined actions of industrialists and the military.

10 The most thorough analysis of the Libres can be found in C. Winston, *Workers and the Right in Spain, 1900–1936*, Princeton, 1985. Winston's study constitutes an apology for the activities of the Libres, often dismissed as a mere 'yellow' trade union. Winston argues that they were a real workers' organization which was forced to take a defensive position when faced by the violence and intransigence of the CNT. He underlines that this trade union achieved a genuine level of workers' support and that by 1922 it could boast more than 120,000 members. Yet Winston destroys his own argument when he recognizes that on a number of occasions after 1920 the Libres participated in terrorist activities and acted as strike-breakers in alliance with the Employers' Federation and the Civil Governor. The Libres enjoyed the official protection of Martínez Anido, who actually became the Honorary chairman of the Libres cooks' trade union.

11 On the spiral of social violence and terrorism of these years see J. M. Farré Morego, *Los atentados sociales en España*, Madrid, 1922; F. Calderón, *La verdad sobre el terrorismo. Datos, fechas, nombres y estadísticas,* Barcelona, 1932; L. Ignacio, *Los años del pistolerismo. Ensayo para una guerra civil*, Barcelona, 1981; A. Balcélls, 'Violencia y terrorismo en la lucha de clases en Barcelona de 1913 a 1923' and F. del Rey Reguillo, 'Ciudadanos honrados y somatenistas. El orden y la subversión en la España de los años 20', both in *Estudios de Historia Social*, July–December 1987, nos. 42–3.

12 Balcélls, *El sindicalisme,* p. 112, argues that Anarchist terrorism increased proportionately in periods of repression and diminished in periods of tolerance and dialogue. Pestaña, *Lo que aprendí*, vol. 1, p. 113, claims that the leadership of the CNT did not back the terrorists but never stood up to them. As terrorism increased, it became more opportunistic and ruthless. Initially, gunmen killed for principles, but later the original Anarchist idealists were joined by other more opportunist characters who regarded assassination as an end in itself.

BIBLIOGRAPHY

Primary sources

Official archives

AD   Eduardo Dato's Papers, Biblioteca de la Real Academia de la Historia, Madrid

ADV   Lluis Durán i Ventosa's Papers, Arxiu Nacional de Catalunya, San Cugat del Vallés, Barcelona

AGA   Foreign Office Papers, Archivo General de la Administración, Alcalá de Henares

AHN   Ministry of the Interior Papers, Serie A, Archivo Histórico Nacional, Madrid

ANR   Natalio Rivas's Papers, Biblioteca de la Real Academia de la Historia, Madrid

AR   Count Romanones's Papers, Biblioteca de la Real Academia de la Historia, Madrid

CAB   Cabinet Office Papers, Public Record Office, Kew
      CAB 23 Cabinet Minutes and Conclusions
      CAB 24 Cabinet Office Papers and Memoranda
      CAB 27 Cabinet Committee on Foreign Policy

DSC   Parliamentary Records, 1914–1918, Biblioteca Nacional de Madrid

FO   Foreign Office Records, Public Record Office, Kew
      FO 371 General Correspondence
      FO 185 Embassy and Consular Archives
      FO 395 General News

Dr Joan Solé i Pla's Papers, Arxiu Nacional de Catalunya, San Cugat del Vallés, Barcelona

Enric Prat de la Riba's Papers, Arxiu Nacional de Catalunya, San Cugat del Vallés, Barcelona

Private collections

AARD   Amaro del Rosal Díaz's Papers, Fundación Pablo Iglesias, Madrid
      AARD-IX National Committee Resolutions 1916–1918
      AARD-330-2 History of the UGT
      AARD-273-2 UGT's Papers

AASM   Papers of the Madrid Branch of the Socialist Party (AASM-LXX-2)
        Fundación Pablo Iglesias, Madrid
AGM   Gabriel Maura's Papers, Fundación Antonio Maura, Madrid
AM   Antonio Maura's Papers, Fundación Antonio Maura, Madrid

Julián Besteiro's Papers, family correspondence (LXV-1), Fundación Pablo Iglesias, Madrid

Newspapers and periodicals

ABC
La Acción
El Correo Español
El Debate
El Día
El Diario Universal
La Época
España
España Nueva
El Heraldo de Madrid
El Imparcial
El Liberal
La Mañana
El Mundo
La Nación
La Publicidad
El País
El Progreso
El Socialista
El Sol
Solidaridad Obrera
La Tribuna
El Universo
La Veu de Catalunya

Memoirs, diaries and theoretical works by protagonists

Albornoz, A. El partido republicano, Madrid, 1918.
—— La tragedia del estado español, Madrid, 1925.
Andrade, J. La burocracia reformista en el movimiento obrero, Madrid, 1935.
Araquistáin, L. Polémica de la guerra, 1914–1916, Madrid, 1915.
—— Dos ideales políticos y otros trabajos, Madrid, 1916.
—— Entre la guerra y la revolución. España en 1917, Madrid, 1917.
Azaña, M. Los motivos de la Germanofilía. Discurso en el Ateneo de Madrid el 15 de Mayo de 1917, Madrid, 1917.
Bajatierra, M. Desde las barricadas. Una semana de revolución en España. Las jornadas de Madrid en agosto de 1917, Tortosa, 1918.
Ballesteros, L. La guerra europea y la neutralidad española, Madrid, 1917.

Burgos y Mazo, M. *Vida política española. Páginas históricas de 1917*, Madrid, 1917.
—— *El verano de 1919 en Gobernación*, Cuenca, 1921.
Buxadé, J. *España en crisis. La bullanga misteriosa de 1917*, Barcelona, 1917.
Cambó, F. *Memorias*, Madrid, 1987.
Cenamor Val, H. *Los españoles y la guerra: neutralidad o intervención*, Madrid, 1916.
Cierva, J. de la. *Notas de mi vida*, Madrid, 1955.
Confederación Regional del Trabajo. *Memoria del congreso celebrado en Sants los dias 28, 29 y 30 de junio y 1 de julio del año 1918*, Barcelona, 1918.
Condena del comité de huelga, Mexico, n.d.
Cordero, M. *Los socialistas y la revolución*, Madrid, 1932.
Cortés Cavanillas, J. *Alfonso XIII. Vida, confesiones y muerte*, Barcelona, 1966; 2nd edn, 1973.
Costa, J. *Oligarquía y caciquismo, colectivismo agrario y otros escritos*, 2 vols, Madrid, 1975.
Datos sobre la guerra submarina, Madrid, 1918.
Discursos en el congreso de diputados. Don Eduardo Dato y Don José Sánchez Guerra (29 y 31 de mayo de 1918), Madrid, 1918.
Domingo, M. *¿Qué espera el Rey?* Madrid, 1930.
Fabra Ribas, A. *El socialismo y el conflicto europeo. ¡El Kaiserismo: He ahí el peligro!*, Valencia, 1915.
Farré Morego, J. M. *Los atentados sociales en España*, Madrid, 1922.
Gutiérrez Ravé, J. *Yo fui un joven maurista*, Madrid, 1944.
Iglesias, P. *Escritos y discursos. Antología crítica*, Madrid, 1984.
Instituto de Reformas Sociales. *Encarecimiento de la vida durante la guerra: Precios de las subsistencias en España y en el extranjero, 1914–1918*, Madrid, 1918.
—— *Informe de los inspectores de trabajo sobre la influencia de la guerra europea en las industrias españolas, 1917–1918*, Madrid, 1918.
—— *Movimiento de los precios al por menor durante la guerra y la posguerra, 1914–1922*, Madrid, 1923.
Largo Caballero, F. *Mis recuerdos. Cartas a un amigo*, Mexico, 1954.
—— *Correspondencia secreta*, Madrid, 1961.
Lerroux, A. *Mis memorias*, Madrid, 1963.
—— *La verdad a mi país. España y la guerra*, Madrid, 1915.
Márquez, B. and Capó, J. M. *Las juntas militares de defensa*, Havana, 1923.
Maura, A. *Tres discursos*, Madrid, 1918.
Maura, G. *Recuerdos de mi vida*, Madrid, 1934.
Maura, G. and Fernández Almagro, M. *Por qué cayó Alfonso XIII. Evolución y disolución de los partidos históricos durante su reinado*, Madrid, 1948.
Maurín, J. *Los hombres de la dictadura*, Barcelona, 1977; first published 1930.
Morato, J. J. *El partido socialista obrero*, Madrid, 1976; first published 1918.
—— *Pablo Iglesias Posse. Educador de muchedumbres*, Barcelona, 1931.
Olivar Bertrand, R. *Repercusiones en España de la primera guerra mundial*, Madrid, 1918.
Pestaña, A. *Lo que aprendí en la vida*, 2 vols, Murcia, 1971.
Posada, A. *Actitud ética ante la guerra y la paz*, Madrid, 1923.
Román, J. *Voces de guerra*, Barcelona, 1916.
Romanones, Conde de. *El ejército y la política*, Madrid, 1920.
—— *Las responsabilidades políticas del antiguo régimen, 1875–1923*, Madrid, n.d.
—— *Notas de una vida, 1912–1931*, Madrid, 1947.

Saborit, A. *Julián Besteiro*, Mexico, 1961.
—— *Asturias y sus hombres*, Toulouse, 1963.
—— *La huelga de agosto de 1917*, Mexico, 1967.
Sainz Rodríguez, P. *Testimonio y recuerdos*, Barcelona, 1978.
Simarro, L. *Los sucesos de agosto en el parlamento*, Madrid, 1918.
Soldevilla, F. *El año político de 1916*, Madrid, 1917.
—— *Tres revoluciones (Apuntes y notas). La junta de reforma. La asamblea parlamentaria. La huelga general*, Madrid, 1917.
—— *El año político de 1917*, Madrid, 1918.
—— *El año político de 1918*, Madrid, 1919.
Vidarte, S. *No queríamos al rey. Testimonio de un socialista español*, Madrid, 1977.

Secondary sources

Abad de Santillán, D. *Contribución a la historia del movimiento obrero español*, 3 vols, Puebla, 1965.
Alonso, J. R. *Historia política del ejército español*, Madrid, 1974.
Alonso Baguer, M. *El ejército en la sociedad española*, Madrid, 1971.
Alvarez Junco, J. *El Emperador del Paralelo. Lerroux y la demagogia populista*, Madrid 1990.
Arana, V. *Clamor ante el trono*, Madrid, 1965.
Arranz, L. and Cabrera, M. 'El Parlamento de la Restauración', *Hispania*, January–April 1995, vol. LV, no. 189
Artola, M. *Partidos y programas políticos, 1808–1936*, Madrid, 1977.
Aubert, P. 'Los intelectuales y la crisis de 1917' in M. Tuñón (ed.) *La crisis del estado español*, Madrid, 1978.
Aunós, E. *Itinerario histórico de la España contemporánea, 1808–1936*, Barcelona, 1940.
Balcélls, A. *El sindicalisme a Barcelona, 1916–1923*, Barcelona, 1965.
—— *Teoría y práctica del movimiento obrero en España*, Valencia, 1977.
—— 'Los Voluntarios Catalanes en la Gran Guerra (1914–1918)', *Historia 16*, May 1986, no. 121.
—— 'Violencia y terrorismo en la lucha de clases en Barcelona de 1913 a 1923', *Estudios de Historia Social*, July–December 1987, nos 42–3.
—— *Historia del nacionalisme catala. Dels origens als nostre temps*, Barcelona, 1992.
Ballbé, M. *Orden público y militarismo en la España constitucional, 1812–1983*, Madrid, 1983.
Balfour, S. *The End of the Spanish Empire, 1898–1923*, Oxford, 1997.
Bar, A. *La CNT en los años rojos: del sindicalismo revolucionario al anarcosindicalismo, 1910–1926*, Madrid, 1981.
Barragán, A. *Conflictividad social y desarticulación política en la provincia de Córdoba, 1918–1920*, Córdoba, 1990.
Baviera, Pilar de and Chapman-Huston, D. *Alfonso XIII*, Barcelona, 1945.
Bernaldo de Quirós, C. *El espartaquismo agrario andaluz*, Madrid, 1974.
Bernís, F. *Consecuencias económicas de la guerra*, Madrid, 1923.
Blinkhorn, M. (ed.). *Fascists and Conservatives. The Radical Right and the Establishment in Twentieth-Century Europe*, London, 1990.
Bookchin, M. *The Spanish Anarchists. The Heroic Years, 1868–1936*, New York, 1978.
Boyd, C. P. *Praetorian Politics in Liberal Spain*, Chapel Hill, 1979.

Brenan, G. *The Spanish Labyrinth*, Cambridge, 10th edn, 1990.

Buenacasa, M. *El movimiento obrero español, 1866–1926*, Barcelona, 1928.

Cabrera, M. 'El testamento político de Maura', *Estudios de Historia Social*, January–June 1985, nos 32–3.

—— 'El conservadurismo maurista en la Restauración. Los límites de la revolución desde arriba', in J. L. García Delgado (ed.) *La España de la Restauración: Política, economía, legislación y cultura*, Madrid, 1985.

Cabrera, M., Comín, F. and García Delgado, J. L. *Santiago Alba. Un programa de reforma económica en la España del primer tercio del Siglo XX*, Madrid, 1989.

Calderón, F. *La verdad sobre el terrorismo. Datos, fechas, nombres y estadísticas*, Barcelona, 1932.

Calero, A. M. 'El papel político de la corona en el reinado de Alfonso XIII: criterios para una revisión' in J. L. García Delgado (ed.) *España 1888–1936. Estructuras y cambio*, Madrid, 1984.

—— 'Los precursores de la monarquía democrática' in J. L. García Delgado (ed.) *La España de la Restauración: Política, economía, legislación y cultura*, Madrid, 1985.

Cardona, G. 'La reforma militar que nunca existió', *Historia 16,* July 1981, no. 63.

—— *El poder militar en la España contemporánea hasta la guerra civil*, Madrid, 1983.

Carnero Arbat, T. 'Política sin democracia en España, 1874–1923', *Revista de Occidente*, April 1988, no. 83.

—— 'Modernització, desenvolupament politic i canvi social: Espanya (1874–1931)', *Recerques*, 1990 no. 23.

Carr, R. *Modern Spain, 1875–1980*, Oxford, 1980.

—— *Spain, 1808–1975*, Oxford, 2nd edn, 1982.

Castillo, J. J. *El sindicalismo amarillo en España*, Madrid, 1977.

Christiansen, E. *The Origins of Military Power in Spain, 1808–1854*, London, 1967.

Comalada, A. *El ocaso de un parlamento*, Barcelona, 1985.

Connelly Ullman, J. *The Tragic Week. Anticlericalism in Spain, 1875–1912*, Harvard, 1968.

Costa, J. *Oligarquía y caciquismo*, Madrid, 1975.

Cruells, M. *Salvador Seguí, el noi del sucre*, Barcelona, 1974.

Delaunay, J. 'España trabajó por la victoria', *Historia 16,* July 1981, no. 63.

Díaz del Moral, J. *Historia de las agitaciones campesinas andaluzas*, Madrid, 1973; first published in 1929.

Díaz Plaja, F. *Francófilos y Germanófilos. Los españoles en la guerra europea*, Barcelona, 1973.

Droz, J. (ed.). *Historia general del socialismo*, 5 vols, Barcelona, 1979.

Elorza, A. 'Los esquemas socialistas en Pablo Iglesias', in *Sistema*, 1975, no. 11.

—— 'Socialismo y agitación popular en Madrid, 1908–1920', in *Historia Social*, 1981, no. 32.

—— 'Nacionalismo económico y renovación política', in J. L. García Delgado (ed.) *España 1898–1936. Estructuras y cambio*, Madrid, 1984.

Elorza, A., Arranz, L. and del Rey, F. 'Liberalismo y corporativismo en la crisis de la Restauración', in J. L. García Delgado (ed.) *La crisis de la restauración. España entre la primera guerra mundial y la II República*, Madrid, 1986.

Espadas Burgos, M. 'España y la neutralidad en la Gran Guerra', *Historia 16*, 1983, no. 5.

Espinos Moltó, V. *Alfonso XIII, espejo de neutrales*, Madrid, 1977.

Fernández Almagro, M. *Historia del reinado de Alfonso XIII*, Barcelona, 1977.

Foix, P. *Los archivos del terrorismo blanco: el fichero Lasarte 1910–1930*, Madrid, 1978.

—— *Apostols y mercaders*, Barcelona, 1970.

Fontana, J. and Nadal, J. 'Spain 1914–1970' in C. M. Cipolla (ed.) *The Fontana Economic History of Europe. Contemporary Economies 2*, 1973.

Forcadell, C. *Parlamentarismo y bolchevización*, Barcelona, 1978.

Forner Muñoz, S. *Canalejas y el partido liberal democrático*, Madrid, 1993.

Fortes Bouza, J. 'La subversión llega a los cuarteles', *Historia 16*, 1980, no. 55.

García Delgado, J. L. 'El ciclo industrial de la economía española entre 1914 y 1922. Capitalismo nacional y crisis política en España (1914–1939)', *Estudios de Historia Social*, January–June 1983, nos 24–5.

—— *España, 1898–1936. Estructuras y cambio. Coloquio de la universidad complutense sobre la España contemporánea*, Madrid, 1984.

—— 'De la protección arancelaria al corporativismo' in J. L. García Delgado (ed.) *España 1898–1936. Estructuras y cambio*, Madrid, 1984.

—— *La España de la Restauración: Política, economía, legislación y cultura*, Madrid, 1985.

—— *La crisis de la Restauración entre la primera guerra mundial y la II República*, Madrid, 1986.

García Delgado, J. L., Roldán, S. and Múnoz, J. *La formación de la sociedad capitalista en España (1914–1920)*, 2 vols, Madrid, 1973.

García Venero, M. *Historia del nacionalismo catalán, 1793–1936*, Madrid, 1944.

—— *Melquiades Alvarez: historia de un liberal*, Madrid, 1974.

—— *Historia de los movimientos sindicalistas españoles, 1840–1922*, Madrid, 1961.

Geary, D. *European Labour Protest 1848–1939*, London, 1984.

Gil Pecharromán, J. '¡Maura al poder!, 1913–1923', *Historia 16*, no. 55.

—— *Conservadores subversivos. La derecha autoritaria alfonsina (1913–1936)*, Madrid, 1994.

Gillespie, R. *Historia del partido socialista obrero español*, Madrid, 1991.

Gómez Llorente, J. L. *Aproximación a la historia del socialismo español*, Madrid, 1976.

González Casanova, J. A. *Federalismo y autonomía. Cataluña y el estado español, 1868–1938*, Barcelona, 1979.

González Hernández, M. J. 'Sobre Antonio Maura: el político, el mito, su política', *Revista de Occidente*, 1987, no. 77.

—— *Ciudadanía y acción. El conservadurismo maurista, 1907–1923*, Madrid, 1990.

Gortazar, G. *Alfonso XIII, hombre de negocios. Persistencia del antiguo régimen, modernización económica y crisis política, 1902–1931*, Madrid, 1986.

Gramsci, A. *Selections from Prison Notebooks*, London, 1971.

Harrison, J. *An Economic History of Modern Spain*, Manchester, 1978.

—— 'The Regenerationist Movement in Spain after the Disaster of 1898', *European Studies Review*, 1979, vol. 9, no. 1.

—— 'The Failure of Economic Reconstitution in Spain', *European Studies Review*, 1983, no. 13.

—— *The Spanish Economy in the Twentieth Century*, London, 1985.

—— 'The Catalan Industrial Elite, 1898–1923', in P. Preston and F. Lannon (eds), *Elites and Power in Twentieth-Century Spain: Essays in Honour of Sir Raymond Carr*, Oxford, 1990.

Herr, R. *An Historical Essay on Modern Spain*, Berkeley, 1971.

Heywood, P. *Marxism and the Failure of Organized Socialism in Spain, 1879–1936*, Cambridge, 1990.

Hobsbawm, E. *Primitive Rebels*, Manchester, 1971.

Huertas, J. M. *Salvador Seguí: El noi del sucre. Materials per a una biografía*, Barcelona, 1974.

Huntington, S. *Political Order in Changing Societies*, Yale, 1968.

Ignacio, L. *Los años del pistolerismo. Ensayo para una guerra civil*, Barcelona, 1981.

Juliá, S. *Los Socialistas en la política española, 1879–1982*, Madrid, 1997.

Jutglar, A. *Historia crítica de la burguesía catalana*, Barcelona, 1984.

Kern, R. W. *Liberals, Reformers and Caciques in Restoration Spain, 1875–1909*, Alburquerque, 1971.

Lacomba, J. A. 'España en 1917. Ensayo de morfología de una crisis histórica', *Valencia*, 1971.

—— *La crisis española de 1917*, Málaga, 1970.

—— 'El hundimiento del artilugio canovista', in *Historia 16*, 1980, no. 55.

Linz, J. J. *El sistema de partidos en España*, Madrid, 1976.

Lleixá, J. *Cien años de militarismo en España*, Barcelona, 1986.

Madariaga, S. de. *Spain,* London, 1942.

Malefakis, E. *Agrarian Reform and Peasant Revolution in Spain*, New Haven 1970.

Martin, B. *The Agony of Modernization. Labour and Industrialization in Spain*, Ithaca, 1990.

Martín, J. *La huelga general de 1917*, Madrid, 1966.

Martín Nogales, V. *Eduardo Dato*, Alava, 1993.

Martínez Cuadrado, M. *Elecciones y partidos políticos, 1868–1931*, 2 vols, Madrid, 1969.

Martínez Fiol, D. 'Lerrouxistas en pie de guerra' in *Historia 16*, October, 1990, no. 174.

—— *Els Voluntaris Catalans a la Gran Guerra, 1914–1918*, Barcelona, 1991.

Martínez Martín, J. A. 'Las elecciones municipales en la crisis de la restauración: Madrid, 1917', in J. L. García Delgado (ed.) *La crisis de la restauración: España entre la primera guerra mundial y la II República*, Madrid, 1986.

Martínez de Sas, M. T. *El socialismo y la España Oficial. Pablo Iglesias. Diputado a cortes*, Madrid, 1975.

Maurice, J. *El anarquismo andaluz. Campesinos y sindicalistas, 1868–1936*, Barcelona, 1990.

Mayer, A. *The Origins of the New Diplomacy, 1917–1918*, Yale, 1959.

—— *The Persistence of the Old Regime,* New York, 1974.

Meaker, G. *The Revolutionary Left in Spain, 1914–1923*, Palo Alto, 1974.

—— 'A Civil War of Words' in H. A. Schmitt (ed.) *Neutral Europe between War and Revolution, 1917–1923*, Charlottesville, 1988.

Montero, E. 'Luis Araquistáin y la propaganda aliada durante la primera guerra mundial', *Estudios de Historia Social*, 1983, nos 24–5.

Morales Lezcano, V. 'La neutralidad española en la guerra del 14' and 'La intelectualidad del 14 ante la guerra', *Historia 16*, 1981, no. 63.

—— *El colonialismo hispano-francés en Marruecos, 1898–1927*, Madrid, 1986.

Moreno Luzón, J. 'Romanones: Conquistador de clientelas. Gran Señor', *Historia Contemporánea*, 1996, nos 13–14.

Mosher, J. R. *The Birth of Mass Politics in Spain. Lerrouxismo in Barcelona, 1901–1909*, New York, 1991.

Muñoz, J., Roldán, S. and Serrano, A. 'La vía nacionalista del capitalismo español', *Cuadernos Económicos del ICE*, 1978, nos 7–8.

Nadal, J. *El fracaso de la revolución industrial en España, 1814–1913*, Barcelona, 1975.

Olaya Morales, F. *Historia del movimiento obrero español (siglo XIX)*, Madrid, 1994.

Pabón, J. *Cambó*, 3 vols, Barcelona, 1952.

Palacio, J. I. 'Crisis política y crisis institucional: la experiencia del Instituto de Reformas Sociales en el periodo 1914–1924', in J. L. García Delgado (ed.) *La crisis de la Restauración entre la primera guerra mundial y la II República*, Madrid, 1986.

Pan-Montojo, J. (ed.) *Más se perdió en Cuba. España, 1898 y la crisis de fin de siglo*, Madrid, 1998.

Payne, S. *Politics and the Military in Modern Spain*, Stanford, 1967.

—— *Ejército y sociedad en la España liberal, 1808–1936*, Madrid, 1976.

Peiráts, J. *Los anarquistas en la crisis política española*, Barcelona, 1976.

Pérez Delgado, R. *Antonio Maura*, Madrid, 1974.

—— *1898. El año del desastre*, Madrid, 1976.

Pérez Ledesma, M. *Pensamiento socialista español a comienzos de siglo*, Madrid, 1974.

—— 'La primera etapa de la Unión General de Trabajadores, 1888–1917. Planteamiento sindical y formas de organización', in A. Balcells (ed.) *Teoría y práctica del movimiento obrero en España*, Valencia, 1977.

Pla, J. *Cambó. Materials per a una historia d'aquesta ultims anys*, 3 vols, Barcelona, 1930.

Petrie, C. *King Alfonso XIII and his Age*, London, 1963.

Preston, P. and Graham, H. (eds) *The Popular Front in Europe*, London, 1987.

Punset, R. 'Maura y maurismo. Perspectiva histórica de la revolución desde arriba', *Sistema*, November 1979, no. 33.

Rama, C. M. *La crisis española del Siglo XX*, Mexico, 2nd edn, 1962.

Ramsden, H. *The 1898 Movement in Spain*, London, 1974.

Reguera, F. *España neutral*, Madrid, 1967.

Rey Reguillo, F. del. 'Ciudadanos honrados y somatenistas. El orden y la subversión en la España de los años 20', *Estudios de Historia Social*, July–December 1987, nos 42–3.

Riquer, B. de. *La Lliga Regionalista: la burguesía catalana i el nacionalisme*, Barcelona, 1977.

—— *Regionalistes i Nacionalistes, 1898–1931*, Barcelona, 1979.

—— 'El fracaso de la asamblea de parlamentarios', *Historia 16*, 1980, no. 55.

Romero Maura, J. 'El *caciquismo*, tentativa de conceptualización', *Revista de Occidente*, October 1973, no. 127.

—— '*La rosa de fuego*'. *El obrerismo barcelonés de 1899 a 1909*, Barcelona, 1974.

—— '*Caciquismo* as a political system', in E. Gellner and J. Waterbury (eds.), *Patrons and Clients*, London, 1977.

Romero Salvadó, F. J. 'Maura, Maurismo and the Crisis of 1917', *Association for Contemporary Iberian Studies (ACIS)*, Spring 1994, vol. 7, no. 1.

—— 'Spain and the First World War: the Structural Crisis of the Liberal Monarchy', *European History Quarterly*, October 1995, vol. 25, no. 4.

Romeu Alfaro, F. *Las clases trabajadoras en España (1898–1930)*, Madrid, 1970.

Ruiz Manjón, O. *El partido republicano radical, 1908–1936*, Madrid, 1976.

Seco Serrano, C. *Perfil político y humano de un estadista de la restauración, Eduardo Dato a través de su archivo. Discurso de entrada en la Real Academia de la Historia*, Madrid, 1978.

—— *Alfonso XIII y la crisis de la restauración*, Madrid, 1979.

—— *Militarismo y civilismo en la España contemporánea*, Madrid, 1984.

Serrallonga, J. 'Motines y revolución. España 1917', in Francesc Bonamusa (ed.) *La huelga general*, *Ayer*, 1991, no. 4.

Serrano, C. *Final del Imperio, España, 1895–1898*, Madrid, 1984.

Smith, J. *The Spanish–American War. Conflict in the Caribbean and the Pacific*, London, 1994.

Suárez Cortina, M. *El reformismo en España*, Madrid, 1986.

Trice, T. G. *Spanish Liberalism in Crisis. A Study of the Liberal Party during Spain's Parliamentary Collapse, 1913–1923*, New York, 1991.

Tuñón de Lara, M. *La España del Siglo XX*, Paris, 1966.

—— *Historia y realidad del poder (El poder y las élites en el primer tercio de la España del Siglo XX)*, Madrid, 1967.

—— *El movimiento obrero en la historia de España*, Madrid, 1972.

—— 'Sobre la historia del pensamiento socialista español entre 1900 y 1931', in A. Balcélls (ed.) *Teoría y práctica del movimiento obrero en España, 1900–1931*, Valencia, 1977.

—— 'Rasgos de crisis estructural a partir de 1917', in Tuñón de Lara (ed.) *La crisis del estado español, 1898–1936*, Madrid, 1978.

—— *La crisis del estado español, 1898–1936*, Madrid, 1978.

—— 'Agosto sangriento', *Historia 16*, 1980, no. 55.

—— 'De la Restauración al desastre colonial', *Historia 16,* June 1982, *Extra XXII: La España de los caciques.*

—— *España: la quiebra de 1898*, Madrid, 1986.

—— *Poder y sociedad en España, 1900–1931*, Madrid, 1992.

Tusell, J. 'La descomposición del sistema caciquil español (1902–1931)', *Revista de Occidente*, October 1973, no. 127.

—— *La política y los políticos en tiempos de Alfonso XIII*, Madrid, 1976.

—— *Oligarquía y caciquismo en Andalucia, 1890–1923*, Barcelona, 1976.

—— *Antonio Maura. Una biografía política*, Madrid, 1994.

Tusell, J. and Avilés, J. *La derecha española contemporánea. Sus orígenes: el maurismo*, Madrid, 1986.

Varela Ortega, J. 'Los amigos políticos: funcionamiento del sistema caciquista', *Revista de Occidente*, October 1973, no. 127.

—— *Los amigos políticos. Partidos, elecciones y caciquismo en la Restauración, 1875–1900*, Madrid, 1977.

—— 'Aftermath of Splendid Disaster: Spanish Politics before and after the Spanish American War of 1898', *Journal of Contemporary History*, 1980, vol. 15.

Vicéns Vives, J. *Historia de España y América*, 5 vols, Barcelona, 2nd edn, 1972.

Vicente Villanueva, L. *Sindicalismo y conflictividad social en Zaragoza, 1916–1923*, Saragossa, 1993.

Vilar, P. *Spain: A Brief History*, Exeter, 1977.

Voltes, P. *La Semana Trágica*, Madrid, 1995.

Winston, C. *Workers and the Right in Spain, 1900–1936*, Princeton, 1985.

Zugazagoitia, J. *Pablo Iglesias: una vida heroica*, Madrid, 1925.

INDEX